Analogy after Aquinas

THOMISTIC RESSOURCEMENT SERIES

Volume 11

SERIES EDITORS

Matthew Levering, *Mundelein Seminary*

Thomas Joseph White, OP, *Dominican House of Studies*

EDITORIAL BOARD

Serge-Thomas Bonino, OP, *Pontifical University of St. Thomas Aquinas*

Gilles Emery, OP, *University of Fribourg (Switzerland)*

Reinhard Hütter, *The Catholic University of America*

Bruce Marshall, *Southern Methodist University*

Emmanuel Perrier, OP, *Dominican Studium, Toulouse*

Richard Schenk, OP, *University of Freiburg (Germany)*

Kevin White, *The Catholic University of America*

Analogy after Aquinas

Logical Problems, Thomistic Answers

DOMENIC D'ETTORE

The Catholic University of America Press
Washington, D.C.

Copyright © 2019
The Catholic University of America Press
All rights reserved

Library of Congress Cataloging-in-Publication Data
Names: D'Ettore, Domenic, author.
Title: Analogy after Aquinas : logical problems, Thomistic answers /
Dominic D'Ettore.
Description: Washington, D.C. : The Catholic University of America
Press, 2019. | Series: Thomisic ressourcement series Volume 11 |
Includes bibliographical references and index.
Identifiers: LCCN 2018028368 | ISBN 9780813234779
(pbk)
Subjects: LCSH: Thomas, Aquinas, Saint, 1225?–1274. | Analysis
(Philosophy) | Reasoning. | Duns Scotus, John,
approximately 1266–1308.
Classification: LCC B765.T54 D4658 2019 | DDC 169—dc23
LC record available at https://lccn.loc.gov/2018028368

For Nicole

Contents

List of Tables	ix
Acknowledgments	xi
List of Abbreviations	xiii
Introduction	1
1. The Objection from John Duns Scotus	18
2. Hervaeus Natalis and Thomas Sutton: The Princes of Primitive Thomism	33
3. John Capreolus: Thomism in Transition	61
4. Flandrensis and Soncinas	89
5. Cajetan	126
6. Early Reception of Cajetan: Chrysostom Javelli and Francis Silvestri of Ferrara	145
Conclusion	181
Selected Bibliography	193
Index	201

Tables

Table 1. Modes of Equivocation by Design according to Boethius	4
Table 2. Development of Conditions for Univocity	66
Table 3. Comparing Aquinas and Boethius on Modes of Analogy	95
Table 4. Natalis to Cajetan on the Three Problems	141
Table 5. Solution to the Equivocation Problem *ad mentem Ferrariensis*	163
Table 6. Thomists on the Three Problems	187

Acknowledgments

This book began with my doctoral dissertation, "Early Thomists on Demonstration through Analogous Terms" (Center for Thomistic Studies, University of St. Thomas, 2012). I became interested in the project while auditing a course on Thomas Aquinas's doctrine of analogy taught by Thomas Osborne Jr. At the time, I was particularly struck by Ralph McInerny's criticism of Cajetan's *De Nominum Analogia* and by Joshua Hochschild's defense of Cajetan. It seemed to me that if McInerny was right about Aquinas's doctrine of analogy, then Scotus was right to reject it. Cajetan seemed to offer a coherent defence of analogy, and I wondered if other Thomists had done so as well. I looked into how some Thomists prior to Cajetan explained why the fallacy of equivocation does not occur when a term is used analogously in a demonstration. This investigation led me toward other related issues in the logic of analogy, which are brought together in this book.

The structure of this book by itself—particularly its unique concern with the relationship between the Thomists' answers to three distinct problems—demanded substantial revision of all previous work. Other changes, of course, emerged owing to revisiting and rethinking the materials in light of further reflection and additional texts. All tables in the manuscript are original to it.

I am especially indebted to Thomas Osborne Jr. for his many

comments on a draft of this work. I would also like to thank the anonymous readers, and the members of my department at Marian University who strongly encouraged me to complete this project.

Most of all, I thank my wife, Nicole, for her loving support.

Abbreviations

AQM	*Acutissimae quaestiones metaphysicales* (Paulus Soncinas)
De Fallaciis	*In Diui Thomae Aquinatis fallaciarum* (Dominic of Flanders)
In SCG	*Commentaria Ferrariensis* (Francis Silvestri of Ferrara)
In Sent.	*Scriptum super libros Sententiarum* (Thomas Aquinas)
OP	*Opera Philosophica* (John Duns Scotus, ed. Andrews et al.)
PL	*Patrologia Latina* (ed. Migne)
QMA	*Quaestiones, In Metaphysicam Aristotelis* (Chrysostom Iavellus)
SDP	*In duodecim libros Metaphysicae Aristotelis* (Dominic of Flanders)
Super Artem	*Expositio Super Artem Veterem Aristotelis* (Paulus Soncinas)
VC	*Opera Omnia* (John Duns Scotus, ed. Scotistic Commission)

Analogy after Aquinas

Introduction

This book takes up several historical interpretations and developments of Thomas Aquinas's doctrine that the key terms of metaphysics, especially in natural theology, are used analogously rather than purely equivocally or univocally. These particular interpretations and developments emerged among Dominican defenders of the thought of Aquinas as answers to objections from John Duns Scotus and his followers, who called the use of analogy in metaphysics and natural theology into question by citing the incompatibility between the semantics of analogy and the demands of the logic of demonstration. This study confines its investigation historically to the period between the opening decade of the fourteenth century, when Dominicans first encountered and answered John Duns Scotus, and the middle of the sixteenth century, prior to the opening of the Council of Trent. This stopping point allows the work to focus exclusively on Dominican Thomists, without needing to branch off into Jesuit contributions to the discussion. The particular Dominican Thomists selected are chosen for a combination of their historical influence on the development of the doctrine of analogy in Thomism and for the purpose of illustrating the range of interpretations to which Thomas's thought has been subjected. I follow the practice of twentieth-century scholarship and treat the late fifteenth- and early sixteenth-century commentator Thomas Cardinal de Vio Cajetan as the most influential contributor on these

2   Introduction

disputed questions. Accordingly, the majority of the Thomists treated here are either direct influences on Cajetan or directly influenced by him.

ANALOGY AND ARISTOTELIAN SCIENCE

The general question that motivates this study is why demonstrations can proceed using terms analogously without falling into the fallacy of equivocation. The debate over demonstration with analogous terms arises in the context of Aristotelian science and its logical tools, one of which is the distinction between univocal and equivocal predication of terms or names. Names themselves are signs of an intellect's concepts, which, in turn, are likenesses of things.[1] A particular name receives its meaning or signification when a speaker uses it to signify a thing. The act of giving a name its signification is called "imposition."[2] The predication of a name about more than

---

1. Aristotle, *De Interpretatione* 1 (16a). See also Thomas Aquinas, *In Peri Hermeneias*, l. 1, lect. 2, in *In Aristotelis Libros Peri Hermeneias et Posteriorum Analyticorum Expositio*, ed. R. M. Spiazzi, 2nd ed. (Turin: Marietti, 1964), 9–12; *Summa Theologiae* I, q. 15, a. 1; and *In 5 Meta.*, lect. 5, in *In Duodecim Libros Metaphysicorum Aristotelis Expositio*, ed. R. M. Spiazzi (Turin: Marietti, 1950), 223b. On the different ways in which a concept can be a likeness of things, see Thomas Aquinas, *In 1 Sent.*, d. 2, q. 1, a. 3. For a discussion of this text, see Gyula Klima, "The Semantic Principles underlying Saint Thomas Aquinas's Metaphysics of Being," *Medieval Philosophy and Theology* 5 (1996): 87–141, esp. 101: "concepts that have as their objects things other than concepts are called first intentions (*intentiones primae*), and, correspondingly, their names are called names of first imposition (*nomina primae impositionis*) ... concepts that have concepts *as such* as their objects are called second intentions (*intentiones secundae*), and, correspondingly, their names are called names of second imposition (*nomina secundae impositionis*)." On the history of the passage, see A. Dondaine, "Saint Thomas et la dispute des attributs divins (I Sent., d. 2, a. 3): authenticité et origine," *Archivum Fratrum Praedicatorum* 8 (1938): 253–62. On the different interpretations of signification between Aquinas, Scotus, and other figures of the thirteenth and early fourteenth centuries, see Giorgio Pini, "Species, Concept, and Thing: Theories of Signification in the Second Half of the Thirteenth Century," *Medieval Philosophy and Theology* 8 (1999): 21–52. See also E. J. Ashworth, "Signification and Modes of Signification in Thirteenth-Century Logic: A Preface to Aquinas on Analogy," *Medieval Philosophy and Theology* 1 (1991): 43–53, and Ria van der Lecq, "Logic and Theories of Meaning in the Late 13th and Early 14th Century Including the Modistae," in *Mediaeval and Renaissance Logic*, ed. Dov M. Gabbay and John Woods (Amsterdam: North Holland, 2007), 2:349–53.

2. On late thirteenth- and early fourteenth-century theories of imposition, see Ria

one thing is either univocal or equivocal. It is univocal when a single name is said about many according to the same signification. That is, the intellect refers one and the same of its concepts to diverse things through one name. By contrast, there is equivocation, when a single name is predicated according to diverse significations; that is, the intellect uses the same name to refer different concepts to different things. Aristotle provides the example of "animal" said of a man and an ox for univocal naming, and the example of "animal" said of a man and a picture of a man for equivocal naming.[3]

Aristotle's *Categories* 1 inspires later authors in the Aristotelian tradition to identify diverse modes of equivocation including analogy. Most importantly for the Latin Scholastics, Boethius divides equivocation into "equivocation by chance" (or pure equivocation) and "equivocation by design." "Equivocation by chance" occurs when there is no relation whatsoever between the diverse meanings of the same name. To give an example from contemporary English, the name "bat" as applied to a mammal and to sporting equipment is equivocal by chance. Equivocation by design occurs when the signification of a name is extended from some first or primary sense to another diverse but related sense of the name. Boethius identifies four variations of equivocation by design: *similitudo, proportio, ab uno,* and *ad unum*. Table 1 illustrates Boethius's fourfold division of equivocation by design with his examples.[4]

Each of Boethius's four modes of equivocation by design matches one or another of Aristotle's treatments of either equivocation or

---

van der Lecq, "Logic and Theories of Meaning," 347–48: "The basic function of language is to signify things, and imposition is the way words acquire their meanings. This is supposed to work as follows: a first *impositor* investigates things and their properties and then decides which sound (*vox*) should be used to signify that object. When this sound has been imposed to signify some thing, it becomes a sign and it has acquired signification." See also van der Lecq's discussion of modes of signification in 354–58. On the controversy over imposition in equivocal and analogous naming, see E. J. Ashworth, "Metaphor and the Logicians from Aristotle to Cajetan," *Vivarium* 45 (2007): 311–27, esp. 325–27.

3. Aristotle, *Categories* 1 (1a).

4. Anicii Manlii Severini Boethius, *In Categorias Aristotelis*, in *Patrologia Latina* (hereafter, *PL*), ed. J.-P. Migne (Paris, 1891), 64:166b–c.

TABLE 1. Modes of Equivocation by Design according to Boethius

Mode	Standard Example
1. Similitudo	"Animal" said of a man and a picture of a man
2. Proportio (Analogia)	"Principle" said of unity for number and of point for lines
3. ab uno	"Medical" said of a book and of a medical tool
4. ad unum	"Healthy" said of medicine, etc., by reference to an animal's health

unity. The first mode, *similitudo*, derives from Aristotle's example of equivocation in *Categories* 1, the name "animal" said of a man and a picture. The second mode, *proportio*, reflects Aristotle's examples of first principles in different genera in the *Metaphysics* and elsewhere.[5] Notably, *proportio* is Boethius's translation of the Greek term *analogia*. The third and fourth modes, *ab uno* and *ad unum*, derive from Aristotle's examples of *pros hen* equivocation, most importantly, those found in *Metaphysics* 4.[6]

Aristotle's *locus classicus* for understanding science is his *Posterior Analytics* 1. Sciences pursue certain knowledge of the proper and necessary causes and attributes of their subject matter. Demonstrated knowledge itself is achieved through necessary principles, which rely ultimately for their certitude on the axioms and other indemonstrable first principles. The subject matter of a given science is some genus. The demonstrated conclusions of a science affirm that all members of genus x, precisely insofar as they belong to genus x, possess property y or principle z, or are caused by w.[7]

Aristotelian science experiences challenges with its logical tools when Aristotle proposes a science that lacks a genus based subject

---

5. See Aristotle, *Metaphysics* 5.3 and 6 (1014b8–9 and 1016b17–35). See also Aristotle, *Posterior Analytics* 1.10 (76b4–5).

6. Aristotle, *Metaphysics* 4.2 (1003a32–b4).

7. For a sustained presentation of Aristotle's approach to scientific demonstration through first principles, see T. H. Irwin, *Aristotle's First Principles* (Oxford: Clarendon Press, 2002). For a medieval interpretation, see Aquinas, *In Aristotelis Libros Posteriorum Analyticorum*, esp. I.1.

matter; namely, wisdom (i.e., metaphysics), the science that studies being as being. "Being" is said in many ways, yet being is not a genus, and being is not predicated univocally of all the things that are studied in the science of being as being.[8] The consequence follows that the name "being" is predicated equivocally within the science of metaphysics. As Aristotle says that there can be no demonstration without univocal terms,[9] a search began among Aristotelians for an explanation of the unity of the science of being sufficient for demonstration. By the Latin Middle Ages, the standard account has become that "being" is said not univocally, nor purely equivocally, in metaphysics, but by analogy, which is somehow between univocity and pure equivocation. Analogy itself is identified with equivocation by design or more explicitly with one or another of the diverse modes of equivocation by design. New modes and alternative divisions are introduced by various medieval authors.[10]

THE LOGIC OF NATURAL THEOLOGY AND
THE FALLACY OF EQUIVOCATION

In the Latin Middle Ages, the challenge of accounting for the nongeneric unity of metaphysics meets the additional problem of predicating names of God and creatures in natural and in revealed theology. The difference between God and creatures requires that no name that signifies a creature in any way could adequately signify God. Yet, Scholastic philosophical theologians, such as Aquinas, agreed with St. Paul that the things of God can be known from God's works, and they believed that Aristotle and others had even succeeded in demonstrating the existence and attributes of the cause of created being through the naturally knowable attributes of its effects.[11]

8. See Aristotle, *Metaphysics* 4.2 (1003b20–31) and 11.3 (1060b–1061b).
9. Aristotle, *Posterior Analytics* 1.11 (77a5–10).
10. A useful history of these divisions is provided by E. J. Ashworth, "Medieval Theories of Analogy," in the *Stanford Encyclopedia of Philosophy*, 2017, available at *plato.stanford.edu/fall2017/entries/analogy-medieval/*.
11. Thomas Aquinas provides short summaries of received positions in his own day

Just as the name "being," as the subject of metaphysics, could not be predicated univocally across the categories of being or of act and of potency, the name "being" and other names signifying the divine attributes could not be said univocally of God and creatures. In both cases, the logical problem arises that if the names are not said univocally, but somehow equivocally, demonstrations using these terms would appear to be instances of the fallacy of equivocation.

Perhaps the most influential medieval treatment of the fallacy of equivocation appears in Peter of Spain's *Tractatus* 7.[12] This work defines the fallacy of equivocation as "deception caused in us from inability to distinguish diverse *rationes* in absolutely the same name."[13] The "second species" of this fallacy occurs "when the same saying [*dictio*] signifies diverse things according to prior and posterior."[14] As a standard example of the second species of the fallacy of equivocation, the text offers the following syllogism: "Everything healthy is an animal, urine is healthy; therefore, urine is an animal."[15] One name "healthy" is predicated of both an animal and urine. The signification of the name as said of an animal is prior in relation to the signification of the name as said of urine, food, diet, etc.[16] This diversity between the prior and posterior *rationes* of the name causes the fallacy in the argument. It becomes a challenge for any Scholastic metaphysics or natural theology to account for why demonstrations

---

in a number of places. See Aquinas, *In 1 Sent.*, d. 2, q. 1, a. 3, and *Summa Theologiae* I, q. 13, aa. 2 and 5.

12. For a discussion of this work's authorship and its influence in the study of logic following its composition in the mid-thirteenth century, see Gyula Klima, "Peter of Spain," in *A Companion to Philosophy in the Middle Ages*, ed. Jorge J. E. Gracia and Timothy B. Noone (Malden, Mass.: Blackwell, 2006), 526–31.

13. See Peter of Spain, *Tractatus* (or *Summule Logicales*), ed. L. M. de Rijk (Assen: Van Gorcum, 1972), 99: "Unde equivocatio sive fallacia equivocationis hoc modo sumpta sic potest diffiniri: fallacia equivocationis est deceptio causata in nobis ex impotentia distinguendi diversas in eodem nomine rationes simpliciter."

14. Ibid., 100: "Secunda species sive secundus modus equivocationis est quando eadem dictio secundum prius et posterius significat diversa."

15. Ibid., 101: "omne sanum est animal urina est sana ergo urina est animal."

16. See ibid., 98–99. The author does not specifically say that the prior meaning is the signification of the name as applied to the animal, but each other meaning is defined by its reference to the health of the animal.

relying on non-univocal predication of the name "being" in metaphysics or other names in natural theology do not fall prey to this second species of the fallacy of equivocation. As will be seen below, the Scotist approach to this problem is to abandon analogy for univocity, and the Thomists look for solutions that preserve both analogy and demonstration.

Aristotle himself is surprisingly unhelpful to the Thomists on this matter. He introduces a science which has merely analogous unity without explaining why this unity is sufficient for demonstration. Aquinas imitates his ancient master on this point very well. An adequate answer to the problem of demonstration through analogous names would show how a term signifying through two analogous *rationes* or one *ratio* analogously is close enough to univocity to share with univocal terms the property of mediating valid reasoning. In various places, including his *De Potentia, Summa Contra Gentiles,* and *Summa Theologiae,* Thomas says that argumentation from creatures to God would be impossible if names were said of them equivocally.[17] Each of these texts proposes analogy as a mean between pure equivocation and univocity, and each gives the same sort of examples of analogy as found in Boethius's account of *ad unum* equivocation by design and in *Tractatus* 7's example of the second species of the fallacy of equivocation. (I will be calling this kind of analogy the "Healthy Model" of analogy.) Not one of Thomas's passages explains why and how analogy avoids the fallacy. To make matters more challenging for Thomists, when Aquinas addresses the issue of the fallacy of equivocation in a specifically logical context, he affirms the need for names to be said according to one and same *ratio* in a demonstration, and he reiterates Aristotle's rejection of the possibility of demonstration using names equivocally.[18]

---

17. See Aquinas, *De Potentia,* q. 7, a. 7, in *S. Thomae Aquinatis Quaestiones disputatae,* ed. P. Bazzi, M. Calcaterra, T. S. Centi, E. Odetto, P. M. Pession (Turin: Marietti, 1965), 2:204a; *Summa Contra Gentiles* I, c. 33 (Leonine, 13:102b); *Summa Theologiae* I, q. 13, a. 5; *Compendium Theologiae* I, c. 27 (Leonine, 42:90–91).

18. See Aquinas, *In Posteriorum Analyticorum, l. 1, lect. 19 (Marietti, 1:211b):* "Et quod oporteat medium demonstrationis esse universale, patet per hoc quod oportet medium

PURPOSE OF THIS BOOK

Explanations from Thomists regarding how analogous terms can function in a valid demonstration first appear in the generation after the death of Thomas, and they are generally presented as responses to John Duns Scotus's criticism of the whole project of basing the unity of a science and its demonstrations on analogy. The object of this book is to relate and evaluate the varied Thomist solutions to the problem of demonstration using analogous terms, beginning with Scotus's contemporaries and proceeding to some of the most notable Thomist figures in the fifteenth and early sixteenth centuries. Three points in particular will be highlighted for marking where Thomas's successors part ways in interpreting the Common Doctor's doctrine.

The first point concerns the question of whether in cases of analogy (and specifically in the cases where demonstration occurs using terms analogously) there is a single *ratio* predicated analogously, or, instead, many *rationes* predicated in ways that are analogous to each other. In other words, does analogy, like pure equivocation, entail two diverse but related impositions of a name, or, instead, does analogy entail a single imposition of a name with a primary and at least one secondary way of signifying its concept? I borrow the name for this problem from George Klubertanz who labelled it *Una ratio vs. diversae rationes*.[19] Klubertanz himself argues that Thomas held the *una ratio* position in his early writings and had emphatically changed his mind by the time he composed his *Summa Contra Gentiles* and *Summa Theologiae* in favor of *diversae rationes*.[20] Besides Klubertanz's

---

demonstrationis esse unum et idem de pluribus predicatum non aequivoce, sed secundum rationem eamdem: quod est ratio universalis. Si autem aequivocum esset, posset accidere vitium in arguendo." On Aquinas's discussions of analogy in demonstration, see Joshua Hochschild, "Did Aquinas answer Cajetan's question? Aquinas's Semantic Rules for Analogy and the Interpretation *of De Nominum Analogia*," in *Proceedings of the American Catholic Philosophical Association* 77 (2003): 273–88.

19. George P. Klubertanz, *St. Thomas Aquinas on Analogy: A Textual Analysis and Systematic Synthesis* (Chicago: Loyola University Press, 1960), 23.

20. Klubertanz, *Aquinas on Analogy*, 24.

brief treatment of this issue, I have not found another analysis in contemporary scholarship directed at the thought of Aquinas himself.

The second point concerns a familiar debated question in contemporary scholarship on Aquinas; namely, the role of analogy of proportionality in Aquinas's metaphysics and the relationship between analogy of proportionality and other modes of analogy (commonly called "analogy of attribution"). The model for analogy of proportionality (sometimes called "proper proportionality") is taken from Aristotle's examples of the term "principle" said by *analogia* of points, lines, springs, foundations, hearts, etc. As noted above, Boethius treats this as the second mode of equivocation by design. Aquinas appears to invoke it as the mode of analogy uniquely suited to metaphysics and natural theology in his (early) *De Veritate*, q. 2, a. 11. Instead of "principle" said of unity, points, hearts, etc., the example is "sight" said of the eye and the soul.[21] It appears again in a prominent role in Aquinas's (late) *Sententia Libri Ethicorum*, l. 1, lect. 7. The model for analogy of attribution in metaphysics or natural theology is taken from Aristotle's example of the term "healthy" said of medicine and an animal; that is, Boethius's fourth mode of equivocation by design. Aquinas applies this mode of analogy in his discussion of being said across the categories and of God and creatures in his *Summa Contra Gentiles* I, c. 34, *Summa Theologiae* I, q. 13, a. 5, and in many other places. The contemporary controversy over interpreting Aquinas's doctrine includes whether analogy of proportionality is a permanent feature of Aquinas's doctrine and whether, and if so how, analogy of proportionality is reducible to analogy of attribution. A recurrent issue in this debate is whether Aquinas holds that, in every case of analogy, the *ratio* of one analogate is in the *ratio* of the other analogate(s), or if analogy of proportionality is an exception to this rule.[22]

---

21. The example comes from Aristotle, *Nicomachean Ethics* 1.6 (1096b29).
22. The standard twentieth- and twenty-first-century interpretations of Aquinas's position on the modes of analogy are laid out and discussed in Joshua Hochschild,

These two points of interpretation relate to a third point, which was introduced above, namely, how it is that analogous terms can mediate demonstrations without falling into the fallacy of equivocation. For clarity and consistency throughout this book, I will call these three points:

- The "*Rationes* Problem" (One or many *rationes*)
- The "Analogy Model Problem" (Healthy versus Principle Model of analogy)
- The "Equivocation Problem" (The fallacy of equivocation)[23]

The focus of this book is the thought of Thomists and only secondarily the thought of Aquinas. It traces a history of Aquinas's disciples' attempts to resolve a set of problems which they inherited from their master and their master's critics. In consequence, there are a number of controversial points in contemporary scholarship that are left out of consideration. For instance, this book will not attempt to resolve any of the questions regarding the development of doctrine between Aquinas's earlier and later writings, including his own positions on the *Rationes* and Analogy Model Problems. These questions are left aside for the simple reason that, however much the

---

"Proportionality and Divine Naming: Did St. Thomas Change His Mind About Analogy?," *The Thomist* 77 (2013): 531–58. Extended treatments include Klubertanz, *St. Thomas Aquinas on Analogy*; Bernard Montagnes, *The Doctrine of the Analogy of Being according to Thomas Aquinas*, trans. E. M. Macierowski, ed. Andrew Tallon (Milwaukee, Wis.: Marquette University Press, 2004); Ralph McInerny, *Aquinas and Analogy* (Washington, D.C.: The Catholic University of America Press, 1996); and John F. Wippel, *The Metaphysical Thought of Thomas Aquinas: From Finite Being to Uncreated Being*, Monographs for the Society for Medieval and Renaissance Philosophy 1 (Washington, D.C.: The Catholic University of America Press, 2000).

23. My terminology for the *Rationes* Problem imitates Klubertanz's "*una ratio* vs *diversae rationes*," and, for the Analogy Model Problem, I adopt the language of Healthy Model versus Principle Model from Lawrence Dewan, "Does Being Have a Nature? (Or: Metaphysics as a Science of the Real)," in *Approaches to Metaphysics*, ed. William Sweet (Dordrecht: Kluwer, 2004), 24. Given the examples of *analogia* in Aristotle's works and in Aquinas's *De Veritate*, q. 2, a. 11, the kind of analogy that I am calling "Principle Model" could equally be called "Sight Model." For clarity's sake, I will remind the reader of this point by calling this kind of analogy "Principle/Sight Model" occasionally when dealing with Thomists who draw heavily on *De Veritate*, q. 2, a. 11.

internal development of Aquinas's thought on analogy has interested twentieth- and twenty-first-century scholars, it does not appear to have interested Thomists writing in the fourteenth through sixteenth centuries. While some of these Thomists were clearly well aware of the variations between what Thomas writes in different parallel passages, they tacitly assume continuity in his doctrine of analogy.

Furthermore, this book does not assess these authors by their relative fidelity to the thought of Aquinas. To do so would be to invert the order of this book's intention. The disputed questions about what Aquinas really thought must be resolved prior to making *ad mentem Thomae* judgments about the Thomists.[24] I hope that someone will be in a better position to write the book that resolves the questions *ad mentem Thomae* as a result of this book's considerations of Aquinas's successors' attempts to understand and defend his doctrine.

CHAPTER SUMMARIES AND BRIEF INTRODUCTION TO THE THOMISTS

As mentioned above, Thomists addressed the problem of demonstration through analogous terms in response to the objections raised by critics of the use of analogy in natural theology and metaphysics, principally, John Duns Scotus (1265–1308). The first chapter sets up the issue for the Thomists by laying out Scotus's objections.[25] It examines the position of Scotus primarily through the lenses of his *Oxford Commentary* and *Commentary on the Metaphysics*. It also draws from contemporary scholars' work on Scotus, especially that of Richard Cross.

---

24. I have benefited greatly from reading the attempts of George Klubertanz, Bernard Montagnes, Ralph McInerny, and John Wippel to produce *ad mentem Thomae* volumes dedicated to analogy or Aquinas's metaphysics in general (cited above). Unfortunately, none of these authors directly attended to the problem of demonstration using analogous terms, and only Klubertanz attended to the *Rationes* Problem.

25. On the life and work of Scotus, see Stephen D. Dumont, "John Duns Scotus," in *Companion to Philosophy in the Middle Ages* (ed. Gracia and Noone), 353–69.

Chapter 2 discusses two prominent early Thomists, Thomas of Sutton (hereafter, Sutton or Thomas Sutton) and Hervaeus Natalis. Natalis (ca. 1250–1323) is perhaps best remembered as the Dominican master general whose efforts produced the canonization of Aquinas and as the defender of the temporal power of the pope. There is some dispute over whether Natalis counts as a Thomist at all. Christiaan Kappes has claimed him as an "eclectic," noting areas where he follows Scotus rather than Aquinas.[26] Perhaps anyone who departs from Thomas *ad literam* makes the purity of their Thomism questionable, but Natalis clearly belongs in the Thomist camp on the issues pertinent to this study. Later Thomists, especially Dominic of Flanders, judge him to be among the best Thomist voices. I follow the tradition (preceding even Suarez) of examining Natalis's *Quodlibet* 2, q. 7, for his understanding of analogy.

Thomas Sutton (ca. 1250–1315) taught at Oxford contemporaneously with Scotus, and has been called the "Prince of the primitive Thomists."[27] He has sometimes been confused with his contemporary English Dominican Thomas Anglicus,[28] whose work will also be mentioned in this book as an influence on Dominic of Flanders. A

---

26. Christiaan W. Kappes, *The Immaculate Conception: Why Thomas Aquinas Denied, while John Duns Scotus, Gregory of Palamas, and Mark Eugenicus Professed the Absolute Immaculate Existence of Mary* (Bedford, Mass.: Academy of the Immaculate, 2014), 234–35. On Natalis's life and works, see Frederick Roensch, *Early Thomistic School* (Dubuque, Iowa: Priory Press, 1964), 107 and 110–17, and Ronald J. Teske, "Hervaeus Natalis," in *Companion to Philosophy in the Middle Ages* (ed. Gracia and Noone), 314–15. The reception of Natalis's doctrine of second intentions by several of the figures appearing in this study is treated in M. Tavuzzi, "Hervaeus Natalis and the Philosophical Logic of the Thomism of the Renaissance," *Doctor Communis* 45 (1992): 132–52.

27. Anton Krempel, *La Doctrine de la Relation chez Saint Thomas: Exposé historique et systématique* (Paris: J. Vrin, 1952), 29. For information about Sutton's place in early Thomism, see Roensch, *Early Thomistic School*, 44–51 and 73–78. Roensch says that Sutton "represents a high point in the progress of Thomism and occupies a position of superiority in matters of doctrinal analysis among his fellow Dominicans" (51).

28. For example, see E. J. Ashworth, "Analogical Concepts: The Fourteenth-Century Background to Cajetan," *Dialogue: Canadian Philosophical Review* 31 (Summer 1992): 404. Ashworth corrects herself on this point in "Analogy and Equivocation in Thomas Sutton O.P.," in *Vestigia, Imagines, Verba: Semiotics and Logic in Medieval Theological Texts (XIIth–XIV Century). Acts of the XIth Symposium on Medieval logic and semantics. San Marino, 24–28 May 1994*, ed. Marmo Costantino (Turnhout: Brepols, 1997), 291.

number of Sutton's works survive and have twentieth-century critical editions.²⁹ Here I follow the example of Przezdziecki, Ashworth, and Henninger by drawing Sutton's doctrine of analogy from his *Quaestiones Ordinariae* 32–33.

Chapter 2 also shows that these English and French Dominicans agree about the *Rationes* Problem but part ways on the Analogy Model Problem. Specifically, Sutton and Natalis agree that there are at least two distinct *rationes* analogous to each other when the same name is said analogously of God and creatures. Sutton, however, argues for Principle Model analogy to explain these predications, while Natalis holds for the Healthy Model. The chapter concludes with an evaluation of the consequences their commitments to the Analogy Model Problem have for their ability to solve the Equivocation Problem.

The third chapter considers the French Dominican John Capreolus (1380–1444). Romanus Cesario calls him "the champion of a small, anti-revisionist movement that, in effect, became a nucleus of the Thomism that during the Italian renaissance flourished in its own circles and even influenced certain secular humanists."³⁰ Cesario adds that Capreolus's *Defensiones Theologiae Divis Thomae Aquinatis* "embodies the first comprehensive presentation of Thomist theology" and "merited Capreolus ... the title *Princeps Thomistarum*, the Prince of Thomists."³¹

Capreolus and the fifteenth-century Italian Thomists familiar with his work set aside the early fourteenth-century Thomists' *diversae rationes* answer to the *Rationes* Problem. Although their explanations vary, prominent fifteenth- and sixteenth-century Thomists held that there is one *ratio* shared in analogously when names are said of God and creatures in natural theology. To make this change work within Thomist principles, Capreolus integrates an understanding

---

29. On the life and works of Thomas Sutton, see Gyula Klima, "Thomas of Sutton," in *Companion to Philosophy in the Middle Ages* (ed. Gracia and Noone), 664–65.

30. Romanus Cesario, *A Short History of Thomism* (Washington, D.C.: The Catholic University of America Press, 2005), 59.

31. Ibid., 61.

both of analogy and of univocity foreign to the earlier Thomists. Chapter 3 traces the origins of Capreolus's revised Thomist understanding of analogy and univocity to the writings of the French Franciscan Peter Auriol (1280–1322).[32]

With respect to the Analogy Model Problem, Capreolus initiates the practice of presenting the division of analogy found in Aquinas (*In 1 Sent*, d. 19, q. 5, a. 2, ad 1) as key for Thomas's understanding of how names are said of God and creatures in natural theology. In that passage, Thomas gives a threefold division of analogy. In the first mode of analogy, Thomas says, "one intention is referred to many by priority and posteriority, although the intention has being [*esse*] in only one." As an example, he points to "health," which "is referred to an animal, urine, and diet in diverse ways, according to the prior and posterior" even though health only exists in an animal. The second mode is analogy "according to being [*esse*] and not according to intention." In describing this mode of analogy, Aquinas gives the example of "body" said of corruptible and of incorruptible bodies and he distinguishes the perspective of the logician from the perspective of the metaphysician or natural philosopher. He says "the Logician, who considers intentions alone, says that the name 'body' is predicated univocally about all bodies, but the being [*esse*] of this nature does not belong to the same *ratio* in corruptible and incorruptible bodies." By contrast, "the Metaphysician and the Natural Philosopher, who consider things according to their being [*esse*]," hold that "neither the name 'body' nor anything else is said univocally about the corruptible and incorruptible." The third mode is analogy "according to intention and according to being [*esse*]." In this mode of analogy, Aquinas says that "it is necessary that the common nature has some being [*esse*] in each one of those things about which it is said, but differing according to a *ratio* of greater and of lesser perfec-

---

32. On the life and work of Peter Auriol, see Lauge O. Nielsen, "Peter Auriol," in *Companion to Philosophy in the Middle Ages* (ed. Gracia and Noone), 494–503. E. J. Ashworth has treated Auriol's position on analogy in the context of the fourteenth-century background to Cajetan. See Ashworth, "Analogical Concepts," 408–9, and *Les theories de l'analogie du XIIe au XVIe siecle* (Paris: Vrin, 2008), 71.

tion." As examples, Aquinas points to being (*ens*) said of substance and accidents and to names such as "truth" and "goodness" said about God and creatures.[33]

Several prominent Scholastic Thomists, including Paul Soncinas (d. 1494), Thomas de Vio Cajetan (1469–1534), and Chrysostom Javelli (ca. 1470/72–ca. 1538), follow Capreolus's lead in giving primacy to this threefold division of analogy. It is less well-known, even among the Scholastic Thomists who cite Capreolus on the threefold division of analogy, that Capreolus also considered this passage to be consistent with Aquinas's other texts which provide twofold divisions of analogy, including both *De Veritate*, q. 2, a. 11, and *Summa Theologiae* I, q. 13, a. 5. *De Veritate*, q. 2, a. 11, divides analogy into analogy of determinate proportion and analogy of indeterminate proportion or proportionality. Examples of determinate proportion include "being" said of substance and accident and "health" said of urine and an animal. Examples of proportionality are "sight" said of bodily sight and intellectual sight "because as sight is in the eye so too understanding is in the mind." Aquinas writes here that names can only be said analogously of God and creatures by proportionality and not by determinate proportion.[34] In *Summa Theologiae* I, q. 13, a. 5, however, Aquinas divides analogy by whether "many have proportion to one" or "one has proportion to another." He gives examples of the way health is predicated for both modes of analogy, but puts names said of God and creatures only within "one-to-another."[35] Chapter 3 concludes by showing how Capreolus's determination to answer the Equivocation Problem moved him to answer the *Rationes* and Analogy Model Problems differently than his Thomist predecessors.

The remainder of the Thomists treated in this book studied or taught at Bologna during the second half of the fifteenth century or

---

33. Aquinas, *In 1 Sent.*, d. 19, q. 5, a. 2, ad 1, in *Scriptum super libros sententiarum*, ed. Pierre Mandonnet and M. F. Moos (Paris: Lethielleux, 1929–47), 1:492.
34. Aquinas, *De Veritate*, q. 2, a. 11 (Leonine, 22.1:79.135–93).
35. Aquinas, *Summa Theologiae* I, q. 13, a. 5.

the first half of the sixteenth century. Chapter 4 takes up the positions of the fifteenth-century Dominicans Paul Soncinas and Dominic of Flanders (1425–79), also called "Flandrensis."[36] These two authors introduce novel variations of Capreolus's answer to the *Rationes* Problem, and they recapitulate in a more complex way the differences between Sutton and Natalis over the answer to the Analogy Model Problem. Texts considered include both authors' books of questions on Aristotle's *Metaphysics* as well as their major logical treatises: Flandrensis's *De Fallaciis* and Soncinas's *Expositio Super Artem Veterem Aristotelis*.[37]

Chapter 5 turns to Thomas de Vio Cajetan. His writings on analogy are certainly the best known and most debated among the figures considered in this study, both in his own day and subsequently.[38] As a student, master, or Dominican master general to Flandrensis, Soncinas, Francis Silvestri of Ferrara (1474–1528), and Chrysostom Javelli, Cajetan serves as a unifying figure for the fifteenth- and sixteenth-century Bologna school Thomists. Cajetan's answers in his *In De Ente et Essentia, De Nominum Analogia*, and *De Conceptu Entis* are repeated here for the sake of clearly indicating points of continuity and departure with the Thomist tradition on the three problems outlined above.

The sixth chapter treats the critical reception of Cajetan's position in the first half of the sixteenth century by Francis Silvestri of Ferrera (hereafter, Ferrariensis) and Chrysostom Javelli.[39] Fer-

---

36. Studies of the metaphysics of Dominic of Flanders which also provide short accounts of his life and works include F. Riva, "L'Analogia Dell'ente in Domenico di Fiandra," *Rivista di Filosofia Neo-Scolastica* 86 (1994): 287–322, and L. Mahieu, *Dominique de Flandre (XVe siècle) sa métaphysique* (Paris: J. Vrin, 1942). On the life and works of Paul Soncinas, see Efrem Jindráček, "Soncino, Paulo Barbo," *Encyclopedia of Renaissance Philosophy*, Springer International Publishing Switzerland, 2015, and "Paolo Barbò da Soncino: la vita ed il pensiero di un tomista rinascimentale," *Archivum Fratrum Praedicatorum* 78 (2008): 79–148.

37. Soncinas's text will be hereafter referred to as *Super Artem*.

38. On the life and works of Cajetan, see Charles H. Lohr, "Renaissance Latin Aristotle Commentaries: Authors C," *Renaissance Quarterly* 28 (Winter 1975): 692–95.

39. On the life and works of Chrysostom Javelli, see Charles H. Lohr, "Renaissance Latin Aristotle Commentaries: Authors G–K," *Renaissance Quarterly* 30 (Winter 1975):

rariensis's *Commentary on the Summa Contra Gentiles of St. Thomas Aquinas* provides a striking hybrid of his predecessors' answers to the *Rationes* and Analogy Model Problems while still maintaining the semantic resources for a principled answer to the Equivocation Problem. More than any of the other authors considered here, Ferrariensis works at integrating the variations in the texts by Thomas Aquinas that generate the Analogy Model Problem. Javelli, for his part, accepts Capreolus's answer to the Analogy Model Problem, and develops Soncinas's solution to the *Rationes* and Equivocation Problems in a unique way intended (seemingly) to address Cajetan's objections to Soncinas's answer to the *Rationes* Problem. For Javelli, I draw primarily from his book of questions on Aristotle's *Metaphysics* and his *In Logicam Aristotelis*, but also from other works including his short work on the transcendentals.

The concluding chapter gives a summary and evaluation of the Thomists' work. It also makes suggestions for further lines of investigation necessary for resolving the three problems.

730–33. On Francis Silvestri, see Michael Tavuzzi, "Silvestri, Francesco (1474–1528)," in *Concise Routledge Encyclopedia of Philosophy* (London: Routledge, 2000).

1

The Objection from John Duns Scotus

Scotus argues for the univocity of "being" and some other names said of God and creatures for the same reason that Aquinas argues against it; namely, to preserve the sciences of theology and metaphysics within an Aristotelian theory of the natural modes of human knowing. For the purposes of understanding Scotus's role in the development of Thomist thought, I follow the convention of looking to Scotus's *Ordinatio* I, d. 3, and *Super Libros Metaphysicorum*, l. 4, q. 1, as the primary expositions of Scotus's understanding of univocity and his objections to analogy in demonstration.

SCOTUS'S DEFINITION OF UNIVOCITY

In both texts, Scotus attempts to avoid unnecessary argument over the use of words by explaining his use of the word "univocal." The reader of Scotus's *Super Libros Metaphysicorum* finds that the debate over whether or not "being" is univocal concerns whether there is a name signifying one concept of being common to the ten categories.[1] By implication, a name is said univocally of many when it

1. Scotus, *Quaestiones Super Libros Metaphysicorum Aristotelis*, l. 4, q. 1, I. Ad quaestionem, nn. 27–28, in *Opera Philosophica*, ed. R. Andrews et al. (St. Bonaventure, N. Y.:

signifies through one and same *ratio* or concept. In his *Ordinatio*, Scotus says that a "univocal concept" satisfies two conditions: (1) it has unity sufficient for it to be a contradiction to affirm and deny it of the same thing, and (2) it has unity sufficient to be used in a demonstration without committing the fallacy of equivocation.[2]

Unfortunately, Scotus's attempt to avoid confusion on the use of the word "univocal" did not prove entirely successful, and has instead generated diverse interpretations (although perhaps not quite so many interpretations as Aquinas's discussions of analogy). One point of disagreement among interpreters of Scotus is over whether satisfying the two conditions mentioned in the *Ordinatio* text is sufficient to make a concept univocal. Ingham, Dreyer, and Dumont regard these as Scotus's sufficient conditions for univocity.[3] Richard Cross, however, regards them as merely necessary conditions. According to Cross: "They merely describe properties that a univocal concept will have. Equally, these two descriptions do not sufficient-

---

Franciscan Institute, 1997) (hereafter, *OP*), 301: "Ad quaestionem istam de univocatione entis dicitur quod quaestio est de significato nominis, quod est ad placitum. Ideo non potest terminari per rationem, sed tantum per auctoritatem vel per usum, quia 'loquendum est ut plures,' II *Topicorum.* Sed contra: quaestio est utrum possit esse aliquis conceptus communis decem generibus, quocumque nomine illud significetur, sive per 'ens' sive per aliud nomen. Posse autem esse talem conceptum vel non, potest argui ratione."

2. Scotus, *Ordinatio* I, d. 3, pars 1, qq. 1–2, n. 26, in *Opera Omnia*, ed. Scotistic Commission (Vatican City: Typis Polyglottis Vaticanis, 1954) (hereafter, *VC*), 3:18: "Et ne fiat contentio de nomine univocationis, univocum conceptum dico, qui ita est unus quod eius unitas sufficit ad contradictionem, affirmando et negando ipsum de eodem; sufficit etiam pro medio syllogistico, ut extrema unita in medio sic uno sine fallacia aequivocationis concludantur inter se uniri."

3. Mary Beth Ingham and Mechthild Dreyer, *Philosophical Vision of John Duns Scotus: An Introduction* (Washington, D.C.: The Catholic University of America Press, 2004), 39–40. Stephen Dumont, "Transcendental Being: Scotus and the Scotists," *Topoi* 11 (1992): 137: "Scotus defines a univocal concept as one whose unity is sufficient to cause a contradiction when asserted and denied of the same thing or, alternatively, one whose unity enables it to function as a middle term in a syllogism. These definitions of univocity, while not incompatible with, differ from the standard one taken from the opening lines of Aristotle's Categories, according to which something is univocal if both its name and essence or definition (*ratio*) are one. Scotus prefers instead to give a functional definition of the univocity he is about to demonstrate, namely, the concept of being will be univocal enough to guarantee the law of noncontradiction and to avoid the fallacy of equivocation in reasoning about God and substances."

ly demarcate univocal concepts from analogous or equivocal ones, although of course satisfying the two descriptions will be *necessary* for univocity."[4]

In other words, Cross believes that the *Ordinatio* treatment of the conditions for univocity should not be taken without the *Super Libros Metaphysicorum* description of univocals in terms of agreement in a single concept. Quoting a more recent article by Cross: "The feature of a single concept—a univocal concept, in Scotus's jargon—is that it has *identity of informational content* wherever it is realized. All simple concepts will count as univocal; analogous concepts include univocal ones."[5]

From Scotus's texts and the contemporary debate over Scotus's own doctrine of analogy and univocity, the reader can deduce that Scotus maintains at least the following as features (if not properties in the strict sense) of univocal terms. Univocal terms have: (1) sufficient unity for a contradiction, (2) sufficient unity for mediating a syllogism validly, and (3) signification through a single concept. The primary point of dispute with the Thomists will be over (2), that is, over whether only univocal terms have sufficient unity for mediating a syllogism without falling into the fallacy of equivocation. The Thomists will maintain that validly mediating a syllogism is not a unique property of univocal terms, but one that can also belong to analogous terms. In subsequent chapters, it will be seen that the Thomists address their dispute with Scotus on this point by arguing that analogous terms (at least some kinds of analogous terms, sometimes) have one or both of the other two characteristics of univocal terms identified by Scotus (sufficient unity for a contradiction, and signification through a single concept).

---

4. See Richard Cross, *Duns Scotus* (Cary, N.C.: Oxford University Press, 1999), 37 and 169n28.

5. Richard Cross, "Univocity and Mystery," in *New Essays on Metaphysics as Scientia Transcendens*, ed. R. H. Pich, Textes et Etudes du Moyen Âge 43 (Louvain-La-Neuve: Fédération Internationale des Instituts d'Études Médiévales, 2007), 119.

Objection from John Duns Scotus

SCOTUS *CONTRA* ANALOGY IN NATURAL THEOLOGY

The direct target of Scotus's *Ordinatio* critique of analogy as a foundation for natural theology is the doctrine of Henry of Ghent (1217–93).[6] Henry of Ghent was one of the great figures at the University of Paris in the closing decades of the fourteenth century and was regent master from 1276 to 1292/93.[7] The richness of the Ghentian's doctrine is passed over here, and is instead treated only as context for Scotus's criticism of analogy in metaphysics.

Henry of Ghent's stance on the *Rationes* Problem is reflected in a passage wherein he explains why some, mistakenly, suppose that one *ratio* or concept applies both to the being of creatures and to divine being.[8] Henry of Ghent explains that a concept of being can be inde-

---

6. On the direction of Scotus's criticism at Henry of Ghent, see Etienne Gilson, *Jean Duns Scot: Introduction à ses positions fondamentales* (Paris: J. Vrin, 1952), 88. See also Alexander Hall, *Thomas Aquinas and John Duns Scotus: Natural Theology in the High Middle Ages*, Continuum Studies in Philosophy (London: Continuum, 2007), 13–26, esp. 17.

7. R. Wielockx, "Henry of Ghent," in *Companion to Philosophy in the Middle Ages* (ed. Gracia and Noone), 296.

8. Henry of Ghent, *Summa questionum ordinarium*, a. 21, q. 2, ad 3, in *Henry of Ghent's Summa: The Questions on God's Existence and Essence (Articles 21–24)* (Leuven: Peeters, 2005), 58–60: "Per hunc ergo modum esse indeterminatum per abnegationem convenit Deo, et per privationem creaturae. Et quia indeterminatio per abnegationem et per privationem propinquae sunt, quia ambae tollunt determinationem, una tamen secundum actum, alia secundum actum simul et potentiam, ideo non potentes distinguere inter huiusmodi diversa pro eodem concipiunt esse simpliciter et esse indeterminatum, sive uno modo sive altero, sive sit Dei, sive creaturae. Natura enim est intellectus non potentis distinguere ea quae propinqua sunt, concipere ipsa ut unum, quae tamen in rei veritate non faciunt unum conceptum. Et ideo est error in illius conceptu. Verus enim conceptus primo concipiendo esse simpliciter indeterminatum quod ratione suae indeterminationis nihil ponit omnino neque determinat, ut ex hoc nihil sit re commune Deo et creaturae positivum, sed negativum solum, et si aliquid sit positivum substratum negationi, illud est alterius et alterius rationis, sicut quod est per essentiam et quod est per participationem, quae consequenter rectus intellectus bene distinguit concipiendo esse indeterminatum vel negative vel privative, et secundum hoc bene processit primum argumentum in oppositum." (Because indetermination through negation and through privation are so close, in that both take away determination—one by act and the other by both act and potency—those not able to distinguish between different things of this kind conceive absolute *esse* and indeterminate *esse* as though they are the same. That individual either conceives both of these in the way that indeterminate being belongs to

terminate in two ways. One way, namely the negative way, is proper to God. The other, the privative way, is proper to creaturely indeterminate being. These indeterminate yet distinct concepts are so similar that a human intellect can mistakenly believe that they are identical.[9] Hence, according to Henry of Ghent, the fact that someone can think that there is one *ratio* through which a name can be signified commonly of God and creatures is an explainable psychological error. The correct answer to the *Rationes* Problem is that there are two diverse, indeterminate *rationes*.

Turning back to Scotus's *Ordinatio*, the question that generates arguments against analogy in natural theology is: "Can the intellect of the wayfarer have a simple concept in which God is conceived?"[10] Scotus observes that if knowledge of God is arrived at discursively, and if discursive knowledge begins with knowledge of creatures, then at the end of the discursive process the reasoner acquires either (1) a concept of God or (2) a concept which is not of God but

---

God or in the way indeterminate being belongs to creatures. This happens because it is the nature of the intellect of someone not able to distinguish things which are close to conceive those things as one, even though in reality those things do not make one concept. There is error in their concept. The true concept, in the one first conceiving absolutely undetermined being [*esse*], posits nothing due to its indetermination. Nor does it determine, as is evident from the fact that there is nothing in reality common to God and creature positively, but only negatively. If there is something positive which is the substrate to a negation, there is still one *ratio* for God and another for the creature, such as "what is through its essence" and "what is through participation." The right intellect makes a good distinction by conceiving indeterminate being as either negative or privative.) All translations are mine, unless otherwise noted.

9. On these points, see also Jos Decorte, "Henry of Ghent on Analogy: Critical Reflexions on Jean Paulus," in *Henry of Ghent: Proceedings of the International Colloquium on the Occasion of the 700th Anniversary of His Death (1293)*, ed. W. Vanhamel (Leuven: Leuven University Press, 1996), 74. For more on Henry of Ghent's notions of privative and negative indeterminacy, see especially his discussion of privatively and negatively indeterminate goodness in *Summa questionum ordinarium*, a. 24, q. 7 (246–48). See also Dumont, "Transcendental Being," 136. For a brief account of unity of "confusion" and Henry of Ghent's understanding of analogy, see Stephen Dumont, "The Univocal Concept of Being in the Fourteenth Century: I. John Duns Scotus and William of Alnwick," *Mediaeval Studies* 49 (1987): 7–8.

10. Scotus, *Ordinatio* I, d. 3, pars 1, qq. 1–2 (*VC* 3:11) "Est ergo mens questionis ista, utrum aliquem conceptum simplicem possit intellectus viatoris habere in quo conceptu simplici concipiatur Deus."

of a creature. If (2), then the reasoner fails in the attempt to achieve knowledge of God from knowledge of creatures.[11] Scotus proceeds in this text to give five reasons why the concept of God which the natural theologian looks for must be univocal to the concept of the creature with which the natural theologian's discursive reasoning begins.[12] I see three of these arguments as particularly pertinent to the Thomist discussion of the three problems.

Scotus's first argument is particularly influential on Thomist answers to the *Rationes* Problem. (In subsequent chapters, this argument will be called the "'Certain and Doubtful' Argument.") The argument begins from the observation that someone's intellect can be certain of one concept and doubtful of others, but no intellect can be both certain and doubtful of the same concept at the same time. It follows that an inquirer can be certain that God is a being while at the same time uncertain or doubtful of whether God is a finite being or an infinite being, a created being or an uncreated being. Consequently, the concept of "being" that the inquirer affirms about God must be distinct from the concepts of finite being or infinite being, created being and uncreated being, which the inquirer refrains from affirming or denying about God.

To support his argument, Scotus describes the situation of a student listening to philosophers disagree about what the first principle is. This student is certain that the first principle is a being, and yet doubtful regarding whether the first principle is fire, water, etc. The student's doubt over what sort of being the first principle is, however, does not cause the student to doubt that the first principle is a being. The student will not lose certainty that the first principle is being even if the student learns that the first principle is not fire, but water, etc.

---

11. Ibid., n. 15 (*VC* 3:7).
12. For a brief summary of all five arguments, see Luis Alberto De Boni, "Duns Scotus and the Univocity of the Concept of Being," in *New Essays on Metaphysics as Scientia Transcendens* (ed. Pich), 102–12. For a fuller description of all five arguments given in the context of Scotus's overall cognitional theory, see Ingham and Dreyer, *Philosophical Vision of John Duns Scotus*, 38–47.

Objection from John Duns Scotus

To this argument, Scotus adds a direct critique of Henry of Ghent's model of analogy through proximity of concepts. Should someone say that the imaginary philosophy student has two very similar concepts rather than one simple concept of being, Scotus warns that this would destroy univocity and at the same time knowledge of common natures, as univocity involves proximate concepts. According to Scotus, by Henry of Ghent's account of analogy, one could just as well say that there is not one concept of "human" for Socrates and Plato, but two concepts that seem to be one because of their great similarity. Scotus implies that any commonly accepted instance of univocal concepts could fit into Henry of Ghent's description of two analogous, indeterminate concepts which have been confused for one concept. Consequently, if the Ghentian's view holds, it is impossible to ever identify an instance of a univocal concept, as one could always argue that there are really diverse, indeterminate concepts mistaken for one concept.[13]

Scotus's second argument disputes the possibility of acquiring an analogous concept which could be used to demonstrate a divine attribute if the reasoner did not already know that God has that attribute. The argument proceeds through an account of knowledge acquired through sense experience. In this life, Scotus observes (with the Aristotelian tradition),[14] that the human intellect acquires concepts naturally only by means of what naturally moves our intellect, and what naturally moves our intellect proceeds through our sense powers and active intellect. Because the active intellect can only produce a concept that is univocal with what is revealed in the sensory image, it is impossible to have any natural knowledge of God by anything other than a univocal concept. That is, because the natural

---

13. For the full text of the argument, see Scotus, *Ordinatio* I, d. 3, pars 1, qq. 1–2, nn. 27–30 (*VC* 3:18–20).

14. On Scotus's Aristotelian theory of cognition, Pasnau writes that "Scotus accepts the general cognitive framework set out by his most distinguished recent predecessors, Thomas Aquinas and Henry of Ghent; where he disagrees, he does so in ways that reinforce the broader contours of the theory." See R. Pasnau, "Cognition," in *The Cambridge Companion to Duns Scotus*, ed. Thomas Williams (Cambridge: Cambridge University Press, 2003), 285.

modes of knowing only provide univocal concepts (and no analogous concepts), if we have natural knowledge of God, the concepts involved are univocal to God and creatures.

Scotus defends his assumption that the human intellect cannot produce analogous concepts from its natural objects on the grounds that the intellect can produce only one of two things from a sense image or intelligible species. Either it produces a proper concept of the object, or it produces a concept of what is essentially or virtually included in the object. As an analogous concept is neither one of the above, the intellect cannot produce an analogous concept naturally.[15]

While the first argument serves Scotus by showing that basing natural theology on analogy (at least as understood by Henry of Ghent) would destroy univocity and thereby knowledge and argument, this second argument serves to show that one simply could not arrive at a concept analogous to God and creature without already knowing both the creature and God. One could not think of two concepts as similar or confuse two concepts as one concept if one did not already possess both concepts. Because recognizing an analogy analogy between God and creatures follows upon comparing what one knows of God and what one knows of creatures, analogy cannot produce demonstrative knowledge of God from creatures. Rather, analogy depends on demonstrative knowledge of God from creatures.

The fourth argument most directly addresses the issue of the fallacy of equivocation. Scotus begins with the premise that either a pure perfection has a *ratio* common to God and to a creature or it does not. If it does not, then either the concept is proper to the creature only and its *ratio* does not belong formally to God, or its *ratio* is altogether proper to God. If the *ratio* is altogether proper to the creature, then one cannot attribute a pure perfection known in a crea-

---

15. For the full text of the argument, see Scotus, *Ordinatio* I, d. 3, pars 1, qq. 1–2, n. 35 (*VC* 3:21–24). See Richard Cross's short summary of this argument in his *Duns Scotus*, 36–37.

ture to God (which is unacceptable to theology and metaphysics). On the other hand, if the *ratio* is altogether proper to God, then it follows that no pure perfection (*perfectio simpliciter*) would be in a creature (which is contrary to experience).

To confirm this argument's reasoning, Scotus argues further that every question concerning any divine attribute supposes there is the same univocal concept of that attribute in God and in creatures. If this were not the case, then the concept through which the name is said of God is distinct from the concept through which the name is said of the creature. And if there are two different concepts or *rationes* for the name said of God and creatures, then there is no more reason to say that God is wise drawing on the *ratio* of created wisdom than there is reason to say that God is a stone drawing on the *ratio* of stones.[16] Scotus's point is that unless the *ratio* signified by a name is the same in both places it occurs in a demonstration, absurd consequences follow. And if the *ratio* signified by the name is the same in both places it occurs in a demonstration, it is predicated univocally. Consequently, if there is to be science of God, it must rely on names said through one and the same *ratio* and, therefore, on univocity and not on analogy.

Metaphysical and Semantic Considerations of Univocity and Analogy in Scotus

Before moving on to the Thomists' attempts to respond to Scotus's objections to analogy in metaphysics and natural theology, some metaphysical and semantic disputes over Scotus's position should be considered for the purposes of more clearly distinguishing and comparing Scotus's position to those of the Thomists responding to him.

Scotus distinguishes in his *Ordinatio* between conceptual and real diversity, saying that God and creatures are not primarily diverse in concepts, although they are primarily diverse in reality because

---

16. For the full text of the argument, see Scotus, *Ordinatio* I, d. 3, pars 1, qq. 1–2, nn. 38–40 (*VC* 3:25–27).

they agree in no reality.¹⁷ In other words, although Scotus holds that God and creatures agree in one univocal concept—including the concept signified through the name "being"—he also says that the concept of being is not answered by a single reality, in the way that, for example, the concept signified by the name "animal" both is said univocally of a man and a horse and corresponds to a reality present in a man and in a horse univocally. Scotus's *Super De Anima* and *Super Libros Metaphysicorum* find him specifically saying that although being has one concept logically that is not the case metaphysically.¹⁸

Texts such as these have provoked debate on whether Scotus restricts the univocity of being (and presumably other names said of God and creatures) to the level of concepts while granting that the realities are metaphysically analogous. In effect, does Scotus hold that being is simply speaking univocal or does he hold that being

17. See Scotus, *Ordinatio* I, d. 8, pars. 1, q. 3, n. 82 (*VC* 4:190). See also Scotus, *Lectura* I, d. 8, n. 129 (*VC* 17:46).

18. See Scotus, *Quaestiones Super Secundum et Tertium De Anima*, q. 21 (*OP* 5:224.10–14): "omnia entia habent attributionem ad ens primum, quod est Deus, vel entia creata ad substantiam; tamen, hoc non obstante, potest ab omnibus istis entibus abstrahi unus communis conceptus significatus nomine entis, qui est univocus logice loquendo, licet non naturaliter vel metaphysice loquendo." (All beings have attribution to the first being, which is God, or created beings to substance. Nevertheless, not withstanding this, one common concept, which is signified by the name "being," can be abstracted from all those beings. This concept is univocal logically speaking, although it is not [univocal] naturally and metaphysically speaking.) See also Scotus, *Super Libros Metaphysicorum*, l. 4, q. 1, n. 70 (*OP* 3:315–16): "Ad quaestionem, concedo quod ens non dicatur aequivoce, quia aequivoce dicitur aliquid de multis quando illa de quibus dicitur non habent attributionem ad invicem; sed quando attribuuntur, tunc analogice. Quia ergo non habet conceptum unum, ideo significat omnia essentialiter secundum propriam rationem, et simpliciter aequivoce secundum logicum. Quia autem illa quae significantur, inter se essentialiter attribuuntur, ideo analogice secundum metaphysicum realem." (To the question, I concede that being is not said equivocally, because something is said equivocally about many things when those things about which it is said do not have attribution to each other. But when the things are attributed [to each other], then [something is said of many] analogously. Therefore, because [being] does not have one concept, it follows that [being] signifies all things essentially according to proper *ratio*, and absolutely equivocally according to the logician. But because the things which are signified have attribution between them essentially, it follows that [being is said about them] analogously according to metaphysical reality.) For a treatment of similar passages from Scotus, see Alexander Hall, "Confused Univocity," *Proceedings of the Society for Medieval Logic and Metaphysics* 7 (2007): 20.

Objection from John Duns Scotus

(as Aquinas said about body) is univocal to the logician although analogous to the metaphysician? Even early Scotists disagree on this very point, with some Scotists contending that univocity extends to the real order and others holding that univocity pertains only to the order of logic.[19] Among contemporary scholars, Ingham and Dreyer cite Scotus's *Super Libros Metaphysicorum*, l. 4, q. 1, and say that Scotus holds there that "the metaphysician (who deals with reality) attributes according to analogy, while the logician would deem this equivocation."[20] Richard Cross, E. J. Ashworth, and Olivier Boulnois agree based on the same text, with Cross also noting the same argument appears in Scotus's *Super Praedicamenta Aristotelis*.[21] Gilson says about *Super Libros Metaphysicorum*, l. 4, q. 1, that it "has been the despair of generations of Scotists, firm partisans of the univocity of being, that they find before them a radical negation of univocity and an express decision of Duns Scotus in favour of analogy."[22] Boulnois has produced a detailed account of Scotus's treatments of univocity and its conditions in his early logical works as well as his commentaries on the *Sentences* and on the philosophical works of Aristotle.[23] He argues that Scotus's position develops over time while remaining the same in some essential points, including that being (*ens*) cannot be logically analogous, and that being can be analogous in reality for the metaphysician.[24]

Contrary to the aforementioned scholars, a note contained in

---

19. For a discussion of this point in the writings of fourteenth-century Scotists, see Dumont, "Transcendental Being," 135–48.
20. Ingham and Dreyer, *Philosophical Vision of John Duns Scotus*, 40n24.
21. Cross, *Duns Scotus*, 169n32: "Scotus clearly allows for analogical senses for terms referring to crucial transcendental attributes such as being." Scotus, *Quaestiones Super Praedicamenta Aristotelis*, q. 4, n. 38 (*OP* 1:285.11–21). E. J. Ashworth, "Analogy, Univocation, and Equivocation in Some Early Fourteenth-Century Authors," in *Aristotle in Britain during the Middle Ages*, ed. John Marenbon (Turnhout: Brepols, 1996), 244–45. Olivier Boulnois, "Duns Scot, Theoricien De L'Analogie de L'Etre," in *John Duns Scotus, Metaphysics and Ethics*, ed. L. Honnefelder, R. Wood, M. Dreyer (Leiden: Brill, 1996), 302.
22. Etienne Gilson, "Avicenne et le point de départ de Duns Scot," *Archives d'Histoire doctrinale et littéraire du Moyen Age* 2 (1927): 105.
23. Boulnois, "Duns Scot," 293–315.
24. Ibid., 314.

Objection from John Duns Scotus

the 1997 critical edition of Scotus's *Super Libros Metaphysicorum* argues that the passage where Scotus supports analogy of being is a marginal note and that the diligent reader can see that it does not reflect Scotus's own opinion. The note adds that this is clear from the fact that the remainder of the column where the argument is found is devoted to proving univocity.[25] The parallel passage cited by Cross in Scotus's *Super Praedicamenta Aristotelis* is open to the same criticism. There too, Scotus describes "being" as analogous to the metaphysician but equivocal to the logician in a column followed by a series of arguments proving that being is univocal. It does not seem unreasonable to suppose that this passage also could be Scotus's note to himself about the position that he is opposing.

There is at least then some ambiguity about the truth of the statement: "Scotus teaches univocity of being." Nevertheless, it is clear that Scotus teaches that "being" is said univocally of God and creatures and that this means the human intellect forms one concept of "being" by which it names God and creatures. It is also clear that he teaches that there must be one univocal concept of being for there to be scientific demonstration of the existence and attributes of God. It is to these positions that we find the medieval and Scholastic Thomists addressing their defenses of Aquinas, while providing their rival developments (or distortions) of Aquinas's doctrine.

Before concluding with Scotus, some remarks on his positive doctrine of analogy are in order. Scotus rejects analogy as a foundation for natural theology, but he does not exclude analogy from natural theology altogether, as has been pointed out recently by Richard Cross in a response to Joshua Hochschild's criticisms of attempts

---

25. See Scotus, *Super Libros Metaphysicorum*, l. 4, q. 1, n. 70 (*OP* 3:315d): "*Sequuntur adnotationes interpolatae*: Haec non est opinio istius Doctoris sicut patet diligenter consideranti. Opinio propria quam tamen non tenet modo. Item nota quomodo tenet analogiam. Alias tamen tenuit univocationem quod in aliis magis manifestat. Item nota solutiones rationum probantes univocationem ulterius per totam columnam. Responsio ad quaestionem quam non tenuit in *Sententiis*." The "in *Sententiis*" texts referred to are *Lectura* I, d. 3, pars 1, qq. 1–2, nn. 97–104 (*VC* 16:261–64), and *Ordinatio* I, d. 3, pars 1, q. 3, nn. 131–51 (*VC* 3:81–94).

to reduce analogous unity to univocity.²⁶ Although I demur from Cross's overall conclusion about the semantics of analogy, I follow his interpretation of Scotus for the following points about Scotus's semantics of analogy.²⁷

According to Scotus, analogy occurs between two or more complex concepts if they agree (or overlap) in one of the simple (or simpler) parts of their definitions. Without overlapping content, any two concepts are altogether diverse or equivocal. But, because all conceptual agreement is univocal, where there is any overlap of content between two concepts, there is univocity. Analogous agreement, then, is a certain kind of univocal agreement. A parallel passage to Scotus's first argument for univocity in natural theology serves as a primary text for Cross's interpretation. See Cross's translation of a passage from *Ordinatio* I, d. 8:

When the intellect is certain, it is certain either of a concept that is one simply speaking, or not, but [certain] of [a concept that is one] by the unity of analogy. If the first—and [it is] not [certain] of either concept (since it is doubtful about each of these in particular)—then it is certain of some third concept that is simply one: which is what is proposed. If the second, it is true to the extent that [the concept] is one in that way [i.e., by the unity of analogy]. But I argue about the [concept] that is thus one, that [the intellect] cannot be certain of what is one by the unity of analogy unless it is certain of the two as they are two: therefore those two do not seem to the intellect to be one, because they are simultaneously conceived as distinct concepts.²⁸

---

26. Cross refers specifically to Joshua P. Hochschild, *The Semantics of Analogy: Rereading Cajetan's De Nominum Analogia* (Notre Dame, Ind.: University of Notre Dame Press, 2010), 135. See Hochschild's discussion of the conditions for "an acceptable theory of analogy" at 134–35. Hochschild follows Yves Simon's "nonreductionist" understanding of analogy. For Simon's position, see his "Order in Analogical Sets," in *Philosopher at Work: Essays by Yves R. Simon*, ed. Anthony O. Simon (Lanham, Md.: Rowman and Littlefield, 1999), 135–71, esp. 140–41.

27. I follow the same practice in Domenic D'Ettore, "The Semantic Unity of the Analogous Concept according to John Capreolus," in *Maimonides on God and Duns Scotus on Logic and Metaphysics (Volume 12: Proceedings of the Society of Medieval Logic and Metaphysics)*, ed. Gyula Klima and Alexander W. Hall (Newcastle upon Tyne: Cambridge Scholars Publishing, 2015), 134–38.

28. Scotus, Ordinatio I, d. 8, pars 1, q. 3, n. 67 (*VC* 4:183), as translated in Richard

Out of this treatment of the semantics of analogous terms we can more clearly see how Scotus would answer the *Rationes* Problem. The signification of one complex *ratio* is analogous to the signification of another complex *ratio* because both share in one common (simple or simpler) *ratio*. In the example given, the complex concepts "infinite wisdom" and "finite wisdom" are analogous concepts because both contain the concept of "wisdom." On the matter raised by this problem, of whether there is one *ratio* somehow common to analogates, Scotus's answer is a definitive "yes." There needs to be one common *ratio* for there to be commonality at all. So, if analogy is a kind of commonality, it relies on a common *ratio* between analogates.

Scotus's semantics of analogy also implies a kind of answer to the Analogy Model Problem. The kind of analogy suited to names said of God and creatures is one which preserves a univocal common content across the analogates. The problem with the models of analogy which Scotus opposes is that they lack the common core content which would provide the single (and thereby univocal) *ratio* necessary for mediating syllogisms. Henry of Ghent's analogates do not share a common *ratio*. They have two *rationes* which are mistaken for one. The Thomist debate over the Analogy Model Problem concerns the comparative unity of *ratio* between the different modes of kinds of analogy. Only an answer which finds a place for a single *ratio* somehow common to the analogates would be amenable to Scotus.

CONCLUSION

Scotus's arguments and semantics point to an insufficiency within Aristotle and Aquinas's explanations of the formation of non-univocal concepts and of their use in demonstrative science. If a Thomist insists that Aquinas's model(s) of analogous naming de-

---

Cross, "Duns Scotus and Analogy: A Brief Note," *The Modern Schoolman* 89, nos. 3–4 (July and October 2012): 151. See also Cross, *Duns Scotus*, 33–39.

mand more than one *ratio*, then the Thomist must explain how this model dodges Scotus's criticism that, without one and only one *ratio for a term*, demonstration is impossible. If a Thomist argues instead that there is one *ratio* involved in analogous signification, then the Thomist must explain the difference between his own position and that of Scotus, either admitting that analogy reduces semantically to univocity or challenging Scotus's definition(s) of univocity and analogy. Scotus's contemporary Thomists, as will be seen in the next chapter, take up the challenge of arguing that demonstration can proceed through terms used analogously even though there is no common *ratio* between them.

2

Hervaeus Natalis and Thomas Sutton
The Princes of Primitive Thomism

As mentioned in the introduction, Hervaeus Natalis and Thomas Sutton were among the most important Thomist contemporaries of John Duns Scotus. They are discussed in this chapter for their answers to the three problems regarding analogy discussed in the introduction. Natalis and Sutton give different, but not opposed answers to the *Rationes* Problem. They disagree on the Analogy Model Problem, and they give significantly different treatments of the Equivocation Problem.

Scholars of Natalis's doctrine of analogy, beginning with his contemporary opponent Peter Auriol and continuing through his fifteenth-century admirer Dominic of Flanders and up to E. J. Ashworth in the twenty-first century, have looked to his *Quodlibet* 2, q. 7, for his doctrine of names said of God and creatures. Roensch dates the composition of *Quodlibet* 2 to 1308.[1] Its content reflects an awareness of the objections of Scotus to analogy in metaphysics and demonstration. The text addresses the distinction between univocal, equivocal, and analogous naming; disjunctive unity; the distinction between what later authors call the "formal concept" and the "ob-

---

1. Roensch, *Early Thomistic School*, 113.

jective concept"; and a justification of demonstration through analogous terms.

Sutton's doctrine of analogy has received more twentieth- and twenty-first-century scholarly attention than Natalis's. In 1959, Przezdziecki noted the fact that Sutton holds analogy of proportionality for names said of God and creatures.[2] Montagnes treated Sutton briefly and critically in his book from the same period.[3] More recent articles by Ashworth and Henninger challenge Przezdziecki for including "being" among the names which Sutton says are predicated by proportionality.[4] These articles focus primarily on Sutton's analysis of the different kinds of analogy and his assessment of their suitability for naming God and creatures.[5] Here I first treat Sutton's understanding of analogous unity before looking into its application to demonstration. Following scholarly convention, I draw from Sutton's *Quaestiones Ordinariae* 32–33.[6]

---

2. Joseph J. Przezdziecki, "Thomas of Sutton's Critique of the Doctrine of Univocity," in *An Etienne Gilson Tribute*, ed. Charles O'Neil (Milwaukee, Wis.: Marquette University Press, 1959), 189–208.

3. Montagnes, *Doctrine of the Analogy of Being*, 119 and 142–43.

4. Mark Henninger, "Thomas Sutton on Univocation, Equivocation, and Analogy," *The Thomist* 70 (2006): 537–75, and Ashworth, "Analogy and Equivocation in Thomas Sutton," 289–303.

5. I discuss the aforementioned work on Sutton's doctrine of analogy in Domenic D'Ettore, "Thomas Sutton's Doctrine of Analogy: Revisiting a Continuator of Thomas Aquinas," *Nova et Vetera* (English Edition) 14 (2016): 831–52.

6. This work is also called *Questiones disputatae* 35. According to Roensch, it dates from 1295 (Roensch, *Early Thomistic School*, 50). Henninger, however, follows Schneider, editor of the 1977 edition of Sutton's *Quaestiones Ordinariae*, and dates them to 1305–10 (Henninger, "Thomas Sutton on Univocation, Equivocation, and Analogy," 540). The apparent references to Henry of Harclay's *Ordinary Questions*, written in 1300–1312 (Mark Henninger, "Henry of Harclay," in *A Companion to Philosophy in the Middle Ages* [ed. Gracia and Noone]), suggest that 1295 is too early. All my citations of Sutton's *Quaestiones Ordinariae* are taken from *Zur Diskussion über das Problem der Univozität in Umkreis des Johannes Duns Skotus*, ed. Michael Schmaus (Munich: Bayerische Akademie der Wissenschaften, 1957). There is a difference in question numbering between Schmaus's edition and the one cited by Przezdziecki. Question 32a in the Schmaus edition is question 33 in the edition cited by Przezdziecki.

NATALIS ON THE *RATIONES* AND ANALOGY MODEL PROBLEMS

Hervaeus Natalis is possibly the first thinker to distinguish explicitly the *ratio* produced in the intellect by the intellect's own act from the *ratio* in *re* which the intellect grasps. The distinction has a foundation in certain texts of Aquinas, such as *In 1 Sent.*, d. 2, q. 1, a. 3. To quote Klima's account of this passage:

> As Aquinas goes on to explain, however, we can also say that the *ratio* is in the thing. But this is not intended in the sense that the concept by which the thing is conceived of would be in the thing, for the concept is in the human mind as in its subject. What this means is that there is something in the thing corresponding to the *ratio*—what Aquinas calls the form or nature of the thing—on account of which the concept applies to this thing at all. For example, if the concept in question is a universal concept of many particulars, as the concept of man is a specific concept that represents humans in abstraction from their accidental, individuating features, then the *ratio* in the mind is this concept itself. But the *ratio* in the thing is what is represented by this concept in the thing, and that is what is referred to as human nature, or humanity, on account of which the thing represented is a human being.[7]

Other fourteenth- and fifteenth-century authors call the *ratio* in the mind the "formal concept," and the *ratio* in *re* the "objective concept." Natalis finds it useful to observe this distinction in order to address two aspects of the *Rationes* Problem. The first concerns his belief that he must deny that there is one *ratio* in any instance of analogous naming at the risk of reducing analogy to univocity.[8] The second aspect concerns strong arguments from Scotus for a single *ratio* of being. Natalis's solution grants greater unity to the *rationes* in the mind than to the *rationes* in *re*.

---

7. Klima, "Semantic Principles," 102–3.
8. See Natalis, *Quodlibet* 2, q. 7, in *Quolibeta Heruei: subtilissima Heruei Natalis Britonis* (Venice, 1513; reprinted in Ridgewood, N.J.: Gregg, 1966), 43Ra: "Univocum dicatur illud nomen quod secundum eandem rationem praedicatur de pluribus." (A name is called "univocal" which is predicated about many things according to the same *ratio*.)

Within the text, the distinction between formal and objective concepts appears in a remark about univocity. Natalis writes:

When it is said that the same *ratio* according to the same name belongs to the univocal name, "*ratio*" can be taken in two ways. In one way, [it can be taken] for the very concept of the mind. In another way, [it can be taken] for the thing understood through such a concept. When therefore it is said that the *ratio* of a univocal is one, "*ratio*" is not taken for the concept of the mind, but for the thing understood through the concept.[9]

The message is that the difference between the unity of univocal naming and the unity of analogous naming has its foundation in the *ratio* present in the things known by the intellect rather than in the product of the intellect's own act. In the case of univocity, the intellect grasps one and the same objective concept present in the things named, that is, in the univocals. In the case of pure equivocation, the objective concepts of the things named are diverse and unconnected. In the case of analogy, the objective concepts are diverse but connected.[10]

The importance of this point for Natalis appears in his rebuttal of Scotus's first argument for the univocity of "being" said of God and creatures and across the categories (i.e., his "Certain and Doubtful" Argument).[11] Natalis cannot admit to Scotus that the intellect has one formal concept of being which refers to the diverse modes of being without surrendering the grounds for denying that there is one objective concept of being answering to that formal concept. That is, if the intellect indeed possesses a single concept of being which signifies the being of God and creatures, substance and accidents, then it would seem that this concept stands over God and creatures,

---

9. Ibid., 43Rb: "Quando dicitur quod nominis univoci est eadem ratio secundum idem nomen, ratio potest dupliciter accipi. Uno modo pro ipso conceptu mentis. Alio modo pro re intellecta per talem conceptum. Quando igitur dicitur quod ratio univocorum est una non accipitur ratio pro conceptu mentis sed pro re intellecta per conceptum."

10. For an instance of this division of univocal from equivocal, and purely equivocal from analogous naming, see Natalis, *Quodlibet* 2, q. 7 (Venice 1513, 46Va).

11. Natalis, *Quodlibet* 2, q. 7 (Venice 1513, 44V).

substance and accidents, in the way that a univocal concept stands over univocals.

Natalis's solution is a disjunctive concept. Natalis acknowledges that an intellect can be certain that something (e.g., a potency) is a being but uncertain regarding whether it is a substance or an accident. But he maintains that this intellect is, in fact, certain that the following disjunction is true—"the being is a substance or an accident"—while it is uncertain which side of the disjunction is true. The intellect's disjunctive concept of being (i.e., substance or accident) is not simply one concept. Rather, it is a composite of two (or more) separate concepts (i.e., the concept of substance and the concept or concepts of the accidents), neither of which relates to the other as genus, species, or difference. Nonetheless, as a disjunction, this concept has sufficient unity to serve as the subject in a judgment of the sort Scotus's argument describes. Natalis uses the example of being uncertain whether Socrates is sitting or standing while being certain that Socrates is either sitting or standing.[12] The disjunctive unity option seems to address Scotus's thought experiment by showing that the experience Scotus describes does not require either one objective concept in the things or one formal concept in the mind which has simple unity. Disjunctive unity suffices.

Turning to the Analogy Model Problem, Natalis divides analogy into "analogy of one to another" and "analogy of two to a third."

12. Natalis, *Quodlibet* 2, q. 7 (Venice 1513, 45Va): "quando dicitur quod de aliquo potest esse certum quod sit ens et dubius utrum sit determinate qualitas vel aliquid aliud hoc non est quia unum dicat unam rationem simplicem univocam essentialem istis predicamentis. Sed hoc est quoniam conceptus disiunctus potest esse certus veritate dubia cuiuslibet partis disiuncti per se acceptae. Unde possumus esse certus quod Sortes vel stat vel sedet et ignorare quae illarum partium sit vera et tamen stare vel sedere non dicit aliquem unum conceptum simplicem essentialiter alicui rei convenientem." (When it is said about anything that one can be certain that it is a being and be doubtful whether it is determinately quality or something else, this is not because one expresses one simple, essential, univocal *ratio* for those categories. Rather, this is because a disjunctive concept can be certain while the truth of each part of the disjunction, taken by themselves, is doubtful. Consequently, we can be certain that Socrates either stands or sits and not know which of part of the disjunction is true, and; nevertheless, "to stand or to sit" does not express any one simple concept belonging to anything essentially.)

The divisions themselves as well as the Healthy Model examples that he provides are derivate of Aquinas's parallel passages in *De Potentia*, q. 7, a. 7, *Summa Contra Gentiles* I, c. 34, and *Summa Theologiae* I, q. 13, a. 5. Names are said of God and creatures by the analogy of one to another, in the way that "healthy" is said of medicine and an animal.[13]

These remarks fit onto the framework of Natalis's answer to the *Rationes* Problem. On the side of the *ratio* in *re*, there is a connection between creaturely wisdom and divine wisdom as there is between an animal's health and the health inducing properties of medicine; namely, the connection of effect to cause. Just as there is not one and the same objective concept (i.e., *ratio* in the thing) present in the effect and in the cause where analogous health is concerned, there is not one and the same objective concept of wisdom present in the creature and in God.

With respect to the formal concept (i.e., *ratio* in the mind), Natalis says nothing directly. Presumably, the intellect forms a concept in the mind of "healthy" signifying the health of an animal and later forms a different concept which signifies the health inducing properties of medicine. In a case where there may be confusion—for example, someone hears or reads "Benelin is healthy" and does not know if Benelin is the name of a person or the name of a drug—the intellect could form a disjunctive concept such as "the healthiness of medicine or the healthiness of an animal." The same would apply in the case of the pure perfections. The intellect's concept that signifies wisdom in Plato and Aristotle is not the same as the concept with which it signifies divine wisdom. Yet the intellect can understand the statement "wisdom is a simple perfection" by using its two *ratio-*

13. See ibid. (46Va): "Dico igitur quod cum in analogo sint duo quorum primum est diversitas rationum significatarum partientium analogum. Secundum est illas res habere connexiones secundum attributionem unius ad alterum, vel ambarum ad aliquam tertiam." (I say, therefore, that there are two features in an analogy. The first is a diversity of *rationes* signifying the parts of the analogy. The second feature is that the things are connected either according to the attribution of one to the other or of both to some third thing.) He gives the standard examples of the way the name "healthy" is said analogously at ibid., 44Rb.

nes of wisdom disjunctively, such that the predicate is taken to refer (non-exclusively) either to human or to divine wisdom.

Here is a brief recap of Natalis's answers to the *Rationes* and Analogy Model Problems. Natalis denies any simple unity of *ratio* for analogous terms. This holds both at the level of the *rationes* in *re* (objective concepts) of the things which receive the names analogously, and at the level of the *rationes* in *mente* (formal concepts) through which the intellect grasps and signifies the thing. The intellect can seem to hold one formal concept for the diverse objective concepts, but that is merely an appearance arising from the composite disjunction of two or more diverse formal concepts. Analogy itself can occur either because two things are related in different ways to a third thing, or because one thing is related to another. God and creatures possess perfections analogously insofar as the perfection in the creature is connected to the greater perfection in God as a deficient effect is connected to its more perfect cause.

NATALIS ON THE EQUIVOCATION PROBLEM

Following Natalis's subtle distinctions on the *Rationes* Problem, his solution to the Equivocation Problem is perhaps disappointingly lacking in nuance. He presents an objection from Scotus to the effect that the terms of a demonstration must be used according to the same *ratio*, otherwise, there would be no difference between demonstrative and fallacious syllogisms.[14] Natalis answers the objection as follows:

I say that there are two ways in which a demonstration can be understood to proceed in an equivocal name. In one way, because by an unknown distinction of the equivocal name, from one sense [of the equivocal name] it is concluded to the other sense [of the equivocal name]. And to proceed thus in an equivocal name is deception and the fallacy of equivocation.

14. Natalis, *Quodlibet* 2, q. 7 (Venice 1513, 44Va): "Omnis demonstratio debet habere terminos eiusdem rationis. Alioquin syllogismus demonstrativus et paralogismus non differrent." (Every demonstration ought to have terms with same *ratio*. Otherwise, a demonstrative syllogism and paralogism would not differ.)

And demonstration does not proceed in an equivocal name in that way. In another way, since it is shown by a known distinction, that which is concluded from an equivocal name belongs to it according to every sense which it is able to have, and most of all where there is connection between the many *rationes* signified through the equivocal or analogous name. And to proceed in this way in an equivocal name is not to be deceived by equivocation, but it is to demonstrate and generate true science, although that demonstration is not as absolutely one as those which proceed in univocal names. On the contrary, it is in some way many. Nevertheless, this does not produce deception, as has been said.[15]

In other words, Natalis grants that an analogous name could bring about the fallacy of equivocation, but it does not do so as long as (1) the distinction between the various senses of the name are known, and (2) there is something which belongs to every sense the name is able to have. These conditions are enhanced when there is connection between the diverse *rationes* of the name. I have not seen this particular part of *Quodlibet* 2, q. 7, discussed in the twentieth-century literature on Natalis, although it is cited by Dominic of Flanders in the fifteenth century.

To this point, I fail to see how Natalis's explanation solves the Equivocation Problem. Awareness of the various senses of a name at best enables someone to avoid being deceived by the fallacy of equivocation. It is not clear what Natalis means by something which "belongs to [an analogous name] according to every sense which it is able to have." He cannot be referring to a single *ratio* which could be abstracted from every thing designated by the name, as that would

15. Natalis, *Quodlibet* 2, q. 7 (Venice 1513, 45Va–b): "Dico quod aliquam demonstrationem procedere in equivoco dupliciter intelligi potest. Uno modo, quia ignota distinctione equivoci ex uno sensu concludatur alterum. Et sic procedere in equivoco est deceptio et fallacia equivocationis. Et isto modo demonstratio non procedet in equivoco. Alio modo quia nota distinctione ostendatur illud quod concluditur de equivoco convenire sibi secundum omnem sensum quem potest habere et maxime ubi est connexio inter rationes plures significatas per terminum equivocum sive analogum. Et sic procedere in equivoco non est decipi secundum equivocationem sed est demonstrare et generare scientiam veram licet illa demonstratio non sit ita simpliciter una sicut illa quae procedit in univoco. Imo est aliquo modo plures. Non tamen hoc facit ad deceptionem, ut dictum est."

make the things univocal with respect to that *ratio*. Alternatively, he could perhaps be reducing analogy semantically to univocity in the way that Scotus does, but this is unlikely and directly opposed to the way in which Natalis distinguishes analogy from univocity.

By something which "belongs to [an analogous name] according to every sense which it is able to have," Natalis could be referring to the *conceptus mentis* (formal concept) of the primary analogate which is also present in the definition of the secondary analogate(s). This would at least be consistent with the semantics of the Healthy Model analogy of one to another which Natalis proposes for names said of God and creatures and of substance and accidents. If, however, the primary analogate's formal concept is what he is referring to, then Natalis's solution is open to the objection that the analogous name used in the textbook case of the fallacy of equivocation (cited in my introduction) have precisely the semantic feature which he is saying should prevent the fallacious syllogism from being an instance of the fallacy of equivocation. If Natalis is referring to something else which is common to the analogates, then he has left his reader in the dark as to what the commonality would be.[16]

A further question is whether Natalis's discussion offers resources which he himself did not employ to solve the Equivocation Problem. I am thinking particularly of the unity of disjunction for the formal concept with which he addressed Scotus's "Certain and

---

16. Ralph McInerny defends a "common core meaning" solution to the Equivocation Problem in a brief article intended to defend Thomas Aquinas's doctrine of analogy against Scotus's criticism. Ralph McInerny, "Scotus and Univocity," *in De doctrina Ioannis Duns Scoti: Acta Congressus Scotistici Internationalis Oxonii et Edimburgi 11–17 sept. 1966 celebrati* (Rome: Commissio Scotisticae, 1968), 120. Taking the familiar example of "healthy" said of an animal and medicine or urine, McInerny proposes that the analogous meanings of "healthy" contain the common core meaning "what relates to health in any way." Presumably, the common core meaning of "wisdom" said analogously of God and creatures would be something like "what relates to wisdom in any way" or "what relates to knowing the highest causes in any way." It seems to me that McInerny's "common core" does not fare any better than Natalis's something that "belongs ... according to every sense." A common core "what relates to x in any way" only appears to limit a syllogism to three terms, as is illustrated by the following: "What relates to health in some way is alive. Food relates to health in some way. Therefore, food is alive."

Doubtful" Argument. A recurrent sample natural theology syllogism is (by one variation or another): "Every simple perfection is in God, and wisdom is a simple perfection; therefore, wisdom is in God." Now consider this syllogism taking the term "wisdom" to be predicated through the disjunctive formal concept "either human or divine wisdom." Thus reformulated, we have "Every simple perfection is in God, and wisdom (either human or divine) is a simple perfection. Therefore, wisdom (either human or divine) is in God." Thus reformulated, the argument clearly employs only three terms and avoids the fallacy of equivocation.

The issue that I see here, however, is that the original argument intends to prove that there is such a thing as divine wisdom. By placing divine wisdom within the minor premise (even as a member of a disjunction), the reformulated argument seems to avoid the fallacy of equivocation at the cost of begging the question.

Furthermore, even if this particular argument succeeded, it is not apparent that unity of disjunction as such serves as a general semantic principle capable of preserving valid demonstration. Consider the "healthy" example again modified with a disjunction: "Everything healthy (either as a subject or as a cause of health) is alive, and medicine is healthy (either as a subject or as a cause of health); therefore, medicine is alive." The addition of the disjunction reduced the number of terms in the original syllogism from four to three, but the premises still produce the same absurd conclusion. It seems that unity of disjunction is not close enough to the mental unity possessed by univocal terms for the purposes of natural theology or any science.

Natalis's solution to the Equivocation Problem invokes a common meaning contained within each analogous use of a name that can be enhanced when there is connection between the analogates. To the extent that Natalis explains these features of analogous terms or the analogates themselves, they do not provide a general solution to the problem which stands up to ready counterexamples. Natalis himself did not invoke his doctrine of disjunctive unity to solve the Equivocation Problem, but even if he had, it too would not adequately address the problem. At best, Natalis's answer to this problem is incomplete and needs further explanation or development.

SUTTON ON THE *RATIONES* PROBLEM

Thomas Sutton is very clear in his answer to the *Rationes* Problem. No *ratio* is common to God and to creatures, or to substance and to accidents. Below are two representative passages, one for analogy across the categories and the other for analogy between God and creatures. The first passage reads as follows:

> Being [*ens*] is common analogously, but not common univocally. The univocally common and the analogously common differ in this respect, that the univocally common has not only the name in common but also a common *ratio* or concept. But the analogously common has only the common name, but not the common concept. Consequently, being, when it is analogous, is not apprehended by the intellect under a *ratio* common to all, but it is always apprehended under some *ratio* of its category, and this can happen in two ways, namely either under this [particular] *ratio* determinately or under this or that [particular *ratio*] indeterminately.[17]

Further on Sutton informs his reader:

> Wisdom or wise, in so far as it is said of a creature, carries some imperfection as the *ratio* of a quality and the *ratio* of a *habitus*[18] and imperfection belongs to quality and *habitus*. But quality and *habitus* are removed from [wise's] signification, in so far as it is said of God, and, therefore, there is

---

17. Sutton, *Quaestiones Ordinariae* 32, ad 12 (Schmaus, 40): "Ens est commune analogum, non autem commune univocum. Differunt autem commune univocum et commune analogum in hoc, quod commune univocum non solum habet nomen commune, sed etiam rationem sive conceptum communem. Sed commune analogum habet solum nomen commune, non autem conceptum communem. Unde ens cum sit analogum, non apprehenditur ab intellectu sub ratione communi ad omnia, sed semper apprehenditur sub aliqua ratione eius praedicamentali et hoc potest esse dupliciter, scilicet vel sub hac ratione determinate vel indeterminate sub hac vel illa." Sutton makes the same point at greater length in the body of the question. See especially ibid., 35–37.

18. Sutton is speaking of *habitus* as one of the divisions of the category of quality rather than of the category *habitus*. Wisdom is a quality, and, specifically as a quality, it is a *habitus*.

one *ratio* of wise in so far as it is said of God and another *ratio* of wise in so far as it is said of a creature.[19]

The univocally common, but not the analogously common, share both a single *ratio* and a single name. As being is analogous to the ten categories, it has ten distinct *rationes* that are analogous to each other.[20] Whenever the intellect conceives categorical being, it conceives it under the *ratio* proper to one of the categories, or the intellect conceives being indeterminately as signifying this or that category. God and creatures are even more diverse than substance and accident,[21] and thus again, God and creatures are never signified through a common *ratio*.

One controversy concerning Sutton's doctrine of analogy concerns whether or not he believes there to be a real or a merely verbal difference between those who say that names such as "being" are analogous and those who say that such names are univocal. In an article on Sutton's contemporary Henry of Harclay (ca. 1270–1317),[22] Armand Maurer places Sutton among those who see only a verbal differences between these two positions.[23] Such an interpretation, however, is inconsistent with Sutton's *Quaestiones Ordinariae* 32, where he writes in the person of an objector that "the controversy is only verbal" (*non est controversia nisi in verbo*). The objector in this passage (presumably Henry of Harclay) asserts that there is a

---

19. Sutton, *Quaestiones Ordinariae* 32a, ad 3 (Schmaus, 58). "Sapientia vel sapiens, prout dicitur de creatura, aliquam imperfectionem importat ut rationem qualitatis et rationem habitus et ista sunt imperfectionis; sed ista removentur a significatione eius, prout dicitur de deo, et ideo alia est ratio eius, prout dicitur de deo, et alia prout dicitur de creatura." See also Sutton, *Quodlibet* 2, q. 3, ad 4, in *Quodlibeta*, ed. Michael Schmaus (Munich: Bayerische Akademie der Wissenschaften, 1969), 183–84.

20. See also the *respondeo* in Sutton, *Quaestiones Ordinariae* 32 (Schmaus, 36).

21. Sutton, *Quaestiones Ordinariae* 32 (Schmaus, 38).

22. On the life and works of Henry of Harclay, see Henninger, "Henry of Harclay," 305–13.

23. See A. Maurer, "Henry of Harclay's Question on the Univocity of Being," in his *Being and Knowing: Studies in Thomas Aquinas and Later Medieval Philosophers* (Toronto: Pontifical Institute of Mediaeval Studies, 1990), 208. See also F. Pelster, "Thomas von Sutton O. Pr., ein Oxforder Verteidiger der thomistischen Lehre," *Zeitschrift für kath. Theol.* 46 (1922): 395n2.

strict sense of univocity and a broader sense of univocity which includes instances where names are said by order and priority.[24] In his response to this objection, Sutton claims that all the philosophers agree on one sense of univocity, which is the sense designated by Aristotle in the *Categories*: "one name and one *ratio* of that name." According to Sutton then (and by his account according to all philosophers), whether there is order and priority in a *ratio* is irrelevant to whether or not it is predicated univocally, there is no distinction between broad and strict univocity, and the controversy over whether "being" is said univocally or analogously is not merely verbal.[25]

A name is said univocally when and only when it is signified of many through one *ratio*. As the quotations given above show, Sutton denies that the name "being" (or other names said across the categories) are said through a single *ratio*. So Sutton must maintain that there is a real disagreement between those who teach the univocity of being and those who teach analogy of being. Further, the real difference between these philosophers is over whether being is signified across the categories and of God and creatures through one or many *rationes*. In Sutton's account, it is a difference over what I am calling the *Rationes* Problem that separates the proponents of analogy from the proponents of univocity. From this point, the reader can see that, whether or not there is a merely verbal difference between Aquinas and Scotus on names said of God and creatures, there is a real difference between Scotus, who insists on a single *ratio* of being and other names said of God and creatures, and Thomas Sutton, who insists on diverse *rationes*.

Unity of disjunction makes a brief appearance in Sutton's answer to the *Rationes* Problem, playing much the same role as it did in the

24. See Sutton, *Quaestiones Ordinariae* 32a, arg. 9 (Schmaus, 52–53), and Henry of Harclay, *Ordinary Questions* 12, n. 28, in *Henry of Harclay: Ordinary Questions I–XIV, XV–XXIX*, ed. M. Henninger, trans. R. Edwards and M. Henninger, Auctores Britannici Medii Aevi (Oxford: Oxford University Press, 2010), 1:472–74.243–51.

25. Sutton, *Quaestiones Ordinariae* 32a (Schmaus, 55–56). E. J. Ashworth gives a short description of this difference between Harclay and Sutton in Ashworth, *Les theories de l'analogie du XIIe au XVIe siecle*, 65.

writings of Natalis; namely, to answer Scotus's "Certain and Doubtful" Argument for the univocity of being. That is, Sutton appeals to unity of disjunction to answer Scotus's argument that there must be a single and therefore univocal concept of being because, although the intellect cannot be both certain and doubtful through the same concept, it can be certain that something is a being without being certain if the thing in question is a substance or an accident, finite or infinite.[26] According to Sutton, as according to Natalis, the analogates really have distinct concepts, and, in the examples Scotus raises, an intellect is certain that one of its distinct concepts applies to the object in question although it is uncertain which one of them.[27] That an object is a being entails that the object is a substance or an accident. Consequently, an intellect can be certain that an object is one or the other (substance or accident), while doubtful about which one, and it is unnecessary to affirm a simple (rather than a disjunctive, and, therefore, complex) concept of being.

SUTTON ON THE ANALOGY MODEL PROBLEM

So far, the positions of Sutton and Natalis agree, although Natalis makes distinctions absent from Sutton's account, principally the distinction between the *ratio* in the mind (the formal concept) and the *ratio* in *re* (the objective concept). In the case of the Analogy Model Problem, however, the agreement between these early Thomist contemporaries ends. Sutton offers a much more extensive account of analogous unity and the different kinds or modes of analogous names than Natalis. Ashworth and Henninger's articles treat the relevant passages from Sutton's *Questiones Ordinariae* 32–33. I note below their disagreements and where I part from their interpretations of Sutton.

---

26. Sutton raises this objection in *Quaestiones Ordinariae* 32, obj. 23 (Schmaus, 29–30).

27. See ibid., ad 23 (Schmaus, 45–46). See also his similar remarks in the body of the article (Schmaus, 32–33).

Sutton presents the diverse modes of analogy in *Quaestiones Ordinariae* 33 on "Whether names, which are said about God and creatures, are said univocally about God and creatures."[28] Sutton begins by dividing names said of many into the univocal (i.e., names said of many by the same *ratio*), and the equivocal (i.e., names said of many by diverse *rationes*).[29] Next, he distinguishes equivocation by chance from equivocation by design,[30] before taking up the argument that there is at least one kind of equivocation by design which is close enough to univocity to explain both (1) how names are said of God and creatures, and (2) why some philosophers mistakenly believe that these names are said univocally. To make this argument, Sutton goes through the properties of the kinds of equivocation by design three times in *Quaestiones Ordinariae* 33, each time providing examples and refining the distinction between his own position and the "common position" about how names are said of God and creatures.

In his first treatment, Sutton gives a division of the modes of analogy or equivocation by design, borrowed from Boethius: (1) *similitudo*, (2) *proportio*, (3) *ab uno*, and (4) *ad unum*.[31] Sutton explains the four modes using Boethius's examples. Hence, Aristotle's *Categories* 1 example of "animal" said of a man and a picture of a man explains *similitudo*; Aristotle's *Metaphysics* 5 example of "unity as the principle of number," "a point as the principle of a line," etc., illustrate *proportio* (i.e., Principle Model analogy); the name "medical" said of a book and a tool explains *ab uno*; and "healthy" said of urine and an animal illustrates *ad unum*. As an aside, Sutton says that *proportio* is the analogy properly speaking and the words *analoga* and *proportio* are the same. He also says here that *ens* is said of substance and of the other categories by the *ad unum* form of analogy.[32] No mention is made of names said analogously of God and creatures.

---

28. Ibid., 33 (Schmaus, 63): "utrum nomina, quae dicuntur de deo et creaturis, dicantur univoce de deo et creaturis."
29. Ibid., 71.
30. Ibid.
31. See the introduction.
32. Sutton, *Quaestiones Ordinariae* 33 (Schmaus, 71–72).

His second presentation of the kinds of equivocation by design or analogy differs from his first by focusing exclusively on *similitudo* and *proportio* through the question of how they could be mistaken for univocity and to what degree they approach univocity. Drawing on Aristotle's *Physics* 7,[33] Sutton notes that sometimes a genus that appears to be univocal hides plurality.[34] According to Sutton, proximity to univocation is manifested either in *similitudo*, agreement in genus, or great agreement in *similitudo* or *proportio* (*magnam convenientiam in similitudine vel proportione*). The first mode of equivocation by design (i.e., *similitudo*) is less distant from univocity than pure equivocation.[35] Logical agreement in genus without "natural" agreement is closer yet to univocity (as in the case of "body" said of heavenly bodies and of corruptible bodies).[36] Where analogates have agreement of *proportio*, they are so close to univocity that some philosophers mistake them for univocals.[37] Sutton's examples include "master" said of the one who teaches in school and of the ruler of a house and "principle" said of unity and of a point.[38]

33. Ashworth suggests that Sutton is influenced here by Aquinas's commentary on *Physics* 7. See Ashworth, "Analogy and Equivocation in Thomas Sutton," 297. See also Aquinas, *In Physic.*, l. 7, lect. 8 (Leonine, 2:354a).

34. See Sutton, *Quaestiones Ordinariae* 33 (Schmaus, 74). See also Aristotle, *Physics* 7 (249a21–25), in *Complete Works of Aristotle*, ed. Jonathan Barnes (Princeton, N.J.: Princeton University Press, 1984), 1:416: "So we have now to consider how motion is differentiated; and this discussion serves to show that the genus is not a unity but contains a plurality latent in it and distinct from it, and that some homonymies are far removed from one another, some have a certain likeness, and some are nearly related either generically or analogically, with the result that they seem not to be homonymies though they really are." Maurer cites this text as a source for the kind of analogy Aquinas calls analogous "physically" but not "logically." See Armand Maurer, "St. Thomas and The Analogy of Genus," in his *Being and Knowing*, 23.

35. Thomas Sutton, *Quaestiones Ordinariae* 33 (Schmaus, 74).

36. Ibid. (74–75).

37. Ibid. (75). See especially: "In proportione autem conveniunt quaedam aequivoca sicut ille, qui docet in schola, dicitur magister, et similiter, qui praeest domui. Sicut enim ille est rector scholarum, ita iste est rector domus et propter hanc propinquitatem proportionis videtur esse univocatio, cum tamen non sit." (However, certain equivocals agree in proportion. For just as the one who is the ruler of a school [relates to a school], so too is the one who is the ruler of a house [in relation to a house], and, because of this nearness of proportion, there seems to be univocation although there is not.)

38. Notice that these examples are identical to the examples given in Aquinas, *In Physic.*, l. 7, lect. 8 (Leonine, 2:354a).

Sutton only directly addresses names said commonly of God and creatures in the question's third discussion of the kinds of equivocation by design. The "common position," he says, is that names are said of God and creatures "by order or respect to one [*ad unum*] just as 'healthy' is said of diverse things by relation to one." Specifically, the common position affirms that names are said analogously of God and creatures by the relation of "one to another," as opposed to a relation of "many to one."[39] The "common position" seems to be none other than the position taken by the likes of Natalis in his *Quodlibet* 2, q. 7, and Aquinas in his *De Potentia*, q. 7, a. 7, *Summa Contra Gentiles* I, c. 34, and *Summa Theologiae* I, q. 13, a. 5.

To argue against the "common position," Sutton draws his reader's attention to the signification of names.[40] God's wisdom causes human wisdom, etc., but the names "wise," "just," etc., are not said about a human because of the order a human has to the wisdom or justice of God.[41] Moreover, these names are not said about God *to signify* his relation to creatures, even though the names are said about creatures first.[42] It follows that neither analogy *ab uno* nor analogy *ad unum* explain naming God and creatures by analogy.[43] It does not make any sense to call medicine "healthy" apart from its relation to the health of an animal. This is not the case, however,

---

39. Sutton, *Quaestiones Ordinariae* 33 (Schmaus, 76–77).

40. See ibid., 77.

41. Ibid.: "Non enim ideo dicitur homo iustus vel sapiens, quia habet ordinem ad iustitiam dei vel sapientiam dei." (For a human is not, therefore, called "just" or "wise," because he has order to the justice of God or the wisdom of God.)

42. Sutton anticipates a possible misinterpretation of his position within his direct discussion of how the name "principle" is said by analogy: "Secundum enim quod res sunt nobis magis notae, secundum hoc prius nominantur. Magnitudo autem est nobis magis nota quam alia et ideo prima pars magnitudinis dicitur principium per prius et in alliis [*sic*] dicitur per posterius." (For insofar as things are more known to us, they are first named. Now magnitude is more known than others and, therefore, the first part of magnitude is called "principle" first and "principle" is said *per posterius* in others.) Sutton, *Quaestiones Ordinariae* 33 (Schmaus, 75). This passage shows that, although *proportio* analogates do not receive their common name in order to signify their relation to each other or to some third, there is order of priority among them with respect to the name, just as there is in the other modes of equivocation by design. This makes Sutton's position consistent with that of Hochschild in "Proportionality and Divine Naming," 547–50.

43. Sutton, *Quaestiones Ordinariae* 33 (Schmaus, 77).

for names such as "being" said of God and creatures, whether God or the creatures serves as the primary analogate toward which and from which the name is said of the secondary analogate. The being of God is not included in the signification of "being" said of a creature, nor is a creature's being contained in the signification of "being" said of God. Finally, Sutton eliminates *similitudo* from serving as the mode of analogy for names said of God and creatures, likewise, on the grounds that the similitude of creatures to God is not the reason why the name is said of creatures.[44]

Sutton concludes his process of elimination by affirming that names are said analogously of God and creatures through the lone remaining option; namely, *proportio* or "analogy properly speaking."[45] He writes:

It remains, therefore, that names said about God and about other things are said in the fourth way, namely, according to proportion, just as the name "principle" is said about unity and about a point and about a spring, as has been said, and this is easy to show regarding individual names. For just as a human knows the highest causes and is, therefore, called wise, so God knows the highest causes perfectly and, therefore, by merit ought to be called wise.... Similarly, just as a human has knowledge of things through their proper cause and, therefore, is called "scientific," so God knows the order of all causes and effects in the most perfect way, and so, because of such proportion, He ought to be called "scientific." ... Similarly, also, just as a human has knowledge of principles without discourse, so too God knows all things without discourse, and, therefore, just as a human is called "intelligent," so too God.[46]

---

44. Ibid. See also Henninger, "Thomas Sutton on Univocation, Equivocation, and Analogy," 566.

45. Ashworth cites this passage as well as one belonging to James of Viterbo as evidence that thirteenth-century authors were aware that their contemporaries' use of the word *analogia* in Latin differed from the original Greek meaning of the term. See E. J. Ashworth, "Suárez on the Analogy of Being: Some Historical Background," *Vivarium* 33 (1995): 55–56.

46. Sutton, *Quaestiones Ordinariae* 33 (Schmaus, 77–78): "Relinquitur igitur, quod nomina dicta de deo et de rebus aliis dicantur quarto modo, scilicet secundum proportionem, prout hoc nomen principium dicitur de unitate et de puncto et de fonte, ut dictum est, et hoc facile est manifestare de singulis nominibus. Sicut enim homo cognoscit altissimas causas et ideo dicitur sapiens, ita deus cognoscit altissimas causas perfecte et

Sutton gives other examples of proportional activities of creatures and God, and he concludes that all names that abstractly signify a perfection are said of God and creatures analogously by *proportio*, and that *proportio* analogous names are the furthest of the equivocals (by design) from pure equivocation and the closest to univocation.[47]

Sutton's rule for determining which kind of analogy is at work is the order of the signification of the names. When a name is said of one thing to signify its relation to another recipient of the same name, then the name is said about both things by analogy *ad unum* (which, by Sutton's Boethian account is identified with the Healthy Model of analogy). When names such as wise, good, etc., are said of creatures, these names do not signify the relation of creatures to God, and, when these same names are said of God, they do not signify God in relation to creatures; therefore, these names are not said of God and creatures by the *ad unum* mode of analogy. The *proportio* mode of analogy (Principle Model as explained by Sutton) alone properly captures the diverse but proportionally similar significations of these names when they are said of God and creatures.

Now one particular name said of God and creatures has been the cause of disagreement among scholars of Sutton's work; namely, the name "being." After observing the uncontentious point that "Thomas Sutton appealed to the analogy of proportionality in the context of the divine names, though he retained the analogy of at-

---

ideo merito debet dici sapiens.... Similiter sicut homo habet cognitionem rerum per propriam causam et ideo sciens dicitur, ita deus omnium causarum et effectuum ordinem cognoscit modo perfectissimo et ita propter talem proportionem debet dici sciens.... Similiter etiam sicut homo habet cognitionem principiorum absque discursu, ita et deus omnia cognoscit absque discursu et ideo sicut homo dicitur intelligens, ita etiam deus." Sutton's examples of proportional naming in *Quaestiones Ordinariae* 33 closely follow Aquinas, *Summa Contra Gentiles* IV, c. 12 (Leonine, 15:47a–b). Each example of proportions that Sutton lists refers to a kind of activity. On the significance of this for understanding analogy of porportionality see Norris Clarke, "Analogy and the Meaningfulness of Language about God," in his *Explorations in Metaphysics: Being-God-Person* (Notre Dame, Ind.: University of Notre Dame Press, 1994), 131, and J. F. Ross, *Portraying Analogy* (Cambridge: Cambridge University Press, 1981), 164.

47. Sutton, *Quaestiones Ordinariae* 33 (Schmaus, 78–79).

tribution for 'ens' as said of substance and accident,"[48] Ashworth goes on to make the controversial claim that Sutton retains analogy of attribution to one (i.e., *ad unum*) for being said of God and creatures. According to Ashworth, Sutton distinguishes at least the following three cases of analogy for metaphysical discourse. The first is analogy of attribution to one for *ens* said of substance and accident. The second is analogy of attribution to one for *ens* said of God and creatures. The third is *proportio* analogy for the divine names other than *ens*.[49]

There is some support for Ashworth's interpretation in the fact that Sutton does not give an example of how *ens* would be said by *proportio* of God and creatures despite the fact that he offers a variety of examples of such names (including "wise," "scientific," "intelligent," "artisan," and "just") and could surely have given an example for *ens* if he intended to do so. Moreover, there is at least one passage

48. See Ashworth, "Suárez on the Analogy of Being," 57. In context Ashworth goes on to say the following: "Medieval logicians, however, did not appeal to the analogy of proportionality in their logical works. Nor did the fifteenth-century authors Capreolus, Dominic of Flanders (outside the area of metaphor) and Soncinas. Cajetan is the first author I know of who not only used the analogy of proportionality but who unambiguously insisted on giving it a privileged position." Chapters 3 and 4 of this study cite texts showing both Capreolus and Dominic of Flanders giving a privileged position to analogy of proportionality.

49. Ashworth, *Les theories de l'analogie du XIIe au XVIe siecle*, 52–53: "He makes a distinction between three cases. The first case is that of the word 'being' said about substance and accident. In this context, the word 'being' is equivocal by design and an example of the analogy of attribution. The second case is 'being' said about God and creatures. In this context, the word 'being' is much further from univocity than the same word as it is said about substance and accidents. God exists through His essence, whereas creatures exist through participation. It follows that there is nothing which can be common to God and creatures. There is no *ratio* which is the same in part and different in part. Rather, one *ratio* is entirely analogous. These remarks suggest the presence of a return to the analogy of imitation. However, the word 'being' said about God and creature always is an example of analogy of attribution. The third case is of the divine names, such as 'wise,' 'just,' and 'good.' Sutton holds that these names are analogous, but, unlike such words as 'being' and 'healthy,' their significations do not contain a relation. One does not say that a human is just because his justice is related to the justice of God, whether by causality or by resemblance. The only type of analogy which is appropriate in this case is the analogy of proportionality. When we say that a human is wise, it is because the human knows the highest causes, and when we say that God is wise, it is because He knows the highest causes perfectly."

in *Quaestiones Ordinariae* 32, as Ashworth points out, where Sutton seems to identify *ens* said of God and creatures with the *similitudo* kind of analogy.[50]

Henninger disagrees. Citing an article by Alessandro Conti,[51] Henninger points out that *Quaestiones Ordinariae* 33

does not explicitly talk of "being," but only of the other divine names, as "wisdom" and "goodness." Nevertheless, he [Conti] is right to treat "being" as a divine name, for as we have seen from their titles, Sutton intends to treat the divine names first in question 33 and then in question 34. Also, in question 33 he extends his use of the analogy of proportion to "all those names which absolutely signify perfection," which I take to include "being."[52]

In effect, Henninger's argument is that it is merely a coincidence that Sutton does not give illustrative examples of *ens* said by Principle Model analogy about God and creatures. Sutton is surely aware that *ens* is one of the divine names. It is reasonable to presume that he does not maintain a separate rule for *ens* from the rules which apply to the other divine names.

Sutton's texts themselves do not definitively resolve the dispute between Ashworth and Henninger. Still, I hold that a consistent reading of Sutton requires that one side with Henninger. If Ashworth is right to say Sutton's account of the analogous predication of *ens* to God and creatures is not *proportio*, then, as will be shown below, Sutton refutes himself through his treatment of demonstrating the divine attributes without committing the fallacy of equivocation.

---

50. Ashworth, *Les theories de l'analogie du XIIe au XVIe siecle*, 52–53. See Sutton, *Quaestiones Ordinariae* 32, ad 11 (Schmaus, 40).

51. See Alessandro D. Conti, "La composizione metafisica dell'ente finito corporeo nell'ontologia di Tommaso Sutton," *Documenti e studi sulla tradizione filosofica medievale* (1991): 326. Conti's treatment of Sutton's *Quaestiones Ordinariae* 32 and 33 is brief. The article focuses on Sutton's treatment of the distinction between essence and existence, the principle of individuation, and the categories.

52. Henninger, "Thomas Sutton on Univocation, Equivocation, and Analogy," 570.

SUTTON ON THE EQUIVOCATION PROBLEM

Thomas Sutton directly raises the Equivocation Problem in two objections in *Quaestiones Ordinariae* 33. Here is the fifth objection:

> Further, just as pure equivocation impedes inference, so does analogy. For just as this is [an example of] the fallacy of equivocation, "Every dog is a land animal, the celestial star is the dog; therefore, the celestial star is a land animal," so too, this is a fallacy through the power of analogy, "Every healthy thing is an animal, medicine is healthy; therefore, medicine is an animal." Therefore, if we assert that those names are predicated analogously about God and creatures, nothing can be proven or known about God through creatures, just as nothing can be if they are said purely equivocally. Therefore, it remains that they are said purely univocally about God and creatures.[53]

The objection is clearly laid out. Using names analogously appears to generate the exact same fallacy as using terms equivocally. "Every healthy thing is an animal, and medicine is healthy; therefore, med-

---

53. Sutton, *Quaestiones Ordinariae* 33, arg. 5 (Schmaus, 65): "Praeterea sicut aequivocatio pura impedit illationem, ita et analogia. Sicut enim haec est fallacia aequivocationis: Omne latrabile est canis, sidus caeleste est canis, ergo sidus caeleste est latrabile, ita et haec est fallacia per vim analogiae: omne sanum est animal, medicina est sana, ergo medicina est animal. Ergo si ponamus illa nomina praedicari de deo et creaturis analogice, nihil potest probari nec cognosci de deo per creaturas, sicut nec potest, si dicantur pure aequivoce. Relinquitur ergo, quod pure univoce dicantur de deo et creaturis." In my translation of "Omne latrabile est canis" I regard *latrabile* as the predicate and *canis* as the subject. I reverse their apparent order in the text for three reasons. First of all, the sentence does not make sense otherwise. Secondly, without this change, the syllogism would fail by the fallacy of undistributed middle even if it did not fail by the fallacy of equivocation. Thirdly, the translation I have made makes the objection consistent with Peter of Spain's *Tractatus* 7 treatment of the first species of the fallacy of equivocation. See Peter of Spain, *Tractatus* (or *Summule Logicales*), 100. See p. 6n15 above to compare Peter of Spain's example of the second species of the fallacy of equivocation with the sample syllogism involving the term "healthy" in Sutton's *Quaestiones Ordinariae* 33, arg. 5. Notice that while Peter of Spain does not mention "medicine" in his example, he does something similar by listing food as cause (*efficiente*) of health among the secondary meanings of "healthy." See also the treatment of the fallacy of equivocation in *De Fallaciis* 6, n. 650, in *Opuscula Philosophica* (Marietti, 228b). The date and authorship of this text once attributed to Aquinas is uncertain. Jean-Pierre Torrell sums up the state of the question in his *Saint Thomas Aquinas, volume 1: The Person and His Work*, revised edition, trans. Robert Royal (Washington, D.C.: The Catholic University of America Press, 2005), 11.

icine is an animal" is no less fallacious by the fallacy of equivocation than "Every dog is a land animal, and a star is a dog; therefore, a star is a land animal."

In objection 25, the objector refers to the argument from motion to the existence of a "first mover." Speaking as the objector, Sutton says that the reasoning of the argument "would be sophistical unless 'mover' were said about God and other movers according to the same *ratio*."[54] Sutton does not name his objector in either passage, but one can see the resemblance between the objections and Scotus's fourth objection to analogy discussed in chapter 1 (above). Unless the terms carry the same meaning when said of God and creatures, then one could just as well argue that God is a stone as argue that God is wise, and, if a term carries the same meaning, then it is said through one *ratio* and (according to Sutton and Scotus) univocally.

Sutton responds to objection 5 by drawing on the distinction between the different modes of analogy or equivocation by design. The objector's argument stands against *ad unum* analogy, as illustrated in the objector's sample syllogism. Presumably, although Sutton is silent on the matter, the objector's argument would also stand against *similitudo* and *ab uno* analogy. But, he maintains, terms "analogous by proportion" can mediate demonstrations. He gives the following example of the use of a name by *proportio* in an argument: "as the heart relates to the whole animal, so the spring relates to the whole river. The heart is the principle of the animal; likewise, the spring is the principle of the river."[55] Sutton says that the same kind of reasoning occurs in natural theology demonstrations:

---

54. See Sutton, *Quaestiones Ordinariae* 33, arg. 25 (Schmaus, 70), especially: "Sed ista ratio esset sophistica, nisi motor diceretur de deo et aliis motoribus secundum eandem rationem." Sutton's example raises the question of whether one could demonstrate God's existence prior to use of analogy. For a twentieth-century scholar's take on this point, see James Anderson, *The Bond of Being: An Essay on Analogy and Existence* (St. Louis, Mo.: Herder, 1949), 161–62.

55. Sutton, *Quaestiones Ordinariae* 33, ad 5 (Schmaus, 81): "Sicut se habet cor ad totum animal, ita se habet fons ad totum flumen. Sed cor est principium animalis, ergo fons est principium fluminis."

Thus, God is whatever is absolutely better that He be than that He not be. But it is altogether better in creatures to be wise than not wise, free than not free, living than not living, just than not just, and so on about other things which carry perfection absolutely without defect. Therefore, God is living, wise, free, just and so forth. For those names signify perfection absolutely, as far as that which is principal in their *ratio*, although they carry some imperfection as regards what is less principal, and, therefore, they are said of God by removing that to which imperfection belongs.[56]

As seen in passages quoted above, being a quality is an imperfection. Hence, the qualitative aspect of the *ratio* of wisdom, etc., must be removed when the names are said about God.[57] The alteration of the *ratio* of a creature necessary to apply the name to God generates a new *ratio*. Although it is no longer said through the same *ratio* when the name is extended to God, the *proportio* between the *ratio* of the name said of the creature and the (distinct) *ratio* of the name said of God suffices to preserve valid demonstration.

Sutton takes the same approach in his response to objection 25: "The name 'mover,' as well as other names, is said about God and other things analogously according to proportion, as has often been said, and in such the proof from creatures to God is effective in all things which principally carry no imperfection, as has been said, because such analogy is near to univocation, on account of which the proof holds just as in univocals."[58] So the demonstration that God is the first mover (and by parity of reasoning other demonstrations

---

56. Ibid. (81–82): "Sic deus est quidquid absolute melius est ipsum quam non ipsum. Sed melius est omnino in creaturis sapiens quam non sapiens, potens quam non potens, vivens quam non vivens, iustum quam non iustum et sic de aliis, quae important perfectionem absolute absque defectu. Ergo deus est vivens, sapiens, potens, iustus et sic de aliis. Ista enim nomina significant perfectionem absolute, quantum ad illud, quod est principale in eorum ratione, quamvis aliquam imperfectionem important, quantum ad id, quod est minus principale et ideo removendo illud, quod est imperfectionis, dicuntur de deo."

57. See also ibid., 32a, ad 3 (Schmaus, 58).

58. Ibid., 33, ad 25 (Schmaus, 87): "Hoc nomen motor sicut et alia nomina dicitur de deo et aliis analogice secundum proportionem, sicut saepe dictum est, et in talibus valet probatio ex creaturis ad deum in omnibus, quae nullam imperfectionem important principaliter, ut dictum est, quia talis analogia propinqua est univocationi, propter quod tenet probatio, sicut in univocis."

of divine attributes) is valid because the *proportio* form of analogy is "near to univocation." As discussed above, Sutton argued in the body of *Quaestiones Ordinariae* 33 that the reason why some mistake instances of *proportio* for univocity is that agreement of proportion is so close to univocal agreement. Sutton's answer to the charge that analogous terms cannot mediate valid demonstrative syllogisms is, then, that they can in the case of *proportio* analogy because of the proximity of proportional agreement to univocal agreement.

The question to consider at this point is the success or failure of Sutton's attempt to solve the Equivocation Problem. Consider a variation of Sutton's own natural theology demonstration: "All simple perfections are in God. Wisdom is a simple perfection. Therefore, wisdom is in God." According to Thomas Sutton, there neither is nor can be a common *ratio* of "wisdom" standing over both creaturely and divine wisdom in this syllogism. Furthermore, Sutton could not hold that "wisdom" in the minor premise signifies the proper *ratio* of God's wisdom because then the demonstration would be redundant, demonstrating God's wisdom through God's wisdom. He also could not hold that "wisdom" in the conclusion signifies through the *ratio* of creaturely "wisdom" without compromising his position that no perfection is in God according to the same *ratio* as it is in creatures. The remaining options are the *ratio* of creaturely wisdom for the word "wisdom" in the minor premise and the *ratio* of divine wisdom for the word "wisdom" in the conclusion. A paraphrase of the syllogism would then be: "All simple perfections are in God. *The quality of knowledge of the highest causes* is a simple perfection. Therefore, *subsistent knowledge of the highest causes* is in God." So far, this shows that Sutton is committed to diverse *rationes* of "wisdom" for the minor premise and to the conclusion and that he cannot reduce the syllogism to three terms.

As indicated by his discussion of the proximity of *proportio* to univocity, the key to Sutton's defense of demonstration using analogous terms is the proportional unity between the analogates. Following the example of Aristotle's *Metaphysics* 5.6, Sutton treats proportional unity as lesser than generic unity, but a true form of unity nonetheless.[59] Among the modes of analogy, only *proportio* carries this form of unity, and, Sutton tells us, a demonstration employing a term through *proportio* analogy retains the proportional unity between its terms just as demonstrations employing terms generically or specifically retain generic and specific unity between their terms. So just as the syllogism "All animals are corruptible, and beavers are animals; therefore, beavers are corruptible" demonstrates that all beavers have one and the same attribute specifically, the syllogism "All simple perfections are in God, and wisdom is a simple perfection; therefore, wisdom is in God" demonstrates that there is something proportionally one and the same in creatures and in God.

SUMMARY AND ASSESSMENT

Natalis and Sutton agree that names said analogously require diverse *rationes*, including the names that are said analogously across the categories and about God and creatures. Although they agree on the *Rationes* Problem, they disagree on the Analogy Model Problem. This disagreement has consequences for their answers to the Equivocation Problem.

Sutton's answer to the Equivocation Problem has a number of advantages, which derive from Sutton's choice of the Principle Model of analogy over the Healthy Model when addressing the Analogy Model Problem. For one, as we have seen, Sutton uses the proportional unity characteristic of the Principle Model to provide an apparently working example of a demonstration using an analogous term from outside of natural theology and metaphysics. It would not be difficult to produce other examples that operate in the same way from either inside or outside these sciences. For instance, "what is falling is going down, the rain and the stocks are falling; therefore,

---

59. Aristotle, *Metaphysics* 5.6 (1016b31–1017a3). The modes of unity are in descending order: numerical, specific, generic, and analogous. Analogous unity is described as two things relating to each other as a third thing relates to a fourth.

the rain and the stocks are going down," "All sharp things have an edge, and both the knife and comedian are sharp; therefore, both the knife and comedian have an edge," or "unity relates to number as a point relates to a line, and unity is a principle of number; therefore, a point is a principle of a line."

Sutton's answer to the Analogy Model Problem also carries the advantage that it follows the precedent set by Aristotle's application of proportional unity in the *Metaphysics* and *Posterior Analytics*. It is a principle of Aristotle's understanding of science that all demonstrative sciences have principles. But demonstrative sciences do not have principles univocally, as illustrated by Aristotle's own discussion of the principles of sciences, and even one and the same axiom applies analogously but not univocally across the sciences.[60]

Furthermore, Sutton's solution is able to explain why it is that some but not all instances of demonstration using analogous terms fall into the fallacy of equivocation; namely, some attempts at demonstration use names in the modes of analogy which fall short of proportional unity. Sutton's solution at least returns the question to the Scotists, who, to preserve their objection, must explain either why proportional unity (which Scotists themselves acknowledge)[61] lacks the semantic unity necessary for use in demonstrations, or why there is, contrary to Sutton's position, really only a verbal difference between Sutton and Scotus.

CONCLUSION

The Princes of Primitive Thomism treated in this chapter both rejected any simple unity of *ratio* in analogy. Natalis used the occa-

60. Aristotle, *Posterior Analytics* 1.10 (76a37–76b2).
61. For Scotus's acknowledgement of proportional unity, see Scotus, *Super Libros Metaphysicorum*, l. 5, q. 4 (*OP* 3:439.2–11). See also the Vives edition of the passage in *Opera Omnia* (Paris: Vives, 1891), 7:208a. Scotus's disciple Antonius Andreas sees no disagreement between Aquinas and Scotus on this particular point. See *In XII Libros Metaphysicorum Aristotelis Expositio* (Vives, 6:43). For the attribution of this *Expositio* to Antonius Andreas rather than to Scotus himself, see the editors' introduction in *Super Libros Metaphysicorum* (*OP* 3:xl–xli).

sion of the *Rationes* Problem to distinguish *rationes* in *mente* from *rationes* in *re*. Sutton made no explicit use of this distinction, but, like Natalis, he applied unity of disjunction to answer Scotus's "Certain and Doubtful" Argument against analogy. Natalis adopted the Healthy Model for the Analogy Model Problem. Sutton criticized the Healthy Model for the Analogy Model Problem on the grounds of signification, but also on the grounds that it lacks the unity necessary to preserve valid demonstration through analogous terms. I have argued that Sutton's answer to the Equivocation Problem advances the debate between Thomism and Scotism over the conditions for natural theology demonstrations by presenting reasons based on the Aristotelian doctrine of proportional unity, backed both by examples and Aristotelian practice, whereas Natalis does not appear to have met the existing objection to demonstration using analogous terms.

Fifteenth-century Thomism renews the fourteenth-century Thomist search for the appropriate unity and types of analogy suited for naming God and creatures and preserving demonstration. As will be seen below, Natalis's distinction between the *ratio* in the mind and the *ratio* in the thing are adopted for purposes other than Natalis's, which significantly changes the course of the discussion of the three problems. Sutton's notion of proportional unity also remerges with modification in fifteenth-century Thomism. Chapter 3 considers the initial synthesis of Natalis and Sutton's ideas in the writings of John Capreolus, the Prince of Thomist Theologians.

3

John Capreolus
Thomism in Transition

Chapter 2 presented the solutions of two prominent early defenders of the doctrines of Thomas Aquinas. It showed that Natalis and Sutton agreed on the *Rationes* Problem, with both taking the side of "many *rationes*" on the grounds that to do otherwise would be to abandon analogous for univocal naming in metaphysics and natural theology. Natalis and Sutton disagreed, however, on the Analogy Model Problem, with Natalis embracing the Healthy Model and Sutton embracing the Principle Model for names said analogously of God and creatures. Chapter 2 showed that Natalis's answer to the Equivocation Problem was inadequate to resolve the existing objections to analogous terms in demonstration, particularly those arising from textbook examples of the second species of the fallacy of equivocation. By contrast, Sutton's answer to the Analogy Model Problem was evidently formed with an eye toward the Equivocation Problem and the susceptibility of the Healthy Model to the fallacy of equivocation. By relying on proportional unity and Principle Model analogy, Sutton offers a more plausible solution to the Equivocation Problem.

I now turn to the work of the great early fifteenth-century defender of Thomas, John Capreolus. In his work *Defensiones Theologi-*

ae Divi Thomae Aquinatis, Capreolus breaks with the early Thomists on the *Rationes* Problem, and argues that names such as "being" are said analogously through one *ratio*. Capreolus takes the side of neither Natalis nor Sutton on the Analogy Model Problem, attempting instead a synthetic position. The significance of this break should not be understated. As noted in the previous chapter, it is precisely this point on which Sutton insisted that there is real disagreement between the proponents of analogy and the proponents of univocity. Capreolus surrenders this ground to the proponents of univocity, and he relocates the difference in the dispute. It will be seen below that Capreolus (1) rejects the Healthy Model for names said of God and creatures by drawing on Aquinas's *In 1 Sent.*, d. 19, q. 5, a. 2, ad 1; (2) embraces the Principle Model for names said of God and creatures as taught by Thomas in *De Veritate*, q. 2, a. 11; and (3) considers Aquinas's *De Veritate*, q. 2, a. 11, to be entirely consistent with passages in *De Potentia*, *Summa Contra Gentiles*, and *Summa Theologiae* that employ the Healthy Model for naming God and creatures. It will be seen that Capreolus's answer to the Equivocation Problem follows directly from (and in part controls) his answers to the *Rationes* and Analogy Model Problems.

The primary point of reference for Capreolus's doctrine of analogy is *Defensiones*, l. 1, d. 2, q. 1, on "Whether God is knowable by us in the present life."[1] Capreolus addresses analogy between God and creatures directly in the question's ninth conclusion, which is that "by the same concept in which the wayfarer conceives the creature, it is able to conceive God, although that concept is not said univocally of God and creature."[2] (The reader of chapter 2 knows that this would be

---

1. This question is treated at length in Dewan, "Does Being Have a Nature?," 23–59, and it is the primary source for Capreolus's doctrine of names said of God and creatures in S. Bonino, "Le concept d'étant et la connaissance de Dieu d'après Jean Cabrol (Capreolus)," *Revue Thomiste* 95 (1995)." I am not aware of any Scholastic or contemporary treatment of Capreolus's doctrine of analogy that draws on other passages from the *Defensiones* than those treated here.

2. John Capreolus, *Defensiones Theologiae Divi Thomae Aquinatis*, ed. C. Paban and T. Pegues (Tours: A. Cattier, 1900–1908; reprinted in Frankfurt: Minerva GmbH, 1967), l. 1, d. 2, q. 1, a. 1 (1:117a, 124a).

a surprising conclusion to Natalis and Sutton.) Capreolus discusses the same issues again in *Defensiones*, l. 1, d. 22 and 35, adding in those passages important and even essential qualifications for understanding his overall answers to the *Rationes* and Analogy Model Problems.

Capreolus's key terms, distinctions, and arguments appear more or less as the occasion for them arises in proofs for his questions' conclusions and in responses to arguments against his conclusions from Scotus, Peter Auriol, and (often unnamed) others. The *ad hoc* appearance of these points makes it more difficult to see the coherence of his position compared to the positions held by the later Renaissance Thomists, who devote specific questions to addressing the distinctions, arguments, and issues which they receive from Capreolus.[3] This chapter takes up the challenge of making Capreolus's occasional remarks into an overall position answering the three problems.

CAPREOLUS ON THE *RATIONES* PROBLEM

Defensiones, l. 1. d. 2, q. 1: Unequal Participation in Formal and Objective Concepts

After a lengthy enumeration of arguments against his ninth conclusion, Capreolus admits that Scotus and others have argued convincingly that there really is one concept of being common to God and creatures and to the ten categories.[4] For Natalis and Sutton, this would be to admit that being is univocal to God and creatures, and to the categories. But Capreolus, and the Renaissance Thomists after him, follow different rules for distinguishing univocal from other forms of predication than their early Thomist predecessors.

---

3. This difference is in large part a function of the later Thomists writing books of questions on topics raised in the works of Aristotle instead of (like Capreolus) presenting their doctrines within a comprehensive work of theology on the model of a commentary on the *Sentences* of Peter Lombard.

4. John Capreolus, *Defensiones*, l. 1, d. 2, q. 1, a. 1 (1:141a): "Ad argumenta Scoti et aliorum... ad omnes ejus probationes, dicitur generaliter, quod itque bene probant quod ens habeat unum conceptum communem Deo et creaturis et decem praedicamentis." See also my treatment of Capreolus on the *Rationes* Problem in Domenic D'Ettore, "The Fifteenth-Century Thomist Dispute over Participation in an Analogous Concept: John Capreolus, Dominic of Flanders, and Paul Soncinas," *Mediaeval Studies* 76 (2014): 246–51.

The practice of qualifying the definition of univocity from Aristotle's *Categories* (i.e., the same name signifying many through the same concept) was not new at the time of Capreolus. Indeed, early critics of Aquinas, including the Franciscans Scotus and Auriol, did so themselves. The reader will recall from chapter 1 that Scotus defines a "univocal concept" as one having (1) unity sufficient for it to be a contradiction to affirm and deny it of the same thing and (2) unity sufficient to be used in a demonstration without committing the fallacy of equivocation, and that Scotus holds that the concept of being is a "distinct concept."[5] Scotus's younger contemporary and admirer Auriol[6] agreed that there is one concept of being, but he denied that it was "distinct."[7] On the contrary, Auriol maintains that the concept of being is altogether indistinct, and that this indistinction is the foundation for its unity.[8] As it does not signify distinctly, Auriol con-

---

5. See Scotus, *Ordinatio* I, d. 3, pars 1, qq. 1–2 (*VC* 3:54–55). See Allen Wolter, *Transcendentals in the Metaphysics of Duns Scotus* (Washington, D.C.: The Catholic University of America Press, 1946), 65–71, for a discussion of Scotus's simple and distinct concept of being containing "one simple intelligible note or *ratio*."

6. References on his life and works are provided in note XX in the Introduction of this book.

7. See Peter Auriol, *Reportatio in I Sententiarum*, d. 2, p. 1, q. 2, ed. Stephen Brown, in *Traditio* 50 (1995), esp. 228.

8. For these points, see especially Auriol's *Scriptum in I Sententiarum*, d. 2, aa. 1–4 (Rome: Vaticana, 1596), 118b–121b. For a brief exposition of Auriol's position, see Stephen Brown, "Scotus's Univocity in the Fourteenth Century," in *De doctrina Ioannis Duns Scoti: Acta Congressus Scotistici Internationalis* (Rome: Scotist Commission, 1968), 35–41. For a more thorough account, see Stephen Brown, "The Unity of the Concept of Being in Peter Aureoli's Scriptum and Commentarium (with a critical edition of the Commentarium text)," PhD diss., University of Louvain, 1964. See also W. Goris, "Implicit Knowledge—Being as First Known in Peter of Oriel," *Recherches de Theologie et Philosophie Medievales* 69 (2002): 33–65. For a comparison of Auriol to Aquinas and Scotus on the concept of being, see especially Goris, "Implicit Knowledge," 41–42: "The innovation in comparison to the traditional conception in the thirteenth century is manifest. According to this conception, the concept of being has a determinate meaning; other concepts are derived from it, adding a proper meaning to the primary meaning of being that is present in each concept. Thomas Aquinas and John Duns Scotus disagree as to the exact character of the meaning that has to be assigned to being. The former seeks the meaning of being in the 'actuality' of things, the latter in the freedom from contradiction on the level of the imaginable. Both, however, agree *that* a determinate meaning has to be assigned to being. Precisely this *communis opinio* is attacked by Peter of Oriol. The unity of the concept of being is not produced by the fact that this concept has a determinate meaning, but rather

cludes that it cannot be univocal. Auriol concludes further that "being" must be said analogously. Specifically, he argues that being must be said analogously in the way that "principle" is said analogously as opposed to the way in which "healthy" is said analogously (on the grounds that "being" is said intrinsically of its analogates).[9] From Auriol, then, the reader is given to understand that a single name signifying through a single concept is an insufficient criterion for univocity, as one must also consider whether that concept is distinct or indistinct. If it is distinct, then the name signifies univocally. But if it is indistinct, then the name signifies analogously. The model of a name that signifies through one indistinct concept is the name "principle" said in the familiar analogous ways.

Capreolus was very familiar with the work of Auriol. It is speculated that a copy of Auriol's *Scriptum in Sententiarum* supplied Capreolus with access to the positions of Scotus, and Auriol's positions appear on nearly every page of the *Defensiones*.[10] In the works of Auriol, Capreolus found an example of a doctrine of analogy which permitted predication through a single concept. He also found that doctrine connected to a rejection of the Healthy Model of analogy in favor of the Principle Model. Although Capreolus does not embrace Auriol's overall position, he does appear to have taken Auriol's idea that univocity requires a distinct concept and modified it to fit into the writings of Aquinas, as will now be seen in Capreolus's distinction between "equal" and "unequal participation" in a concept.

According to Capreolus, Scotus's arguments that there is a single concept of being fail to prove that "being" is said univocally across

---

by the fact that this concept does not have a meaning, is not univocal or determinate, but rather confused and indeterminate. As far as this concept builds an unity, this totality is constituted by the concept's indetermination and not by any coherence from the side of its parts. Hence, other concepts do not relate to the concept of being in such a way that they would add their proper meaning to it; instead, they determine this indetermined and wholly implicit concept and render it explicit."

9. See Auriol, *Reportatio in I Sententiarum*, d. 2, p. 1, q. 1 (Brown, 213 and 219–20), and *Scriptum in I Sententiarum*, d. 2, p. 1, a. 5 (Vaticana, 132a).

10. For Capreolus's reliance on Auriol, see Bonino, "Le concept d'étant, esp. 111–12, and Tavuzzi, "Hervaeus Natalis," 140.

TABLE 2. Development of Conditions for Univocity

Author	Condition for Univocity
Aristotle	One name said of many through the same *ratio*
John Duns Scotus	One name said of many through the same *ratio* with sufficient unity to establish a contradiction and to mediate a syllogism
Peter Auriol	One name said of many through one distinct *ratio*
John Capreolus	One name said of many through one *ratio* equally participated

the categories and about God and creatures because univocal predication requires not only a single *ratio* or concept, but also that the one concept is participated in equally. A *ratio* is participated in unequally when it belongs to one recipient of a name more perfectly than it belongs to another recipient of the name. Leaving out any mention of Auriol as even an indirect source for this doctrine, Capreolus justifies his distinction instead through Aquinas's *In 1 Sent.*, d. 19, q. 5, a. 2, ad 1.

Capreolus explains that when Aquinas writes there that "truth and goodness, and other things of this kind said analogously of God creatures" are "in God and creatures according to a *ratio* of greater and lesser perfection," what Aquinas means is: "those intentions have a more perfect foundation in God than in creatures even though it remains the case that they represent God more imperfectly than they represent creatures because they are immediately taken from creatures and not from God."[11] The foundation for unequal participation is the real natures and perfections of the analogates. The wisdom, etc., in God is more perfect than the wisdom, etc., in creatures. Consequently, the creatures can be said to unequally participate in wisdom, etc., relative to God. Nonetheless, the human intellect's conceptual representation of wisdom, etc., in creatures is

11. Capreolus, *Defensiones*, l. 1, d. 2, q. 1, a. 1 (1:125a): "licet illae intentiones perfectius fundamentum habeant in Deo quam in creaturis; cum hoc tamen stat quod imperfectius repraesentant Deum quam creaturas: quia scilicet sunt immediate sumptae a creaturis et non a Deo."

John Capreolus 67

more perfect than its representation of wisdom, etc., in God. And so, the human intellect's conceptual representation of wisdom, etc., is also unequal, being a more perfect representation of the creature's wisdom, etc., than it is of divine wisdom, etc. A consequence of this inequality of being outside the mind and the corresponding unequal representation is that the names cannot be said univocally, but only analogously, of God and creatures, even though (as Capreolus admits that Scotus had shown) the names are predicated through the same concept.

Capreolus goes on to clarify his distinction between the foundations in things and the foundation in the intellect for unequal participation in a *ratio*. He calls the foundation *ex parte intellectus* the "formal concept" and the foundation *ex parte objecti* the "objective concept." This same distinction appeared in the previous chapter's treatment of Natalis.[12] In Capreolus's own words, the formal concept is the "conception the intellect forms when it conceives,"[13] and the objective concept "is not other than the intelligible which is made the object of the intellect belonging to the one forming the said conception."[14] Capreolus explains with an example. Human na-

12. See also ibid., a. 2 (1:133a–b), where Capreolus cites Aquinas, *In 1 Sent.*, d. 2, q. 1, a. 3, at length to explain what he himself understands by *ratio entis*. For the text of Aquinas, see Mandonnet, 1:66–67.

13. Capreolus, *Defensiones*, l. 1, d. 2, q. 1, a. 2 (1:141a): "Sumendo conceptum pro conceptione quam intellectus format dum concipit."

14. Ibid.: "Si autem loquamur de conceptu objectali, qui non est aliud quam intelligibile quod objicitur intellecti formanti dictam conceptionem." The full Latin text is quoted in note 16 below. See Ashworth, "Suárez on the Analogy of Being," 70: "Capreolus explains that the formal concept is the conception that the intellect forms when it conceives something, and that the objective concept is the intelligible thing which serves as object for the intellect forming such a conception." See also E. J. Ashworth, "Petrus Fonseca on Objective Concepts and the Analogy of Being," in *Logic and the Workings of the Mind: The Logic of Ideas and Faculty Psychology in Early Modern Philosophy*, ed. Easton Patricia (Atascadero: Ridgeview, 1997), 55–56. For further explanation of the distinction between the formal and objective concept in the writings of Capreolus, see Dewan, "Does Being Have a Nature?," 33. As Bonino explains in "Le concept d'étant," 117: "The formal concept is an intramental noetic reality. It is a form produced by the intellect in the act of intellection. Subjectively, the formal concept is an accident, a form-quality whose subject is the intellect. Objectively, it represents and expresses the known object in an intelligible way. The term '*ratio*'—which is far too ambiguous—can express this last aspect of the formal concept. As to the objective concept—clearly an unfortunate

ture is an objective concept insofar as it serves as the foundation for the intellect's formal concept of *homo*.[15] The unity of the objective concept is guaranteed by the unity in form or nature of whatever reality the intellect knows. The unity of the formal concept is established through the intellect's own act. A single "formal concept" is a single accident existing in an intellect representing an "objective concept."

Insofar then as many things possess a common foundation for a single formal concept to represent them in *mente*, many possess one and the same objective concept in *re* which can be represented. When Capreolus denies an equal foundation in God and creatures for a name, he denies that they participate equally in one objective concept. When he denies that the perfections of God and creatures can be equally represented by a human intellect, he denies that the analogates' equally participate in a formal concept.

Thus far, we find that Capreolus answers the *Rationes* Problem by affirming a single *ratio* for the key terms of metaphysics and for names said analogously of God and creatures. He explains that this answer does not surrender Aquinas's doctrine of analogy to the univocity theory of Scotus because the single *ratio* is participated in unequally, and this unequal participation is found both at the mental level of the formal concept and at the real level of the objective concept. Capreolus next needs to explain in what respect these unequally participated in formal and objective concepts are one, and yet not univocal.

He does this by drawing a distinction between the unity belonging to an objective concept when a name is said univocally and when a name is said analogously. Within *Defensiones*, l. 1, d. 2, q. 1, Capreolus grants that the formal concept for "being" and other names said

---

expression due to the fact that this 'concept' is not a concept in the usual sense of the term—, it is 'nothing other than the intelligible which is placed before the intellect which forms the said (formal) concept. For example, human nature is the objective concept of the intellection by which human is understood as such.' As such, the objective concept is the foundation of the truth of the formal concept."

15. Capreolus, *Defensiones*, l. 1, d. 2, q. 1, a. 2 (1:141a).

analogously of God and creatures must be one. The difference between univocals and analogates depends upon the unity of the objective concept. Unlike the objective concepts of univocals, which have a unity of "one form participated by many," the objective concepts of analogates have a lesser unity which Capreolus calls "unity of imitation" or "attribution." Returning to the example of "being" said of God and creatures and across the categories, Capreolus informs his reader that "Creatures are called beings from imitation and attribution to God, and accident from imitation of substance and attribution to substance."[16] To understand more fully what Ca-

16. See ibid., 141a–b: "Unde, ad omnes ejus probationes, dicitur generaliter, quod utique bene probant quod ens habeat unum conceptum communem Deo et creaturis et decem praedicamentis, sumendo conceptum pro conceptione quam intellectus format dum concipit ens. Si autem loquamur de conceptu objectali, qui non est aliud quam intelligibile quod objicitur intellectui formanti dictam conceptionem, sicut natura humana diceretur conceptus objectalis illius intellectionis qua intelligitur homo inquantum hujusmodi, tunc distinguendum est de unitate. Quia, vel potest intelligi de unitate attributionis, eo modo quo multa, habentia attributionem ad unum, dicuntur unum attributive; vel potest dici de unitate, quae attenditur penes aliquam formam vel naturam quae participatur a multis, qualis est unitas generis vel speciei. Humanitas enim, in omnibus est una forma; non quidem actu, nec potentia, extra intellectum, sed aptitudine; sic quod non stat, ex parte illius formae, quin sit una, sed ex alio, scilicet ex principiis individuantibus illam, vel ex differentiis dividentibus eam. Si loquamur de primo modo unitatis, sic conceditur quod ens habet unum conceptum communem Deo et creaturis objectalem: unum quidem, non per indivisionem alicujus formae in eis participatae, sed unum per attributionem: quia creaturae dicuntur entia, ex imitatione et attributione ad Deum; et ulterius accidens, ex imitatione substantiae, et attributione ad illam. Et ideo ille conceptus objectalis non est unus tanta unitate quanta conceptus objectalis generis dicitur unus, vel conceptus speciei, sed multo minori." (Hence, to all its proofs, it said generally, that, yes, they prove well that being has one concept common to God and to creatures, and to the ten categories, by taking "concept" for the conception which the intellect forms while it conceives being. But if we are speaking about the objective concept, which is not other than the intelligible which is the object belonging to the intellect in the act of forming the said conception, as human nature is called the objective concept of the act of intellection by which human [nature] is understood as such, then a distinction must be made regarding unity. For either it can be understood from the unity of attribution, in which way many things that have attribution to one thing are said to be one attributively; or, it can be said from the unity which is found within any form or nature which is participated in by many things. Such is the unity of a genus or a species. For humanity, in all things, is one form. Now it is not one form in all actually or potentially outside the intellect, but aptitudinally, such that it does not stand on the part of the form itself that it is one, but from another, namely from the principles individuating it or from the differences dividing it. If we speak about the first mode of unity, then it is conceded that

preolus means in distinguishing the unity of the formal concept in an analogy from the unity of the objective concept, the reader must turn to *Defensiones*, l. 1, d. 22, q. 1, where Capreolus goes back to the question of whether names are predicated univocally or analogously about God and creatures.

Defensiones, l. 1, d. 22, q. 1: Formal Concepts of God and Divine Attributes

Capreolus clarifies the relationship between the formal concept proper to the creature and the intellect's conception (i.e., formal concept) of the creator in *Defensiones*, l. 1, d. 22, q. 1.[17] The question proposed is "whether God can be designated by any name properly."[18] Conclusion 4 maintains that "No name imposed by us signifies God according to a concept of him which is simple and proper to him alone,"[19] and conclusion 5 that "No name imposed by us is said univocally of God and creature."[20] In the course of defending these conclusions, Capreolus presents the single formal concept through which a name is said of God and creatures as (1) the proper concept of the creature and (2) a component part of the complex formal concept proper to God. Capreolus writes in his defense of conclusion 4:

---

being has one concept common to God and to creatures objectively. It is truly one, not by the lack of division of any form participated by them, but by attribution, because creatures are called beings from imitation and attribution to God; and, again, an accident [is called being] from imitation of substance and attribution to it. And, therefore, that objective concept is not one by as great a unity as the objective concept of a genus or the concept of a species is called one, but much less.) See also the *ad secundum* below (ibid., 141b): "licet conceptus entis prima impressione imprimatur in anima, sumendo conceptum ex parte intellectus, non tamen oportet quod objectalis conceptus habeat aliquam unitatem, nisi attributionis aut imitationis." (Although the concept of being is impressed by the first impression in the soul, taking "concept" from the side of the intellect; nevertheless, it is not necessary that the objective concept has any unity other than of attribution or of imitation.)

17. See also my treatment of this passage in D'Ettore, "The Semantic Unity," 140–45.

18. Capreolus, *Defensiones*, l. 1, d. 22, q. 1 (2:169b): "utrum Deus possit aliquo nomine proprie designari."

19. Ibid., 171b: "Quarta conclusio est quod nullum nomen a nobis impositum, significat Deum secundum ejus simplicem et proprium ei soli conceptum."

20. Ibid., 172a: "Quinta conclusio est quod nullum nomen a nobis impositum, dicitur univoce de Deo et creatura."

For our intellect, in the state of the way [i.e., in this life], does not understand God in any concept unless it is a concept of a creature, such as the concepts of perfections exemplared [*conceptus perfectionum exemplatarum*] from divine perfection; or at least composed from such concepts as is the case with the concepts: first cause, infinite being, and the like. But we signify as we understand. Therefore, no name imposed by us is attributed to God by us in such a way that the concept would signify God and no other, not even its [i.e., the concept's] parts. These things are clear from what has been said. And it is confirmed. Because if there were any such name expressing any concept proper to God alone, this would seem most of all to be the name "God." But it is not so about the term "God." Hence, [it is the case] about none. The minor premise is clear. Because although the name "God" signifies the divine nature, nevertheless, it does not express a concept belonging to God alone; on the contrary, [it expresses] a complex concept from many concepts, which belong separately to creatures. For "God" signifies divine nature under the concept "universal provider" or "first cause," or "first mover," or something of this kind. But it is certain that the parts of these complex concepts belong to many creatures. And so, the conclusion is clear. With which it stands that although many names, such as wise, good, and the like, express simple concepts; nevertheless, [they are] common to God and creatures.[21]

The human intellect forms its concepts through experience of creatures. Consequently, any and every name said about God properly, including the name "God," is signified through a composite con-

21. Ibid., 171b–172a: "Probatur conclusio ista ex praedictis. Nam intellectus noster, in statu viae, non intelligit Deum in aliquo conceptu, quin ille sit conceptus creaturae, sicut sunt conceptum perfectionum exemplatarum a divina perfectione; vel saltem compositus ex talibus conceptibus, sicut sunt isti conceptus: causa prima, ens infinitum, et hujusmodi. Sicut autem intelligimus, ita significamus. Ergo nullum nomen a nobis impositum, sic est Deo a nobis appropriatum, quod Deum significet et nihil aliud significet iste conceptus, nec ejus partes. Ista omnia patent ex praedictis. – Et confirmatur. Quia si esset aliquod tale nomen exprimens aliquem conceptum soli Deo proprium, hoc videretur esse potissime hoc nomen, Deus. Sed non sic est de hoc termino, Deus. Ergo de nullo. Minor patet. Quia hoc nomen, Deus, licet naturam divinam significet, tamen non exprimit conceptum soli Deo convenientem; immo conceptum complexum ex multis conceptibus, qui divisim creaturis conveniunt. Significat enim divinam naturam sub hoc conceptu, universalis provisor, vel causa prima, vel primus motor, vel hujusmodi. Constat autem istorum conceptuum complexorum partes convenire multis creaturis. Et sic patet conclusio. Cum qua stat quod multa nomina exprimunt conceptus simplices, communes tamen Deo et creaturis, sicut sapiens, bonus, et hujusmodi."

cept that is formed from concepts that properly signify creatures. In Capreolus's example of the name "God," the intellect begins with its concepts of "first" and "cause." Both of these concepts are acquired by the natural acts of a human's intellect. To supply Capreolus with an example, one can think of an intellect deriving its concepts of "first" and "cause" from judging something to be "the first domino to fall" and "the cause of the second domino falling." Combining these two concepts, the intellect forms the complex concept, "first cause." Insofar as the name "God" signifies through the complex concept "first cause," and the simpler parts of this concept take their signification from the intellect's proper concepts of creatures, the name "God" cannot be signified without employing formal concepts that properly signify creatures.[22]

This passage establishes that the proper formal concept of the creature must carry over into the signification of the name as predicated of God. If it is entirely absent, then nothing would be signified about God at all. Still, the proper formal concept of the creature does not pass into the signification of God altogether without modi-

---

22. Capreolus provides a detailed example of what he means by forming a complex concept of God in *Defensiones*, l. 1, d. 2, q. 1, a. 1, conclusion 7 (1:123a–b): "Verb gratia: ex motu coeli, quem videmus sensu, concludimus coelum moveri ab aliquo alio; et ultra, per alias rationes, quod illud quod movet coelum est substantia. Item, ex eo quod movetur circulariter, arguimus quod substantia movens coelum est intelligens; et quia ille motus semper videtur durare, ulterius concluditur quod illud movens est incorporeum et immateriale. Et ex omnibus istis colligimus quod est aliquod ens quod est substantia immaterialis incorporea, qui conceptus est proprius substantiae separatae. Ulterius autem per alias rationes concludimus quod est aliquod ens quod est substantia immaterialis incorporea et prima omnium substantiarum separatarum, qui est conceptus proprius Dei, in quo conceptu ex post cognoscimus Deum." (For example: from the motion of the heavens, which we see by sense, we conclude that the heavens is moved by some other thing. Through other reasons, we conclude further that the other thing which moves the heavens is a substance. Then, from the fact that it is moved in a circle, we argue that the substance moving the heavens is intelligent; and, because that motion seems to endure always, it is further concluded that the substance doing the moving is incorporeal and immaterial. From all those conclusions, we gather that there is some being which is an immaterial, incorporeal substance, which is the concept proper to separate substance. We conclude further through other reasons that there is some being which is an immaterial, incorporeal substance and the first of all separate substances, which is the concept proper to God, in which concept from that time we know God.)

fication. Yet even the modifications it receives must be through concepts that are themselves proper to creatures.

Capreolus further clarifies this point when addressing an argument from Auriol. The Franciscan argued that, although the human intellect cannot produce a proper concept of God through abstraction, it can nonetheless produce a concept proper to God through analogous reasoning from three unknowns to a known. Auriol's argument appeals to Aristotle's account of the discovery of prime matter. The intellect does not abstract a concept of prime matter from a phantasm. Rather, it arrives at a concept of prime matter through analogous reasoning from three knowns. In the same way, the intellect cannot abstract a concept of God from phantasms, but it can arrive at a concept of God by engaging in analogous reasoning from three knowns.[23]

Capreolus writes in response: "I say that the wayfarer can have the fourth concept; but that concept will not be properly of God and simple, but [it will be] the concept of being or some composite concept."[24] Capreolus continues his rebuttal as follows:

> It is doubtful to me if we have a simple concept of prime matter. For it seems that prime matter is always conceived by a certain complex concept, composed from an absolute concept and a relative concept with respect to form. And whatever may be [the case] about this, no effect of God can lead the wayfarer to knowing God in himself, that is, by a simple concept proper to Him, by which no other thing is conceived. Nor does any concept held by creatures represent him as he is in himself, but always in another, whether [it represents] by negation, as the concept of infinite, or by causality, as first cause, [or] first being, or by the way of eminence, as super-good, super-just, and the like; for our concepts either are likenesses of sensible creatures, or composed from them or with them, or drawn from them.[25]

---

23. Capreolus, *Defensiones*, l. 1, d. 22, q. 1, a. 2 (2:172b–173a). See Auriol, *Scriptum in I Sententiarum*, d. 22, a. 2 (Vaticana, 522b).
24. Ibid., 175a: "Ad tertium dico quod viator potest habere illum quartum conceptum; sed ille non erit proprius Dei et simplex, sed conceptus entis vel aliquis conceptus compositus."
25. Ibid.: "Sed dubium tamen mihi est, si nos habeamus simplicem conceptum proprium materiae primae. Videtur enim quod semper concipitur quodam conceptu complexo,

Capreolus does not criticize Auriol's comparison between reasoning to God's existence and attributes and reasoning to the existence and attributes of prime matter. Both are admittedly instances where reason must go beyond the imagination and sensory experience. Both, likewise, require the intellect to modify its concepts for them to be signified about the "fourth" object.[26] Rather, Capreolus's point is that, even through the kind of reasoning Auriol describes, the intellect does not produce a simple concept that properly signifies God. That is, the human intellect in this life does not produce a concept that signifies God without first signifying creatures. The human intellect does not even produce a concept that properly signifies prime matter (apart from signifying formed matter). Even the concepts of negations, causality, and eminence are derivative from experience of creatures. Hence, the complex formal concept with which a human intellect signifies God (or prime matter) is only able to perform its act of signifying God (or prime matter) because its parts properly signify creatures (or composites of substantial form and prime matter).

Having placed formal concepts that are proper to creatures into the complex concept that properly signifies God, Capreolus still

---

composito ex conceptu absoluto et conceptu relativo, per respectum ad formam. Et quidquid sit de hoc, nullus effectus Dei potest viatorem deducere ad cognoscendum Deum in se, id est, conceptu sibi proprio simplici, quo nulla alia res concipiatur. Nec aliquis conceptus habitus a creaturis, sive per negationem, ut conceptus infiniti, sive per causalitatem, ut causa prima, ens primum, sive per viam eminentiae, ut superbonus, superjustus, et hujusmodi, repraesentat eum ut in se est, sed semper in alio; conceptus enim nostri, vel sunt similitudines creaturarum sensibilium, aut compositi ex illis, vel cum illis, aut ab illis extracti."

26. Capreolus acknowledges that, in cases such as Auriol's example of bread, someone with a sufficient prior knowledge of a thing's accidental features or effects could reason by analogy to a quidditative concept of the thing. Ibid., 175a: "quando per accidentia rei vel effectus ejus sufficienter homo ducitur in notitiam quod quid est, sicut exemplificat de materia et de pane; tunc enim, in illo casu, quis potest habere conceptum simplicem, proprium, et distinctum de quidditate rei, puta panis, si habeantur tales tres conceptus, de quibis iste loquitur." (When through the accidents of a thing or its effects a human is led into quidditative knowledge. This is exemplified by [prime] matter and by bread. For then, one can have a simple, proper, and distinct concept of the quiddity of the thing—such as bread—if one possesses three concepts of the sort he [i.e., Auriol] speaks.)

John Capreolus 75

needs to address the question of why this solution does not reduce analogy to univocity.²⁷ He does this in his defense of *Defensiones*, l. 1, d. 22, q. 1, a. 5, conclusion 5: that no names signify God and creatures univocally. In the objections to conclusion 5, Capreolus restates in detail Scotus's "Certain and Doubtful" Argument, including the following:

Every intellect certain about one concept and doubtful about different things has one concept about which it is certain, [which is] other than the concepts about which it is doubtful. But the intellect of the wayfarer can be certain about God, that he is a being, while being doubtful about [whether God is] a finite or infinite being, created or uncreated. Therefore, the concept of being about God, is other than the concept about the latter and the former [i.e., finite being and infinite being; created being and uncreated being], and so [the concept of being is] neither [the latter nor former concept] in itself and is included in both of them.²⁸

In chapter 2, we saw that Natalis and Sutton responded to this objection by employing the unity of disjunction and by steadfastly denying any simple unity to the concept of being.²⁹ Consistent with his remarks in *Defensiones*, l. 1, d. 2, q. 1, here Capreolus admits simple unity to the concept of being while denying its univocity through appeal to the distinction between equal and unequal participation in a *ratio*. He writes:

To the first argument of Scotus against the fifth conclusion, with all its confirmations, it is said that it does not suffice for some name to be said univocally about two things that it signifies one concept, common to those two in any way; but it is required that that concept is participat-

---

27. The reader should recall here Cross's interpretation of Scotus's semantics of analogy discussed in chapter 1, which also involves seeing the same concept in one or more complex concepts.
28. Capreolus, *Defensiones*, l. 1, d. 22, q. 1, a. 2 (2:173a): "Omnis intellectus certus de uno conceptu, et dubius de diversis, habet conceptum de quo est certus, alium a conceptibus de quibus est dubius. Sed intellectus viatoris potest esse certus, de Deo, quod sit ens, dubitando de ente finito vel infinito, creato vel increato. Ergo conceptus entis de Deo, est alius a conceptu illo et isto, et ita neuter ex se, et in utroque istorum includitur. Ergo est unicus."
29. Capreolus is likely aware of Auriol's criticism of the unity of disjunction response to this argument. See Auriol, *Reportatio in I Sententiarum*, d. 2, p. 1, q. 1 (Brown, 210–12).

ed by them equally, and not more perfectly by one than by the other; so that, if that concept is more perfectly a likeness of one than of the other, on account of this, a name signifying that concept will not be univocal to those two about which it is said. Yet, so it is for every concept which the wayfarer has about God. For every concept formed by [the wayfarer that is] common to God and to creature represents God more imperfectly than the creature. For the concept of wisdom represents created wisdom more perfectly than uncreated; because it is taken immediately from created wisdom; and, therefore, it represents it more distinctly, as regards itself and its modes, than uncreated wisdom; therefore this name "wisdom" is not properly univocal. Unless you say that for univocation one concept of any kind suffices; but then it is a question about the name; because then that which I call analogous, you call univocal.[30]

Repeating his points from *Defensiones*, l. 1, d. 2 about the human intellect's concepts representing creatures more perfectly than they represent God, Capreolus insists once again that inequality of representation prevents univocal predication. Following Auriol, he

30. Capreolus, *Defensiones*, l. 1, d. 22, q. 1, a. 2 (2:175b): "Ad primum Scoti contra quintam conclusionem, cum omnibus confirmationibus suis, dicitur quod ad hoc quod aliquod nomen dicatur univoce de duobus, non sufficit quod significet conceptum unicum, communem illis duobus quocumque modo; sed requiritur quod ille conceptus aequaliter participetur ab eis, et non perfectius ab uno quam ab alio; ita quod si conceptus ille sit perfectius similitudo unius quam alterius, non, propter hoc, nomen significans illum conceptum erit univocum illis duobus de quibus dicitur. Sic autem est de omni conceptu quem habet viator de Deo. Nam omnis conceptus ab eo formatus, communis Deo et creaturae, imperfectius repraesentat Deum quam creaturam. Conceptus enim sapientiae repraesentat perfectius sapientiam creatam quam increatam; quia est immediate sumptus a sapientia creata; et ideo repraesentat eam distinctius, quoad se et modos ejus, quam sapientiam increatam; ideo hoc nomen sapientiae non est proprie univocum. Nisi dicas quod ad univocationem sufficit unicus qualiscumque conceptus; sed tunc est quaestio de nomine; quia tunc illud quod ego dico analogum, tu dicis univocum." Besides the texts already quoted to make this point, see also the response to the second objection from Scotus to the fifth conclusion (ibid.): "Dico tamen quod intellectus viatoris potest formare conceptum compositum de sapientia divina, puta concipiendo actum sapientificandi, independentem, non inhaerentem, etc. Et tamen ille conceptus adhuc esset, secundum unam partem sui, similitudo sapientiae creatae, superexcellens; et ideo nunquam esset univocus isti et illi." (Nevertheless, I say that the intellect of the wayfarer can form a composite concept of divine wisdom. This could be done, for example, by conceiving the act of acting wisely, independence, and non-inherence, etc. And nevertheless, that concept would still be a superexcelling likeness of created wisdom, according to one its parts. And, therefore, it would never be univocal to created wisdom and divine wisdom.)

finds the single concept "of any kind" criterion for univocity to be insufficient. He accepts an overlap of semantic content between the concepts through which the intellect signifies wise creatures and divine wisdom. Yet he denies that this overlap is enough to produce univocity, because it is participated in unequally.

Summing up this section, Capreolus argues that when names are said by analogy about God and creatures, the intellect expresses the name through a formal concept that is perfectly one, even though the foundation for the name in God and in creatures (i.e., the objective concept) has only the lesser unity of imitation or attribution. The formal concept is perfectly one because it represents God imperfectly by representing the creature that imperfectly imitates God. God and creature participate unequally in the formal concept or formal *ratio* insofar as this *ratio* represents the creature more perfectly than it represents God. God and creature participate unequally in the objective concept or objective *ratio* unequally insofar as the creature is an inadequate imitation of God. Capreolus concedes to Scotus true unity for the formal concept while maintaining that the objective concept has the lesser "unity of imitation or attribution," which is what ultimately prevents univocal naming.

Unlike Sutton, Capreolus is willing to grant a merely verbal difference with the Scotist if by "univocal" the Scotist designates any name said of many through a single *ratio*. However, Capreolus thinks that such a use of the term overlooks the distinction between equal and unequal participation in a *ratio*, and that the name "univocal" ought to be restricted to cases of equal participation in a *ratio*. Precedent for this approach can be found in Auriol's critique of Scotus, and Capreolus presents it as the doctrine of Aquinas in *In 1 Sent.*, d. 19.

CAPREOLUS ON THE ANALOGY MODEL PROBLEM

Defensiones, l. 1, d. 2, q. 1: A Threefold Division of Analogy

John Capreolus's rejection of the Healthy Model of analogy for names said of God and creatures could hardly be more thorough and explicit, but his embrace of the Principle Model has been largely overlooked in the scholarly literature. His initial rejection the Healthy Model appears in his threefold division of analogy in *Defensiones*, l. 1, d. 2, q. 1, a. 2:

There is a threefold mode of analogy according to what was said in the proof of the Ninth Conclusion. The first occurs when the analogous term expresses one *ratio* principally, and besides this expresses a relation or proportion to that *ratio* as occurs in the case of "healthy." Sometimes it expresses the form of health, sometimes the relation of cause to health. An analogous term of such a kind expresses diverse *rationes* actually and explicitly. The second mode of analogy occurs when the analogous term expresses only one *ratio* and that *ratio* has diverse and not uniform *esse* in the analogates. For example, "body" when it is said about heavenly and lower things. Thirdly, there is the analogous term which expresses one *ratio* actually in which the analogates are not made equal, and they are not made equal in their *esse* either. For example, "being" said of God and a creature, or of substance and accident. Only the first mode of analogy renders a proposition ambiguous.[31]

31. Ibid., d. 2, q. 1, a. 2 (1:142a): "Triplex est enim modus analogiae, secundum quod dictum est in probatione nonae conclusionis. Primus est quando analogum dicit unam rationem principaliter, et praeter hoc dicit habitudinem vel proportionem ad illam rationem; sicut sanum, quandoque dicit formam sanitatis, quandoque habitudinem causae ad sanitatem; et sic tale analogum dicit diversas rationes in actu et explicite. Aliud est analogum quod non dicit nisi unam rationem, quae tamen diversum esse habet in analogatis, et non uniforme, sicut corpus cum dicitur de caelestibus, et inferioribus. Aliud est analogum quod dicit unam rationem actu, in qua tamen non parificantur analogata, nec in esse illius, sicut ens dictum de Deo et creatura, de substantia et accidente. Et solum primus modus analogiae reddit propositionem multiplicem." On this passage, see Bonino, "Le concept d'étant," 119: "In the second and third modes of analogy, the analogous term or concept reflects a single unique *ratio*. The difference is taken from the manner in which this *ratio* is based in the analogates, that is to say, the difference is at the level of the objective concept." In the second and third modes of analogy, the analogates share in one formal concept. The formal concept represents the analogates of the second mode equally,

The structure of this threefold division and the examples for each mode of analogy come from Aquinas's *In 1 Sent.*, d. 19, q. 5, a. 2, ad 1 (the same text that Capreolus uses to justify his understanding of univocity requiring equal participation in a *ratio*). The first mode of analogy employs Healthy Model examples. Principally, the name "healthy" signifies the "form of health" in an animal. It also signifies "the relation of cause" toward health in an animal. According to Capreolus, it follows that the name "healthy" and other names said analogously in the first mode express "diverse *rationes* actually and explicitly." Notice here that he does not say that they express one *ratio* participated in unequally, or that they express an objective concept that has only the unity of attribution. Quite to the contrary, Capreolus denies that analogates in this mode have one *ratio* even by the unity attribution or imitation. He does not go into detail, but presumably he considers the difference in *re* between what is signified in a proposition such as "every healthy thing is alive" and what is signified in a proposition such as "medicine is healthy" to be so great with respect to the form or nature signified by the term "healthy" that they do not participate in one objective concept even by the unity of attribution. By implication, urine's capacity to signify health in an animal, medicine's capacity to affect an animal, and an animal's good physical disposition are so different objectively that the name "healthy" is predicated of each one through its own separate formal concept, and there is not one formal concept which even imperfectly represents the health found in each of them. Capreolus notes that

---

even though these analogates are not equal in their mode of being. The formal concept does not represent analogates of the third mode equally. See also the remarks of Dewan on the passage: "I do wonder whether Capreolus goes too far (though it is a side-issue) in saying that *only* the first mode of analogy makes for ambiguity; it would seem that the second mode could also do so" (Dewan, "Does Being Have a Nature?," 57n53). Dewan does not give an example, but I assume he is imagining something like the following syllogism (or paralogism): "Bodies are solid. Fire is a body. Ergo, fire is solid." If so, I do not think that the problem is ambiguity on the word "body," but either a false or ambiguously distributed major premise, or else an ambiguity on the term "solid." Dewan is the only author who I have seen suggest that the second mode of analogy is unsuited for demonstration. See also my remarks in D'Ettore, "John Capreolus on Names Said Analogously of God and Creatures," *The Thomist* 77 (2013): 408–12.

this first mode of analogy "renders a proposition ambiguous," which entails that it would render a syllogism using the ambiguous term invalid by the fallacy of equivocation.

The second mode of analogy—"when the analogous term expresses only one *ratio* and that *ratio* has diverse and not uniform *esse* in the analogates"—does not concern the Analogy Model Problem because it is logically univocal, and, consequently, it does not apply to the analogy between God and creatures. Following Aquinas's example, Capreolus concludes that names are said of God and creatures by the third mode of analogy. In this mode, in Capreolus's words, "the analogous term ... expresses one *ratio* actually in which the analogates are not made equal, and they are not made equal in their *esse* either." Capreolus explains the unity of *ratio* in the third mode of analogy and its suitability for use in demonstration in the following two awkward sentences:

> But a name said analogously which expresses only one *ratio* explicitly, granting that it is one by only unity of attribution speaking of the objective concept, because it also expresses only one intention of the intellect representing the objective *ratio*, although not equally as regards to all the things contained under such a *ratio*, such a name said analogously, I say, does not make a proposition ambiguous. But being is of this kind.[32]

In other words, in the third mode of analogy, the analogates possess an objective concept that has unity of attribution or imitation. This lesser unity at the level of the objective concept is sufficient for one single formal concept to represent the diverse analogates unequally.

It is then the objective concept's unity which makes the third mode of analogy singularly suitable among the modes of analogy for use in the demonstrations of metaphysics and natural theology.

---

32. Capreolus, *Defensiones*, l. 1, d. 2, q. 1, a. 2 (1:142a): "sed analogum quod dicit unam solam rationem explicite, licet illa sit una, sola unitate attributionis, loquendo de ratione objectali, quod etiam dicit unam intentionem intellectus repraesentantem rationem objectalem, quamvis non aeque quantum ad omnia contenta sub tali ratione, tale, inquam, analogum non facit propositionem multiplicem. Hujusmodi autem est ens ..." Sometimes Capreolus refers to the "objective concept" and sometimes to the "objective *ratio*." This is explained by the fact that the objective concept is the *ratio* as it exists in the thing known.

The first mode has too little objective unity to be represented by one formal concept, and so it leads to the fallacy of equivocation if used in a demonstration. The second mode has too much objective unity to be logically analogous, and, while it may be useful for the demonstrations of physics (such as when properties are demonstrated of heavenly and lower bodies alike), it does not capture the way that "being" is said across the categories or the way that names, including "being," are said analogously of God and creatures. The third mode alone has neither too much objective diversity for demonstrative use nor too much objective unity for the key terms of metaphysics and natural theology. Based on this text alone, Capreolus appears to have completely rejected the Healthy Model as the explanation for how names are said analogously of God and creatures. It does not, however, address whether he endorses the Principle Model or some other third alternative model of analogy distinct from the Healthy Model and the Principle Model. To fully understand Capreolus's position on the Analogy Model Problem, I turn now to passages where he yet again takes up the topic of names said analogously of God and creatures, and interprets a wider set of texts from Aquinas.

Defensiones, l. 1, d. 35, q. 2, a. 2: The Primacy of
De Veritate, q. 2, a. 11

A second passage where Capreolus treats the Analogy Model Problem is *Defensiones*, l. 1, d. 35, q. 2, a. 2. There he quotes at length the body of *De Veritate*, q. 2, a. 11. As discussed above, Aquinas explains in this passage that names are said of creatures and the creator by "proportionality." Specifically, Thomas states that *scientia* is said of God and creatures just as "seeing" is said of the mind and the body. Thomas distinguishes names said by proportionality from names said proportionally. His example of the latter is "healthy" said of urine in relation to the health of an animal.[33] Having given this text

---

33. Ibid., d. 35, q. 2, a. 2 (2:398b–399a). See also ibid., d. 43, q. 1 (2:533a–b), where Capreolus repeats *De Veritate*, q. 2, a. 11's discussion of the proportionality between God and creatures in his own words.

as Aquinas's answer to the question of how names are said of God and creatures, Capreolus adds without further qualification that Aquinas says the same thing about names said analogously of God and creatures in the *De Potentia*, q. 7, a. 7, *Summa Contra Gentiles* I, cc. 33 and 34, *Summa Theologiae* I, q. 13, a. 4 and 5, and *In 1 Sent.*, d. 35, q. 1, a. 1.[34] Capreolus could have been much clearer on how he understands the reconciliation of these apparently conflicting passages and on his own understanding of analogy of proportionality. Indeed, Montagnes—relying exclusively on the *Defensiones*—considered Capreolus to represent a line of Thomism in opposition to the Principle Model of analogy proposed by Sutton for names said of God and creatures.[35]

Besides the citation of *De Veritate*, q. 2, a. 11, in *Defensiones*, l. 1, d. 35, Capreolus also mentions proportionality in passing in *Defensiones*, l. 1, d. 45.[36] But, as in his discussion of the single *ratio* common to God and creatures, Capreolus leaves to the reader the work of piecing together his overall position on the diverse kinds of analogy and the divine names.[37]

This work can be accomplished by considering Capreolus's sparse nontheological (and nonmetaphysical) examples of pro-

---

34. Ibid., 399a: "Eamdem sententiam ponit, *de Potentia Dei*, q. 7, art. 7. – Item, 1 p., q. 13, art. 4 et 5. – Item, 1. *Contra Gentiles*, cap. 33 et 34; et 1. *Sentent.*, dist. 35, q. 1, art. 4." Capreolus does not discuss the chronology of Aquinas's texts. G. Emery's catalogue puts *De Veritate* between 1256 and 1259 and the *prima pars* of *Summa Theologiae* between 1265 and 1268. See Emery's catalogue in Torrell, *Saint Thomas Aquinas*, 1:332–61.

35. Montagnes, *The Doctrine of the Analogy of Being according to Thomas Aquinas*, 119–20. See also Bonino, "Le concept d'étant," 129.

36. Responding to an argument from Auriol regarding the will, Capreolus writes: "quia intelligit divinum velle non in se, sed sub conceptu quem format intellectus de actu nostrae voluntatis, cui est adjuncta illa imperfectio, scilicet quod non subsistit sed elicitur a voluntate nostra. Et ideo oportet quod proportionaliter intelligat velle divinum." (Because the intellect [of the wayfarer] does not understand the divine will in itself, but under a concept which the intellect forms about the act of our will, to which an imperfection is adjoined, namely the imperfection that the act of the will does not subsist but is chosen from our will. And, therefore, it is necessary that the intellect [of the wayfarer] understands divine willing by proportionality.) *Defensiones*, l. 1, d. 45, q. 1 (2:571b).

37. I made an initial attempt to piece these texts together in D'Ettore, "John Capreolus on Names said Analogously of God and Creatures," esp. 408–15.

portionality and of more or less perfect participation in a *ratio*. The search for such examples leads the reader back to *Defensiones*, l. 1, d. 2, q. 1, a. 1, but this time to its conclusion 7, which affirms that the human intellect in this life can achieve a qualified immediate knowledge of God.[38] Capreolus writes: "in any concept God is conceived, the creature is conceived through the whole concept or through part of such a concept"[39] and, further,

> it must be known that when I say that God cannot be seen immediately or understood by the one in this condition [i.e., the one in this life], I understand this as follows: when I know God in this life, the intellect has a twofold medium, namely, one on the side of the one knowing, which is the intelligible species, the other on the side of the thing known, namely, some creature which is represented though that species, not God alone. It is as though I know Hercules by seeing his stone statue.[40]

Just as the museum visitor only sees the stone image of Hercules (or Julius Caesar) and not the man himself, the human intellect in this life only sees a creaturely imitation of the divine essence, not the divine essence itself. Just as Hercules himself is seen by the one viewing the image of Hercules (or Caesar is seen by the one viewing the image of Caesar), the human intellect understands God insofar as its medium for understanding God is an image of God. It follows that

---

38. Capreolus, *Defensiones*, l. 1, d. 2, q. 1, a. 1 (1:122b): "Septima conclusio: quod Deus potest in via immediate cognosci, ita quod cognitio viatoris attingit in ipsum, licet per media transeat; dum autem Deum attingit, potest de ipso immediate cogitare, sic quod ex tunc ad cogitandum de Deo non oportet praecogitare de alio." (The seventh conclusion is that God can be known immediately in this life, such that the knowledge of the wayfarer attains God Himself, even though it crosses through media. But when it attains God, it is able to know about Him immediately, such that from that time it is not necessary to know about another in order to know about God.)

39. Ibid., 123b: "quocumque conceptu concipiatur Deus, concipiatur creatura per totum conceptum vel per partem talis conceptus."

40. Ibid.: "Sciendum etiam quod cum dico Deum pro isto statu non videri immediate vel intelligi, hoc sic intelligo, quod quando Deum cognosco in via, intellectus habet duplex medium, scilicet unum ex parte cognoscentis, quod est species intelligibilis, aliud ex parte cogniti, scilicet aliqua creatura, quae repraesentatur per illam speciem, non solum Deus; et est simile sicut si cognoscam Herculem videndo ejus statuam lapideam." On the Thomist debate over the intelligible species' relationship to things and to concepts, see Pini, "Species, Concept, and Thing," 21–52.

the human intellect can only represent God by representing a creature.[41] Although the words "unequal participation" do not appear in this passage, the connection between his remarks here in conclusion 7 to his remarks in conclusion 9 is apparent. The *ratio* (specifically the formal concept) through which the creature represents God is the same (at least in part) as the concept through which the creature represents God. That *ratio* represents the creature more perfectly, as it was derived from creatures in the first place. Yet it still represents God to the extent that God is imitated by the creature.

Aquinas's *De Veritate*, q. 2, a. 11, example of proportionality—quoted by Capreolus in *Defensiones*, l. 1, d. 35, as cited above—is "seeing" or "vision" said of the act of the eye and the act of the intellect. Applying what Capreolus wrote about the stone Hercules to this example, Capreolus would hold that through one *ratio* (i.e., through one formal concept) the intellect represents both the seeing of the eye and the proportionally similar seeing of the intellect. The *ratio* properly representing the eye's activity at once represents imperfectly the intellect's seeing.[42]

I see no problem in applying this same interpretation to Capreolus's theological examples. Just as the statue imitates and participates in the perfection of the exemplar, the creature imitates and participates in the perfections belonging to God. This participation and imitation founds a proportionality between a creature's perfection and the divine perfection. The proportionality between the imitating effect and the imitated cause entails that what answers in reality to the intellect's conception of a perfection in a creature has a like-

---

41. Capreolus denies that the intellect has any concept of God that is not the concept of a creature in *Defensiones*, l. 1, d. 2, q. 1, a. 1 (1:121b), defense of conclusion 5.

42. Imperfect-to-perfect representational relationships can also work in the reverse. For example, someone who had seen Caesar, but not his statue, would represent the statue imperfectly in his or her representation of Caesar. The man born blind would have some (very imperfect) understanding of what it is to see based on the experience of applying the word "seeing" to the experience of the act of understanding. The second example better captures the human intellect's understanding of God by analogy to creatures insofar as the blind person does not know directly what it is to see with eyes, and the natural theologian does not acquire quidditative knowledge of the divine essence.

ness of proportionality to the divine perfection. An objective concept that is one by the unity of imitation belongs proportionally in a creature and in the creator. Although the divine perfections are inaccessible in themselves to the human intellect insofar as the human intellect has no direct access to God, the human intellect can acquire an imperfect formal concept of God through its concepts abstracted from creatures. For example, the wisdom of God and the wisdom of creatures are different insofar as the reality signified by the name of "wisdom" in creatures is only similar by proportionality to the reality signified by the name of "wisdom" in God. But from the foundation in creatures (that is, the objective concept) from which the intellect abstracts "wisdom," the human intellect can in one formal concept perfectly represent the wisdom of a creature and imperfectly represent the wisdom of God insofar as the wisdom of the creature is proportionally similar to the wisdom of God that it imitates.

From this consideration, it seems possible to make sense of Capreolus's claim that Aquinas says the same thing in *De Veritate*, q. 2, a. 11, and the relevant passages in *De Potentia*, *Summa Contra Gentiles*, and *Summa Theologiae*. Although Aquinas appears to endorse the Healthy Model answer to the Analogy Model Problem in these passages by affirming that names are said analogously of God and creatures by analogy of one to another and using "healthy" examples, Aquinas is in fact only endorsing one aspect of what the "healthy" examples illustrate. Specifically, Aquinas is pointing to the non-univocal cause-and-effect relationship whereby what exists in the cause exists differently and deficiently in the effect. The medicine's health-inducing properties make the animal healthy by passing over into the animal, but these properties do not exist in the animal in the same way that they existed in the medicine. Similarly, God gives being, etc., to creatures, but these do not exist in creatures in the same way that they exist in God.

Capreolus's answer to the Analogy Model Problem, then, can be read as either dividing the Healthy Model or subsuming Boethius's second mode of analogy (i.e., *proportio*; the Principle Model according to Boethius and Sutton) into Boethius's fourth mode of analogy (i.e., *ad unum*; the Healthy Model according to Boethius and Sutton) as one of this mode's species. Drawing Capreolus's use of *In 1 Sent.*, d. 19, into this synthesis, analogy of one to another (*ad unum*) is suited to naming God and creatures, but not to the kind of *ad unum* analogy that expresses diverse *rationes* actually and explicitly. Rather, the kind of analogy *ad unum* in which one formal concept represents objective concepts that have unity of imitation is suited to naming God and creatures. And this kind of analogy *ad unum* can be identified with analogy of proportionality or Principle Model analogy.

This concludes my attempt at a synthesis *ad mentem Capreoli* of Capreolus's remarks on the Analogy Model Problem. The following section considers the relation between Capreolus's solutions to the *Rationes* and Analogy Model Problems and his solution to the Equivocation Problem.

CAPREOLUS ON THE EQUIVOCATION PROBLEM

In the previous chapter, we saw that Sutton defended demonstration using analogous terms by arguing that the Principle Model of analogy was close enough to univocity to preserve demonstration. Capreolus stands with Sutton in maintaining analogy of proportionality for names said of God and creatures, but Capreolus never points directly to proportionality as even a part of the solution to the Equivocation Problem. Instead, as we have seen in the first two sections of this chapter, Capreolus points to the unity of the formal concept as that which preserves validity in demonstration.

Consider again, now, our sample natural theology syllogism: "All simple perfections are in God, and wisdom is a simple perfection; therefore, wisdom is in God." Capreolus acknowledges that Scotus correctly insists that there is one concept for names said of God and creatures in natural theology because a valid demonstration requires a single concept for each mediating term. According to Capreolus, this syllogism avoids the fallacy of equivocation for the name "wisdom" in the minor premise and in the conclusion because both times it is signified through one and the same *ratio* (or formal concept). The name "wisdom" is not univocal here because the proportionally similar recipients of the name (i.e., creatures in the minor premise and God in the conclusion) participate unequally in the *ratio* of the name, and a name is only predicated univocally when the name is said of many according to one *ratio* equally participated. The *ratio* is unequally participated because there is only proportional likeness between what is objectively in the creature and what is objectively in God. The formal concept representing what is objectively in the creature at once represents the creature perfectly and God imperfectly. Indeed, that formal concept necessarily represents God proportionally insofar as there is a proportional likeness between the creature and what it imitates. The unity of the formal concept here is guaranteed because a formal concept cannot represent something without at once proportionally representing whatever else is proportionally similar to it. At the end of an argument from perfections in creatures to the being or some other perfection of God, one knows that there is something in God answering proportionally to what one knows in creatures.

Capreolus's doctrine of naming God and creatures by analogy requires a single formal concept proper to the creaturely analogate to serve as the imperfect representation of the divine analogate. The concept of the creaturely analogate has to serve as the concept of the divine if the divine is to be known and signified at all. Even in the nontheological cases of analogy of proportionality, the formal concept that properly signifies one analogate is the imperfect formal concept of the other, and vice versa. That is, just as we can only very imperfectly know what it means for the intellect to see if it is explained to us by reference to the act of eyes, or what it means for stocks to fall if it is explained to us by reference to falling rocks, we can only know very imperfectly what it is for God to be wise by reference to Socrates's wisdom.

If Capreolus's position holds, then the imperfect likeness that establishes the unity of imitation or attribution between the objective concepts in analogates saves both demonstration through analogous terms from the fallacy of equivocation and Capreolus's doctrine of analogy from reduction to univocity. It saves valid demonstration by providing a sufficient foundation for a single formal concept to be signified in both analogous uses of the term in a syllogism. It prevents reduction to univocity (at least by Capreolus's standards) by ensuring that the formal concept represents the analogates unequally.

CONCLUSION

Capreolus's solution to the *Rationes* and Equivocation Problems surrenders more to the Scotists than the solutions of his fourteenth-century Thomist predecessors Natalis and Sutton. As we have seen, his concessions on the *Rationes* Problem forced Capreolus to move away from the definition of univocity present in Aquinas's *De Principiis Naturae*. However, by departing from Aquinas's words in this text, Capreolus joins Aquinas in others where the Common Doctor himself also speaks of a single *ratio* for analogates. Perhaps more difficult for the historically attentive Thomist, Capreolus uses chronologically prior texts (*In 1 Sent.*, d. 19, q. 5, a. 2, ad 1, and *De Veritate*, q. 2, a. 11) to interpret later ones in providing his *ad mentem Thomae* answer to the Analogy Model Problem. The justification for this move, however, is worthy of consideration. Capreolus could not see how he could do otherwise without conceding the Scotist position that demonstration in natural theology depends on univocal terms, as the Healthy Model that characterizes many later texts of Aquinas requires diverse formal *rationes* or concepts, and even analogously diverse formal concepts have too little unity to preserve valid demonstration. In the following chapters, it will be seen that some of Capreolus's Renaissance Thomist successors would partially agree and partially disagree with Capreolus's one *ratio* solution to the *Rationes* Problem, and they would not look back to Natalis and Sutton's insistence on diverse *rationes*. Capreolus's answer to the Analogy Model Problem, especially his use of *In 1 Sent.*, d. 19, q. 5, a. 2, ad 1, and *De Veritate*, q. 2, a. 11, would prove no less influential.

4

Flandrensis and Soncinas

Chapter 3 considered the early fifteenth-century Thomist John Capreolus. I noted his revolutionary answer to the *Rationes* Problem, whereby he accepted that Scotus had succeeded in establishing a single *ratio* for being and other names said across the categories and about God and creatures, and yet argued that a single *ratio* for a name is insufficient for univocity. The chapter also highlighted Capreolus's adoption of the distinction between formal and objective concepts (first discussed in the treatment of Hervaeus Natalis in chapter 2). On the Analogy Model Problem, it was seen that Capreolus adopts the Principle Model as the mode of analogy suited to expressing a name through a single *ratio* unequally participated. It was shown that Capreolus relied primarily on his answer to the *Rationes* Problem to answer the Equivocation Problem. According to Capreolus, demonstrations can be made about God from creatures because their proportional likeness permits the same name to be predicated about both through one and the same formal concept, which perfectly signifies the creature and thereby imperfectly signifies God.

The present chapter engages the thought of a teacher and his student at the Dominican Studium at Bologna during the latter portion of the fifteenth century. Both student and teacher engage the thought of Capreolus in their metaphysical treatises, although only the student explicitly adopts portions of Capreolus's thought into his own solution to the three problems. The first section of the chapter considers the thought of the teacher, Dominic of Flanders, on the *Rationes* and Analogy Model Problems, illustrating how he adopts Capreolus's one *ratio* answer to the *Rationes* Problem, but not Capreolus's understanding of unequal participation. The second section considers the reaction of the student, Paul Soncinas, noting especially how Soncinas develops and parts from the position of Capreolus.[1] The third section compares and contrasts Flandrensis and Soncinas's solutions to the Equivocation Problem, drawing both from their books of questions on Aristotle's *Metaphysics* and from their logical treatises.

DOMINIC OF FLANDERS ON THE *RATIONES* PROBLEM

Dominic of Flanders raises and answers the three problems in his *Quaestiones in duodecim libros Metaphysicales Aristotelis secundum expositionem Angelici Doctoris*, l. 4, q. 2.[2] The question itself consists of a series of nine articles relating to the extension of metaphysics' consideration of being, and its articles 2 through 6 bear on the problems considered in this study. Articles 2 through 4 take up whether being is predicated about substance and accidents equivocally (a. 2), univocally (a. 3), or analogously (a. 4). Article 5 takes up the

---

1. See also the comparison of Capreolus and Soncinas on what I am calling the *Rationes* Problem in F. Riva, *Analogia e univocità in Tommaso de Vio "Gaetano"* (Milan: Vita e Pensiero, 1995), 149–59.

2. This text is also called *Summa Divinae Philosophiae*, and will hereafter be referred to as SDP. All SDP citations are taken from Dominic of Flanders and Cosmas Morelles, *In duodecim libros Metaphysicae Aristotelis, secundum expositionem eiusdem Angelici Doctoris, lucidissimae atque utilissimae quaestiones* (Cologne: Ordo, 1621). This text was first published in 1496 and republished in 1621. See also my discussion of Flandrensis in D'Ettore, "The Fifteenth-Century Thomist Dispute," 257–64, and "Dominic of Flanders' Critique of John Duns Scotus's Primary Argument for the Univocity of Being," *Vivarium* 56 (2018): 176–99.

question of whether there is an equivocal or analogous concept of being separate (or prescinding) from the concept of substance or of accident. Article 6 asks whether being signifies one concept disjunctively.[3]

To answer the *Rationes* Problem, Flandrensis, like Capreolus, maintains that in cases of analogy (including those that pertain to the key terms of metaphysics and natural theology) there is always one *ratio* that is shared in different ways by the analogates. As will be seen below, however, Flandrensis so thoroughly reinterprets "unequal" or "diverse" participation as to make his own position radically different from his predecessor's.

That Dominic of Flanders takes the *Rationes* Problem in a different direction from Capreolus can be seen by considering a representative text from his *SDP*, l. 4, q. 2, explaining the distinction between univocity, equivocation, and analogy:

> Just as healthiness relates to all healthy things and medicativeness to all medicative things, likewise, being relates to all beings. Yet "healthiness" is not said univocally, nor equivocally but analogously of all healthy things because [it is said] according to the same *ratio* participated in diverse ways. For everything is called healthy [by relation] to the same health: it is the same health which an animal acquires, and urine signifies, medicine causes, and diet conserves, although it is participated in diverse ways. For the *ratio* of health, insofar as it is said about diet, consists in conserving health, but, insofar as it is said about medicine, in making health, and, insofar as it is said about urine, inasmuch as it is a sign of health, but, insofar as it is said about an animal, its *ratio* is insofar as it is receptive [of health]. Similarly, something is called medicative either because it has the art of medicine, like the skilled physician, or because it is well disposed for having the art of medicine, like those who are well disposed for that art, or because it is an instrument of medicine itself. Nevertheless, it is the same art of medicine which the skillful physician has and to which some are well disposed, and to which some things coincide instrumentally. Consequently, it is clear that [names] of this kind are predicated analogously,

---

3. Dominic of Flanders, *SDP*, l. 4, q. 2 (141a–b)/(143a–b). In the 1621 edition of Flandrensis's *SDP*, pages 143 and 144 are mislabeled 141 and 142. The "(141a–b)/(143a–b)" above indicates that the quotation appears on a page marked as 141 which should be labelled 143.

because [they are predicated] not according to a *ratio* [which is] through and through the same or through and through diverse, but according to one *ratio* participated in diverse ways.[4]

The contrast between Flandrensis's position and Capreolus's could hardly be stronger. Capreolus's example of analogy without unequal participation in a *ratio* is Flandrensis's example of analogy with unequal or diverse participation in a *ratio*. In Dominic of Flanders's hands, the Healthy Model of analogy, by illustrating ordered *per prius et posterius* signification, serves as the primary example of "diverse" or "unequal" participation. But, as was seen in chapter 3, Capreolus refers to examples of analogous "health" as the counterexamples of unequal participation in a *ratio*, saying that they express diverse *rationes* "actually and explicitly."

Remaining within *SDP*, l. 4, q. 2, the reader finds Flandrensis clarifying his own understanding of a pair (or set) of analogates' one *ratio*. The passage is intended to distinguish analogous predication from univocal and purely equivocal predication:

Something is predicated of diverse things in many ways. Sometimes it is predicated of many according to a *ratio* altogether the same. And then it is said to be predicated of them univocally, as "animal" [is predicated] of

    4. Dominic of Flanders, *SDP*, l. 4, q. 2, a. 1 (142a)/(144a): "Sicut enim se habet sanatiuum ad omnia sana, et medicatiuum ad omnia medicatiua, ita ens se habet ad omnia entia: sed sanatiuum non dicitur vniuoce, nec aequiuoce, sed analogice de omnibus sanis: quia secundum eandem rationem diuersimode participatam. Omne enim sanatiuum, dicitur ad eandem sanitatem: eadem autem sanitas est, quam animal suscipit, et vrina significat, medicina facit, et dieta conseruat, licet diuersimode participetur. Nam ratio sani, secundum, quod dicitur de dieta, consistit in conseruando sanitatem, secundum vero quod dicitur de medicina, in faciendo sanitatem, et secundum quod dicitur de vrina, in quantum est signum sanitatis, secundum vero quod dicitur de animali, ratio eius est, secundum quod est susceptiuum. Similiter aliquid dicitur medicatiuum, vel quia habet artem medicinae, sicut peritus medicus, vel quia est bene aptum ad habendam artem medicinae, sicut homines bene dispositi ad illam artem, vel quia est instrumentum ipsius medicinae, tamen est eadem ars medicinae, quam medicus peritus habet, et ad quam aliqui bene sunt dispositi, et ad quam aliqua instrumentaliter concurrunt. Vnde patet, quod huiusmodi, analogice praedicantur: quia non secundum rationem penitus eandem, neque penitus diuersam, sed secundum vnam rationem diuersimode participatam. Cum ergo ens, similiter se habeat ad omnia entia: sequitur quod analogice praedicabitur de omnibus, vt clarius postea patebit."

a man and a cow. Sometimes [something is predicated of many] according to altogether diverse *rationes*. And in such cases, it is said to be predicated of them equivocally as "dog" [is predicated] of a star and an animal. Sometimes [something is predicated of many] according to *rationes* which are diverse in part and one in part. [They are] diverse insofar as they carry different relations. [They are] one insofar as those diverse relations are referred to something one and the same. We say in this way [something said of many] is predicated analogously, that is proportionally, inasmuch as each one [to which something is predicated] is referred according to its relation to that one [and the same thing].[5]

Flandrensis provides an identical account of the difference between univocity, analogy, and equivocation in his *De Fallaciis*, c. 9.[6] On the one hand, then, Flandrensis maintains Capreolus's qualified understanding of univocity. Names are said univocally only when the *ratio* is predicated of many equally or in exactly the same way.[7] On the other hand, whereas Capreolus restricts unequal participation in a *ratio* to certain kinds of analogous naming, Flandrensis regards unequal participation in a single *ratio* as a general feature of analogous names, regardless of which mode of analogy they fall into.

---

5. Dominic of Flanders, *SDP*, l. 4, q. 2, a. 2 (145b): "vt hic dicit Doctor Sanctus, aliquid praedicatur de diuersis, multipliciter. Quandoque quidem, secundum rationem omnino eandem. Et tunc, de eis dicitur vniuoce praedicari. Sicut animal, de homine, et boue. Quandoque vero secundum rationes omnino diuersas, et tunc dicitur, de eis aequiuoce praedicari, sicut canis de sidere, et animali. Quandoque vero, secundum rationes, quae partim sunt diuersae, et partim vna. Diuersae quidem, secundum quod diuersas habitudines important. Vna autem, secundum quod ad vnum aliquid, et idem, istae diuersae habitudines referuntur. Et hoc dicimus, analogice praedicari, id est proportionabiliter, prout vnumquodque, secundum suam habitudinem, ad illud vnum refertur." This presentation closely follows that given in Aquinas, *De Principiis Naturae*, c. 6 (Leonine, 43:46b.18–35).

6. See notes 55 and 56 below.

7. See also Flandrensis's treatment of three different uses of the term "univocal." Dominic of Flanders, *SDP*, l. 4, q. 2, a. 3 (148b–149a). Flandrensis notes that, "in his present discussion," he is concerned with the sense of univocity whereby it refers to "what is predicated about many things according to one and the same *ratio* equally participated, which *ratio* is the whole essence or part of the essence of those things about which it is predicated." See ibid.: "In praesenti autem disputatione, loquimur de vniuoco, tertio modo accepto, pro eo scilicet quod praedicatur de multis, secundum vnam, et eandem rationem aequaliter participatam, quae ratio est tota essentia, vel pars essentiae eorum de quibus praedicatur."

Turning to *SDP*, l. 4, q. 2, a. 4, the reader finds that Flandrensis (uniquely among the Thomists considered in this study) cites Aquinas's *Sententia libri Ethicorum*, l. 1, lect. 7, for his version of the modes of analogy. In this passage, Aquinas himself divides analogy according to the different ways in which a name can be said about many "according to *rationes* which are not totally diverse but which agree in something one" (*secundum rationes diversas non totaliter, sed in aliquo uno convenientes*).[8] According to Flandrensis, this passage reveals three different ways names can be said of many analogously by an ordered relation of signification to one: namely, "analogy of some things to one effective principle," "analogy of some things to one end," and "of some things to one subject."[9] Following the pattern set by Aquinas, Flandrensis informs his reader that "medicative" serves as an example of the first mode of analogy, "healthy" as an example of the second, and "being" as an example of the third.[10]

8. For the full passage from Aquinas, see his *Sententia libri Ethicorum*, l. 1, lect. 7 (Leonine, 47.1:26–27.168–213). The division that Aquinas gives in this text is comparable to the fourfold division of equivocation by design produced by Boethius and adopted by Sutton. The example that Aquinas gives of "one proportion to diverse subjects" is taken from Aristotle in the passage that Aquinas is commenting on (i.e., *Nicomachean Ethics* 1.6), and it also serves, as noted above, as Aquinas's example of proportionality in *De Veritate*, q. 2, a. 11. See table 3 for a comparison of Aquinas's modes of analogy in *Sententia libri Ethicorum*, l. 1, lect. 7, with Boethius's modes of equivocation by design.

9. Dominic of Flanders, *SDP*, l. 4, q. 2, a. 4 (153b): "illa quae dicuntur de aliquibus, ordine quodam, per respectum ad aliquod vnum, praedicantur analogice." (Those things are predicated analogously which are said about some things by a certain order, through relation to something one.)

10. Ibid.: "Et talis analogiae, triplex est gradus, vt innuit philosophus hic lect. 1 et in 1 Ethic., lect. 7. Nam quaedam est analogia aliquorum ad vnum principium effectiuum. Alia est analogia aliquorum ad vnum finem. Tertia vero est aliquorum ad vnum subiectum. Exemplum primi, est de medicatiuis. Exemplum secundi est de sanatiuis. Exemplum tertii est de entibus." (And of a such analogy, there is a threefold grade, as the Philosopher suggests here in lect. 1 and in *Ethics*, l. 1, lect. 7. For there is, first, the analogy of some things to one effective principle, second, the analogy of some things to one end, and the third is [the analogy] of some things to one subject. An example of the first kind is medicative things, an example of the second is healthy things, and an example of the third is beings.) The reader will notice that Flandrensis reduces the third and fourth modes of analogy in Aquinas's text to one division in which the analogates have reference to one subject. Cornelio Fabro gives the same interpretation in his *Participation et causalite selon S. Thomas d'Aquin* (Louvain: Publications universitaires de Louvain, 1961), 526–27.

TABLE 3. Comparing Aquinas and Boethius on Modes of Analogy

Mode of Analogy (lect. 7)	Thomas's Example	Corresponds to Boethius's
Reference to one principle	Something such as a sword is called "military" because it is the instrument of a *miles* (i.e., a solidier)	*Ab uno*
Reference to one end	Medicine called "healthy" because it makes something healthy	*Ad unum*
Diverse proportions to the same subject	Quality and quantity called "being" because the fomer is a disposition of a substance and the later is a measure of a substance	No direct correspondence to Boethius's divisions
One proportion to diverse subjects	Sight relates to the body as understanding relates to the soul	*Proportio*

Flandrensis explains analogy and its different modes by listing and giving examples of the different ways in which a name can be said of many things by priority about one thing and by posteriority about other things. Nevertheless, he denies that all kinds of priority in naming produce analogy. "Number," for example, is not said analogously of double and quadruple, although double has priority over quadruple in the genus of number. The same holds in general for priority within a genus.[11] Similarly, there can be priority at the level of efficient causality and yet a name can still be said univocally of the prior and the posterior. For this point, he gives the example of "body" said about inferior and superior bodies. Although the

11. Dominic of Flanders, *SDP*, l. 4, q. 2, a. 3, ad 10 (151b–152a): "Nec valet dictum eorum quando dicunt, quod diuersa participatio rationis, secundum prius, et posterius, variat vniuocationem: aliter numerus non diceretur vniuoce de suis speciebus: quia binarius praecedat trinarium: licet enim binarius praecedat trinarium, si considerentur secundum proprias eorum rationes, non tamen si considerentur secundum participationem rationis illius numeri communis, vt innuit Doctor Sanctus in 1 Perihermenias." (They do not speak well when they say that diverse participation of a *ratio*, according to prior and posterior, alters univocation. In that case, "number" would not be said univocally about its species, because twofold precedes threefold, if they are considered according to their proper *rationes*, but not if they are considered according to participation in the common *ratio* of number, as the Holy Doctor suggests in Perihermenias, l. 1.) See also Aquinas, *Expositio Libri Peryermenias*, l. 1, lect. 8 (Leonine, 1:40a–b.53–72).

inferior bodies causally depend on the superior, the name "body" is said univocally of both. Flandrensis limits analogy to those cases alone wherein one imposes a name "to signify one principally, and the other secondarily."[12]

Connecting analogy to *per prius et posterius* order of signification echoes the thought of both Natalis and Sutton, who also rejected the reduction of analogy to *per prius et posterius* order without qualification. The observation that causal priority—such as the priority of heavenly bodies over terrestrial bodies—by itself does not make analogy is consistent with Capreolus's use of Aquinas's "second mode" of analogy (*In 1 Sent.*, d. 19), which is not analogous to the logician but only to the physician and metaphysician.

As mentioned above, *SDP*, l. 4, q. 2, a. 5, takes up the question of whether there is a separate concept of being from the concepts of

---

12. Dominic of Flanders, *SDP*, l. 4, q. 2, a. 3, ad 29 (153a): "Ad Vigesivm Nonvn dicendum, quod substantia, et accidens habent connexionem ad inuicem: ideo inter ipsa est analogia, non autem ad talem connexionem, quae facit analogiam, sufficit connexio in esse reali, secundum causalitatem: alioquin corpus, diceretur analogice de corporibus superioribus, et inferioribus: quod falsum est, sed requiritur connexio, quantum ad rationem significandi, et impositionem nominis, vnam scilicet impositionem, ex parte ipsius imponentis, ita quod analogum debet significare vnum principaliter, et aliud secundario, quod non conuenit corpori, respectu corporum superiorum et inferiorum." (To the twenty-ninth argument, it must be said that substance and accident have a connection to each other. Therefore, there is an analogy between them. However, a connection in real being is not a sufficient connection for making an analogy. If it were, "body" would be said analogously about the bodies above and below, which is false. Rather, a connection is required regarding the *ratio* of signifying, and the imposition of the name; namely, one imposition on the part of the one imposing, such that the analogous name ought to signify one thing principally and another secondarily, which is not how "body" agrees with bodies above and below.) Dominic of Flanders does consider the fact that creatures receive what God gives deficiently to be a reason why names cannot be said univocally of God and creatures. See Dominic of Flanders, *SDP*, l. 4, q. 2, a. 3 (149a). The names are said analogously, however, because when the name is imposed it primarily signifies God and secondarily signifies creatures. See a. 3 (151a): "Ens enim quod praedicatur de Deo, omnia alia nomina, significant primo, et proprie diuinam essentiam, participatiue vero perfectiones creaturarum. Similiter ens reale creatum, quod diuiditur in decem praedicamenta, significat primo, et principaliter, et immediate ipsam substantiam, et ex consequenti, siue secundario ipsum accidens." (For "being" which is predicated about God, [and] all other names, signifies first and properly the divine essence, but participatively the perfections of creatures. Similarly, real created being, which is divided into the ten categories, signifies substance itself first, principally, and immediately, and accident itself consequently or secondarily.)

substance and accident. According to Flandrensis, some Thomists had taken Scotus's "Certain and Doubtful" Argument to establish that there is a separate concept of being, but that concept is analogous and not univocal.[13] In article 5, Flandrensis himself completely rejects, on a variety of grounds, the existence of a separate concept.[14] In article 6, he argues that his understanding of analogy as entailing a *per prius et posterius* order of signification is the best way of denying the existence of a "third separate concept" of being among the three methods proposed by Thomists.

Here is Flandrensis's account of those three ways. Speaking about the first way in which Thomists deny a separate concept of being, Flandrensis refers to Natalis's unity of disjunction solution to Scotus's "Certain and Doubtful" Argument:

There are some who say that "being" signifies a disjunctive concept, which concept is one by the unity of proportion or analogy. For according to them "being" signifies "substance or accident," such that [the statement] "substance is being" is "substance is substance or accident." And they say that the intellect can be certain that something is a being, that is, that it is a substance or accident, while the intellect is unaware of whether it is determinately substance or determinately accident. Hervaeus is of this opinion. From which it follows that [these Thomists] deny a simple concept of being.[15]

13. See Dominic of Flanders, *SDP*, l. 4, q. 2, a. 5, ad 14 (159a). Flandrensis attributes this position to Antonius de Carlensis (d. 1460) but does not provide a textual citation. For a brief discussion of Antonius de Carlenis's life and works, including references to other points of criticism from Flandrensis, see the introduction in Steven J. Livesey, *Antonius de Carlenis, O.P.: Four Questions on the Subalternation of Sciences*, Transactions of the American Philosophical Society 84 (Philadelphia: American Philosophical Society, 1994), ix–xxxv.

14. See Dominic of Flanders, *SDP*, l. 4, q. 2, a. 5 (156a–159b).

15. Ibid., a. 6 (160a): "Respondeo dicendum, quod in praesenti schola Doctoris Sancti hodiernis temporibus, est triplex modus dicendi, secundum diuersos Doctores in doctrina Doctoris Sancti peritissimos, negantes tertium conceptum praecisum. Quidam enim dicunt quod ens significat conceptum disiunctum, qui conceptus est vnus, vnitate proportionis, siue analogiae. Ens enim, secundum eos significat, substantiam vel accidens, ita quod sit sensus, substantia est ens, id est, substantia est substantia, vel accidens. Et dicunt quod intellectus potest esse certus de aliquo, quod sit ens, id est substantia, vel accidens, ignorando vtrum esset substantia, determinate, vel accidens determinate. Et huius opinionis est Heruaeus." On the position of Natalis, see also chapter 2 and Natalis, *Quodlibet* 2, q. 7 (Venice 1513, 44v, 45v). For Sutton's similar answer to Scotus's

This particular Thomist way of denying a separate concept is somewhat anachronistic, insofar as Natalis (and Sutton) did not address the argument specifically against an analogous yet separate concept of being. Natalis was arguing against any single concept of being, whether separate or not, because any such concept would be univocal and not analogous. Still, insofar as Scotus did consider a univocal concept to be separate, it is not unreasonable for Flandrensis to bring up his predecessor's unity of disjunction based rebuttal of an argument from Scotus for univocity.

The second Thomist way of denying a separate concept of being is drawn from Dominic of Flanders's own teacher, the fifteenth-century commentator John Versor:[16]

> But there are others who say that "being" does not signify a disjunctive concept, but signifies ten concepts immediately inasmuch as there are ten categories, for example, Versor in [his *Questions on the Metaphysics of Aristotle*], l. 4, q. 1. For they say that there are as many concepts of being as there are first genera, and from these [many concepts of being] there is one concept merely by the unity of analogy and of proportion to one [concept of being] which is included in the concepts of the others.[17]

Unlike Natalis's appeal to disjunctive unity,[18] Versor's argument in the passage cited by Flandrensis was indeed directly aimed at those

---

"Certain and Doubtful" Argument, see Sutton, *Quaestiones Ordinariae* 32, ad 23 (Schmaus, 45–46).

16. On the thought of John Versor (d. after 1482), see Pepijin Rutten, "'*Secundum processum et mentem Versoris*': John Versor and His Relation to the Schools of Thought Reconsidered," *Vivarium* 43 (2005): 293–336. Rutten argues that Versor is neither a Thomist nor an Albertist, and maintains that Versor offers and was known by his contemporaries to offer his own distinct position. Although Rutten identifies Dominic of Flanders as one of Versor's students (ibid., 295n9), Rutton does not comment on the fact that Flandrensis himself includes Versor among the Thomists.

17. Dominic of Flanders, *SDP*, l. 4, q. 2, a. 6 (160a): "Ex quo patet quod negant intellectum simplicem entis. Alii vero sunt qui dicunt quod ens non significat vnum conceptum disiunctum, sed significat decem conceptus immediate: secundum quod sunt decem praedicamenta, vt patet per Versorem in hoc 4, q. prima, dicunt enim quod tot sunt conceptus entis, quot sunt genera prima, et ex illis sit conceptus vnus, dumtaxat vnitate analogiae, et proportionis ad primum, quod clauditur in conceptibus aliorum."

18. For remarks on unity of disjunction in Aquinas's works, see E. J. Ashworth, "Analogy and Equivocation in Thirteenth-Century Logic: Aquinas in Context," *Mediaeval Studies* 54 (1992): 132.

apud ponentes analogiam entis who propose a separate concept of being. According to Versor, the correct position is that the many proper concepts of being corresponding to the diverse genera are all united by analogy because one of these concepts of being is contained in all of the others, that is, the concept of being proper to substance.[19]

The third position among Thomists rejecting a separate concept of being proposes that "being" properly signifies substance, and that, by signifying substance primarily, "being" also signifies the other categories as ordered to substance secondarily:

Still others [i.e., other Thomists] say that the concept of "being" is equally one and somehow diverse. It is one because of the attribution of the others [i.e., of the secondary analogates] to the primary [analogate] which is enclosed in the concept of the others. It is in some way diverse because "being" is said of the first being according to itself and of other beings by their order to the first being. And these [Thomists] propose that "being" should signify substance and accident by one concept and by one imposition. For it signifies substance with relation to accident, but the relation cannot be signified, because it cannot be understood, without that to which it is determined. Therefore, it signifies accident secondarily. And such a concept of "being" is not separate from the concept of "substance" but it is the proper concept of "substance," although by another way of signifying and conceiving; namely, in the concrete and with relation to accident.[20]

Thomists holding the second and third positions agree that the concept of one mode of being is contained in the concepts of the other modes of being. Where they disagree is over whether the other

---

19. Johannes Versor, *Quaestiones super metaphysicam Aristotelis*, l. 4, q. 1 (Cologne, 1494; reprinted in Frankfurt am Main: Minerva GmbH, 1967), 25Vb.

20. Dominic of Flanders, *SDP*, l. 4, q. 2, a. 6 (160a–b): "Alii vero dicunt quod conceptus entis, est aequaliter vnus, et aliqualiter diuersus. Vnus quidem: quia aliorum est attributio ad primum, quod clauditur in conceptu aliorum. Aliquo modo diuersus: quia de primo ente dicitur ens, secundum se, et de aliis vero, secundum ordinem ad ipsum. Et isti volunt quod ens significet, vnico conceptu, et vnica impositione, substantiam, et accidens. Significat enim substantiam cum habitudine ad accidens, habitudo autem non potest significari: cum non possit intelligi, sine eo. Ad quod determinatur: ideo significat secundario accidens. Et talis conceptus entis, non est praecisus a conceptu substantiae, sed est proprius conceptus substantiae, cum alio modo significandi et concipiendi, videlicet cum concretione et habitudine ad accidens."

modes of being besides substance strictly speaking have proper concepts of their being. By Versor's account, there is a concept of being for substance, another for quantity, etc. These diverse concepts are analogously one by the presence of the concept of substantial being in the rest. By the third position, there is really just one concept of being; namely, the concept of substantial being. This concept, which primarily signifies substantial being, secondarily signifies accidental being. Flandrensis judges the third position as "more plausible" than the others,[21] and it is the position he has already laid out in the preceding articles of the question (as seen above).[22]

In these texts addressed to the semantics of analogy, Flandrensis explains to his readers that there is always diverse or unequal participation in a *ratio* when a name is predicated analogously. Diverse participation in a *ratio* consists in the *per prius et posterius* order of the signification of a name. In the examples and explanations Flandrensis offers in *SDP*, l. 4, this kind of signification occurs when a name is imposed which carries both a primary signification to one (primary) analogate and a secondary signification extending to analogates that contain the primary analogate in their definition. Based on what Flandrensis writes in *SDP*, l. 4, q. 2, the reader may fairly conclude that Flandrensis follows a strict reading of Aquinas's *Summa Theologiae* I, q. 13, a. 6, where he writes:

---

21. Ibid., 160b: "Licet enim duo modi praedicti, videantur pluribus probabiliores, hic tamen tertius videtur esse verisimilior." (For although the aforementioned two modes seems more probable to many; nevertheless, this third seems to be more plausible.)

22. On this passage, see Ashworth, "Suárez on the Analogy of Being," 68–70, esp. 70: "Clearly he believes that to be one by the unity of analogy and proportion is not to be genuinely singular. View three is that the concept is partly one, by virtue of attribution, and partly diverse, by virtue of the different ways *ens* belongs to substance and accidents. The word '*ens*' signifies both substance and accidents by one concept and one imposition, but it does not signify anything separate from substance. In fact, it is a proper concept of substance but with another mode of signifying and conceiving. It signifies substance as it is related to and joined with accidents, and thus it is that accidents are signified secondarily. The references to conceiving suggest that the source of the concept's unity is the mind's activity rather than reality, a view which Suárez was later concerned to reject."

It must be said that in all names which are said about many analogously, it is necessary that all are said by relation to one, and, therefore, that it is necessary that one is asserted in the definition of the other. And ... it is necessary that that name is said *per prius* about that which is asserted in the definition of the others, and *per posterius* about the others ... as the "healthy" which is said about an animal falls in the definition of the "healthy" which is said about medicine, which is called "healthy" inasmuch as it causes health in an animal.[23]

It will be seen below, however, that Flandrensis's *SDP*, l. 4, offers only an incomplete vision of his understanding of unequal participation.

As an answer to the *Rationes* Problem, Flandrensis's account is partly the same and partly different from the answer given by Capreolus. Both Flandrensis and Capreolus acknowledge a single *ratio* in analogous names. Both likewise acknowledge a kind of primary and secondary signification for the single *ratio* in analogy. In Capreolus's account, the one formal *ratio* or concept primarily signifies what it represents more perfectly, and it secondarily signifies what it represents less perfectly. As the formal concept of "healthy" that signifies the health of an animal does not represent the health of medicine at all, and vice versa, the healthiness of an animal and the healthiness of medicine do not participate in one formal concept, even though one analogate appears in the definition of the other. Furthermore, Capreolus maintains that unequal participation in a *ratio* occurs in analogy of proportionality, even though, according to Capreolus (citing Aquinas's *De Veritate*, q. 2, a. 11, ad 6), one analogate does not appear in the *ratio* of the other in this kind of analogy.[24] When addressing the *Rationes* Problem in *SDP*, l. 4, Flandrensis appears to have none of Capreolus's reservations about the Healthy Model of analogy. Indeed, he takes the Healthy Model as a paradigmatic case of diverse participation in a *ratio*, on the grounds that when the name "healthy" is imposed on an animal primarily, at once, it signifies the healthiness of urine, medicine, etc., secondarily.

23. Aquinas, *Summa Theologiae* I, q. 13, a. 6.
24. See Capreolus, *Defensiones* l. 1, d. 35, q. 2, a. 2 (2:399b), and Aquinas, *De Veritate*, q. 2, a. 11, arg. 6 and ad 6 (Leonine, 22.1:77–78.44–59 and 80.251–59).

The difference between Capreolus and Flandrensis on the *Rationes* Problem seems to reside in the unity of what Capreolus calls the "objective concept." Capreolus denies a single formal concept over healthy animals and healthy medicine on the grounds that there is not even unity of imitation or attribution between the healthiness of the animal and the healthiness of the medicine. That is, there is not even proportional unity between the analogates in the real order, and consequently there is insufficient unity outside the mind for the intellect to represent the analogates through the same formal concept. This lack of even proportional unity outside the mind does not appear to prevent Flandrensis from affirming the presence of a common, although diversely participated in, *ratio* between the analogates. On the contrary, for there to be diverse participation in a *ratio*, it is enough that the name itself is attributed to some because of their relation to something which receives the name in its own right. It will be seen below, however, that when addressing names said analogously of God and creatures specifically, Flandrensis qualifies his doctrine of diverse participation in a *ratio* in a way which leads him away from the strict interpretation of *Summa Theologiae* I, q. 13, a. 6, and closer to Capreolus's position and to Thomas's *De Veritate*, q. 2, a. 11, ad 6, remarks on whether the *ratio* of one analogate necessarily appears in the definition of the others.

DOMINIC OF FLANDERS ON THE ANALOGY MODEL PROBLEM

Flandrensis's words in *SDP*, l. 4, and in his *De Fallaciis* offer unconditional support for the Healthy Model as an answer to the Analogy Model Problem. They inform the reader that analogy is *per prius et posterius* signification of one *ratio* to many, which occurs when the proper *ratio* of one appears in the definitions of the other analogates. Flandrensis's remarks in *SDP*, l. 12, reveal a more complex doctrine.[25]

25. I overlooked this complexity in my treatment of Flandrensis in D'Ettore, "The Fifteenth-Century Thomist Dispute."

Flandrensis and Soncinas 103

Taking up the topic of divine knowledge (*cognitio*) in *SDP*, l. 12, q. 8, Flandrensis says that it is Aquinas's position that the *ratio cognitionis* belongs *per prius* to one analogate. Flandrensis qualifies this priority using *De Veritate* and other texts from Aquinas that distinguish analogy involving determinate proportions from analogy of proportionality, which involves indeterminate proportions.[26] When

26. Dominic of Flanders, *SDP*, l. 12, q. 8, a. 4, ad 3 (778a–b): "Ad tertium dicendum, secundum Doctorem Sanctum, in de veritate quest. 2 art. 11 in corpore, quod cognitio non dicitur mere aequiuoce, neque mere vniuoce, de cognitione Dei, et cognitione nostra, sed analogice: quia ratio cognitionis, per prius conuenit vni, quam alteri. Haec ille. Pro cuius declaratione considerandum est, secundum eundem ibidem, ad secundum, quod philosophus in secundo topicorum, capite quarto, ponit duplicem modum similitudinis. Vnum, qui inuenitur, in diuersis generibus. Et talis similitudo, attenditur secundum proportionem, vel proportionalitatem, et non secundum identitatem, siue adaequationem. Vt quando alterum proportionabiliter se habet ad alterum, sicut aliud ad aliud. Alium modum ponit in his, quae sunt eiusdem generis, vt quando idem diuersis inest. Similitudo autem analogiae, non semper quaerit determinatam habitudinem modi similitudinis, quae primo modo dicitur, sed solum, quae secundo modo dicitur. Vnde primus modus similitudinis potest competere Deo, respectu creaturae, licet non secundus. Haec ille in solutione ad secundum. Ex quibus patet, quod analogia est duplex, scilicet determinatae habitudinis, sicut inter substantiam, et accidens. Et de hac loquitur etiam Doctor Sanctus, in prima parte, quaestione decimatertia, art.6 et art.10 in corpore. Et in Tertio sententiarum, dist. 33, quaest. 1, art. 1, q. 2, ad 1. Et primo contra gentiles, ca. 33, ad sextum, vbi dicit, quod primum in analogis, oportet poni in definitione omnium aliorum. Et tamen non dicit in omnibus, sed loquitur indefinite. Secunda est analogia proportionalitatis eorum, quae in infinitum distant, sicut inter Deum et creaturas. Et in his primum non ponitur in diffinitione aliorum: quia diffinitio, non esset per notius, sed solum primo modo." (To the third it must be said that, according to the Holy Doctor in the body of *De Veritate*, q. 2, a. 11, "cognition" is said neither merely equivocally, nor merely univocally, about the knowledge of God and our knowledge, but analogously. This is because the *ratio* of knowledge belongs to one prior to the other. He says these things. For a clarification of which, according to *De Veritate*, q. 2, a. 11, ad 2, one should consider "that the Philosopher affirms a twofold mode of likeness in the second book of the *Topics*. One of these is the mode found in diverse genera. This kind of likeness is attained according to proportion or proportionality, and not according to identity or adequation, as when one relates to another proportionally, just as another thing relates to another thing. The other mode [of likeness] affirms in things that they belong to the same genus, as when the same thing is in diverse things. Likeness of analogy (which is predicated in the first mode [of likeness]), however, does not always require a determinate relation, but [a determinate relation] is only predicated in the second [mode of likeness]. Hence, the first mode of likeness can belong to God in relation to creature, but not the second." Thomas says these things in the solution to argument 2. From which it is clear that analogy is twofold; namely, [one kind is analogy] of determinate relation, as between substance and accident. And the Holy Doctor also speaks about this kind in the body of

names are said analogously of God and creatures, they are said by the indeterminate form of analogy. Flandrensis's model for this form of analogy is the example found in Aristotle and Aquinas of "sight" said of the eye's act and of the intellect's.

In *SDP*, l. 12, q. 9, Flandrensis explains that the agreement between the analogates in the analogy of proportionality "is not of two things between which there is a proportion, but more of two proportions to each other."[27] That is, there is not simply speaking any particular relationship between the analogates themselves which provides the grounds for the common name, as there is in the modes of analogy characterized by the example of "healthy" said by priority about an animal that has health and said secondarily of other things that contribute to or indicate health in an animal. Rather, the agreement (*convenientia*) between the analogates is found in the (at once similar but different) characteristics or activities of the analogates themselves. The eye and the intellect's acts of seeing are not related to each other,[28] but "just as sight is in the eye, so too understanding is in the mind."[29] By parity of reasoning, a foundation and a point

---

Summa Theologiae I, q. 13, aa. 6 and 10; and in *In 3 Sent.*, d. 33, q. 1, a. 1, q. 2, ad 1; and in *Summa Contra Gentiles* I, c. 33, where he says that the first among analogates must be in the definition of all the others. And nevertheless, he does not say in all, but he speaks indefinitely. The second [kind of analogy is] the analogy of proportionality of those things which differ infinitely, as between God and creatures. And in these the first is not affirmed in the definition of the others because the definition would not be through the more known. [The definition of the first is in the definition of all] only in the first kind [of analogy].) See also Flandrensis, *SDP*, l. 12, q. 9, a. 1, ad 3 (779b–780b), where he repeats the same points in greater detail. The example of "vision" appears on 780a. This latter passage is cited in Mahieu, *Dominique de Flandre (XVe siècle) sa métaphysique*, 99.

27. Dominic of Flanders, *SDP*, l. 12, q. 9, a. 1, ad 3 (780a): "Alia est conuenientia, quae est non duorum, inter quae est proportio, sed magis duarum ad inuicem proportionum ... est conuenientia proportionalitatis."

28. The act of sight does, of course, contribute to the inner senses' formation of the phantasm on which the agent intellect performs the intellectual act of abstraction. But strictly speaking, the eye's act is not called "seeing" due to its effect on the intellect's act of understanding, and the intellect's act of understanding is not called "seeing" because it has any causal relation to the eye's act. Consequently, Flandrensis maintains that neither analogate of "seeing" is defined by reference to the other. See discussion of this point below.

29. Dominic of Flanders, *SDP*, l. 12, q. 9, a. 1, ad 3 (780a): "sicut visus est in oculo, ita intellectus est in mente."

are not related to each other, but there is a *convenientia* between a foundation's relation to a house and a point's relation to a line. Given the absence of a determinate relation between the analogates, Flandrensis concludes that one analogate does not appear in the definition of the other(s) in proportionality or indeterminate proportion.

Flandrensis's remarks in *SDP*, l. 12, represent, if not a contradiction, at least an extension of the understanding of unequal participation in a *ratio* that he presented in *SDP*, l. 4, where he characterizes analogy in general as involving unequal participation in one *ratio* through *per prius et posterius* signification. Whereas in l. 4 he explains that analogy occurs when the *ratio* proper to one analogate appears in the definition of the others (e.g., the *ratio* properly signifying the health in an animal appears in the *ratio* properly signifying the healthiness of medicine), in l. 12 he says that names are said analogously of God and creatures even though the *ratio* proper to one analogate does not appear in the definition of the other (e.g., the *ratio* properly signifying Socrates's wisdom does not appear in the *ratio* properly signifying divine wisdom or vice versa).

Either Flandrensis changed his mind after writing *SDP*, l. 4, or the determinate Healthy Model examples of diverse participation in a *ratio* offered in this text merely indicated one way, but not the only way, in which a *ratio* can be diversely participated. Flandrensis indicates to his reader that, in his own judgment, these two texts are consistent by referring the reader of *SDP*, l. 12, back to *SDP*, l. 4, q. 2, for his position on analogy between God and creatures and the *analogia entis*.[30] For these two texts to be consistent, there must be one *ratio* that has both a primary and secondary signification in both the determinate (Healthy Model) and indeterminate (Principle/Seeing Model) modes of analogy. Consequently, Flandrensis's consistency requires that there be a different way for a *ratio* to be signified primarily and secondarily than the determinate way, whereby the proper *ratio* of one analogate appears in the *ratio* of the other.

Flandrensis does not explain to his reader what other way or

30. Ibid. (780b).

ways a *ratio* can be shared in diversely besides the way illustrated by the Healthy Model, and this leaves his interpreter to wonder what he would say to resolve the differences between his remarks in *SDP*, l. 4 and l. 12. One hint toward a resolution appears in his reason for why the definition of one analogate does not appear in the definition of the other in names said analogously of God and creatures: "because the definition would not be through the more known."[31] The more known to us is the creature.[32] So if the definition of one is to appear in the definition of the other, it seems, according to Flandrensis, that the one would have to be the creature because definitions are made through the more known to us. I do not find Flandrensis saying, however, that the definition of the name said of the creature falls in the definition of the name said of God, and it seems reasonable

31. See citation above of Flandrensis, *SDP*, l. 12, q. 8, a. 4, ad 3 (778a–b).
32. See *SDP*, l. 4, q. 2, a. 4 (153b), for his recitation of Aquinas's distinction between the order of being and the order of knowing in analogy. Citing *Summa Contra Gentiles* I, c. 35, Flandrensis states that in the case of names said of God and creatures, the thing signified belongs *per prius* to God although in the order of knowing, the name is said first of creatures through which we discover the divine attributes. Flandrensis here compares this way names are said of God and creatures to the way "healthy" is said of an animal and medicine: "Quando vero id quod est prius, secundum naturam est posterius, secundum cognitionem, tunc in analogis non est idem ordo, secundum rem, et secundum nominis rationem, sicut virtus sanandi, quae est in sanatiuis, prior est naturaliter sanitate, quae est in animal, sicut causa effectu: sed quia hanc virtutem, per effectum cognoscimus: ideo etiam, ex effectu nominamus. Et inde est, quod sanatiuum est prius, ordine rei, sed animal per prius, sanum dicitur, secundum nominis rationem. Sic igitur: quia ex rebus aliis, in Dei cognitionem peruenimus, res nominum de Deo, et de aliis rebus dictorum, per prius sunt in Deo, secundum modum suum, sed ratio nominis per posterius." (But when that which is naturally prior is posterior in knowledge, then the order of reality and the order of the *ratio* of the name are not the same in analogates. For example, the power of healing, which is in a healing thing, is naturally prior to the health which is in the animal, as a cause [is prior] to an effect. But because we know this power through the effect, it follows that we also name from the effect. And so it is that the healing thing is prior in the order of reality, but the animal is called "healthy" prior in the order of the *ratio* of the name. Accordingly, because we arrive at knowledge of God from other things, the realities of the names said about God and other things are prior in God, according to His mode, but the *ratio* of the name is posterior [in God].) I find the use of the example of analogous "healthy" in this passage strikingly different from the other appearances of the example even in Flandrensis's own texts. Indeed, he seems to be drawing a proportionality between the way that "healthy" is said of medicine and animals and the way that it is said of God and creatures: just as medicine is called "healthy" from its effect in an animal, God is called "being," etc., from his effects in creatures.

to presume that Flandrensis accepts Aquinas's position that when a name is said of God essentially (as opposed to metaphorically or causally) the creature does not appear in the definition of name said of the creator.[33] So the conclusion follows that neither analogate appears in the definition of the other, and Aquinas's statements to the effect that in analogy one analogate always appears in the definition of the other are not to be taken universally.

What I think this hint points to in terms of understanding unequal participation in the analogy of proportionality is that the unequal participation is not to be found in the intellect's conception at all, as occurs in the other, determinate forms of analogy where the proper *ratio* of one analogate appears in the definition of the other analogate. Rather, the unequal participation must be found exclusively in the realities themselves signified (although diversely) through the analogous name. The reality that is divine wisdom, with its proportion between the divine intellect and the highest causes, is participated in, although deficiently, by Socrates with the proportion between his intellect and the highest causes. To use the nontheological example in Aquinas and Flandrensis, the proper *ratio* of "sight" said of an eye's act—that is, formal reception of color through a material medium—is not contained in the proper *ratio* of "sight" said of an intellect's act. But when "sight" is predicated of an intellect—for example, Socrates discovering what justice really is—then the term signifies an activity which itself involves a proportion similar to the proportion of the seeing eye to its object. Because the intellectual activity is more perfect through its immateriality than the sensory activity, I presume that Flandrensis would hold that the sensory activity participates in the *ratio* of "seeing" less perfectly than the intellectual activity. To employ terms omitted by Flandrensis himself, the

---

33. See for example, Aquinas, *Summa Theologiae* I, q. 13, a. 6: "Respondeo quod in omnibus nominibus quae de pluribus analogice dicuntur, necesse est quod omnia dicantur per respectum ad unum: et ideo illud unum oportet quod ponatur in definitione omnium." (I answer that in all names which are said about many by analogy, it is necessary that all are said by relation to one, and, therefore, that one is necessarily placed in the definition of all.)

diverse participation in analogy of proportionality does not occur through the formal concept but only through the objective concept.

To sum up Dominic of Flanders's position on the one concept of being unequally or diversely participated: it is not a separate concept in the sense of being a third concept distinct from the proper concepts of the analogates, such as substance and accident, God and creature. But it is still one concept; indeed, it is the concept of substance. Dominic of Flanders honors the tradition that uses unity of disjunction to answer some objections, but he himself does not found the unity of the concept of "being" or other analogues on a unity of disjunction.[34] Rather, he grounds it on a name signifying both one thing primarily and other things secondarily because of their relation to that one. That relation can be a direct and determinate relation between the analogates, as in the case of "healthy" said of medicine and urine, or that relation can be an indirect or indeterminate relation between two proportions, as in the case of names said analogously of God and creatures.

Although Dominic of Flanders used the same example to illustrate diverse participation in a single *ratio* as Capreolus used to illustrate the kind of analogy in which a name explicitly signifies many *rationes*, I find the positions of Flandrensis and Capreolus on the *Rationes* and Analogy Model Problems to be similar in key respects. Both require a single *ratio* or concept in some qualified way for the key terms of metaphysics and natural theology. Both invoke Aquinas's *De Veritate*, q. 2, a. 11, division of analogy into determinate proportion and indeterminate proportion (proportionality) to reject the Healthy Model of analogy for names said analogously of God and creatures. Neither one admits the "separate concept" of being proposed by Flandrensis's student Soncinas.

---

34. See Dominic of Flanders, *SDP*, l. 4, q. 2, a. 4 (151a). Flandrensis presents the disjunctive concept as Hervaeus Natalis's answer to Scotist arguments for univocity.

PAUL SONCINAS ON THE *RATIONES* AND
ANALOGY MODEL PROBLEMS

Soncinas's greatest work is his 1495 *Acutissimae quaestiones metaphysicales*, an extensive commentary on Aristotle's *Metaphysics* 4, 10, and 12.[35] Soncinas follows Flandrensis's example and presents his doctrine of analogy in his questions on *Metaphysics* 4. Also following Flandrensis, Soncinas has questions regarding whether there is a separate concept of being (*AQM*, l. 4, q. 2), whether being explicitly expresses one disjunctive concept (q. 3), and whether "being" is said univocally of substance and accidents, God and creature (q. 4). Unlike Flandrensis, however, Soncinas adopts and applies the distinction between formal and objective concepts (q. 1).[36] Soncinas also discusses some of these issues in his earlier work *Expositio Super Artem Veterem Aristotelis*.[37] I notice no significant variation in doctrine between these two texts on the three problems.

Soncinas agrees, at least verbally, with both Capreolus and Flandrensis that univocal naming requires equal participation in a *ratio*. As he writes in his *Super Artem*: "Whatever is predicated is predicated either according to the same name and many concepts, and then there is equivocal predication, or [it is predicated] according to the same voice and the same concept participated in the same way, and then there is univocal predication."[38] He reinforces the point in the

---

35. *Acutissimae quaestiones metaphysicales* will hereafter be referred to as *AQM*. See Jindráček, "Soncino, Paulo Barbo."

36. Readers of the 1579 edition should be aware that *AQM*, l. 4, q. 1, is mislabled as q. 2.

37. All references to this text are taken from Soncinas, *Elegantissima Expositio Super Artem* (Venice, 1499). See also my treatment of Soncinas's doctrine of unequal participation in D'Ettore, "The Fifteenth-Century Thomist Dispute," 264–71. There I drew only from Soncinas's *AQM*.

38. Soncinas, *Super Artem* (18va): "Quicquid praedicatur: aut praedicatur secundum idem nomen et plures conceptus et sic est praedicatio equiuoca. Aut secundum eandem vocem et eundem conceptem eodem modo participatum et sic est praedicatio vniuoca." See also Soncinas, *AQM*, l. 4, q. 4, ad 4 (9a): "dico quod ad vniuocationem non sufficit quod praedicatum sit quidditatiuum, siue essentiale subiecto: sed praeter hoc requiritur quod ratio eius aequaliter repraesentet omnia de quibus dicitur, quod non conuenit rationi entis." (I say that it is not sufficient for univocation that the predicate is

same text saying, "I say ... all univocals equally participate the concept and nature which the univocal term signifies immediately."³⁹

Soncinas's explanation of what he calls alternatively the "modes" or "grades" of analogy and the distinction between those which do or do not express many *rationes* appears in the form of his adaptation of Aquinas's *In 1 Sent.*, d. 19, threefold division of the way names are said according to analogy. Describing the first mode of analogy, Soncinas writes:

The first mode [of analogy] is when an analogue [i.e., a name said analogously] in the mind signifies many *rationes*, both formal and objective, of which one has to another proportion or analogy (or attribution because it is the same). And "healthy" is an analogue in this way. For it signifies the health of an animal, and of medicine, and of urine, concerning which "health" is said according to diverse *rationes*. For the *ratio* of the health of an animal is "to be the balance of the humors," and the *ratio* of the health of medicine is "to be causative of health in an animal," and the *ratio* [of "healthy" said] of urine is "to be a sign [of health in an animal]."⁴⁰

About the next mode, he says: "The second grade [of analogy] is when the analogous term signifies one *ratio* which has diverse being [*esse*] in the analogates. In this way, 'body' is said analogously of corruptible and incorruptible [bodies]. For it signifies three dimensional which is of the same *ratio* in each body. But, in the corruptible body, it has corruptible being [*esse*], whereas it has incorruptible being [*esse*] in the heavenly [body]."⁴¹

---

quidditative or essential to the subject, but, besides this, it is required that its *ratio* equally represents all the things about which it is said, and this requirement is not met by the *ratio* of being.)

39. Soncinas, *Super Artem* (19ra): "Dico secundo quod omnia vniuocata eque participant conceptum et naturam quam immediate significat terminus vniuocus."

40. Soncinas, *AQM*, l. 4, q. 4, ad 1 (9a): "Triplex enim est analogia. Primus modus, est quando analogum in mente significat plures rationes tam formales quam obiectiuas, quarum vna ad alteram habet proportionem siue analogiam: siue attributionem quod idem est. Et hoc modo sanum est analogum. Significat enim sanitatem animalis: et medicinae, et vrinae: de quibus dicitur sanitas secundum diuersas rationes. Ratio enim sanitatis animalis, est esse adaequationem humorum, et ratio sanitatis medicinae est esse causatiuum sanitatis in animali, vrinae vero ratio, est esse signum."

41. Ibid.: "Secundus gradus est quando terminus analogus significat vnam rationem, qui habet diuersum esse in analogatis: et hoc modo corpus dicitur analogice de

Concerning the third mode, which is the one suited to metaphysical discourse, he writes:

> The third grade [of analogy] is when the analogous term signifies one *ratio* in which the analogates are not made equal, nor are they even [made equal] in being [*esse*]. And in this way, "being" [*ens*] is an analogue. For entity [*entitas*] has being [*esse*] in substance and accident, but more perfectly in substance than in accident, and, therefore, the formal conception of "being" [*entis*] is in substance and accident as in the foundation of its truth, and it has a more perfect foundation in substance than in accident. Now the *ratio* of "being" [*entis*] is "to be that to which it belongs to be [*esse illud, cui contingit esse*]." And because of this, the Philosopher and Commentator say in *Metaphysics* 7 ..., that all those things are called "being" [*ens*] which have being [*esse*] in any way.[42]

With this threefold division of analogy into two modes that signify through one *ratio* unequally and one mode that explicitly signifies through many *rationes*, Soncinas adopts the position of Capreolus in opposition to Flandrensis, who, as we saw above, treated all forms of analogy as instances of unequal participation in a single *ratio*. Soncinas also here accepts Capreolus's grounds for rejecting the Healthy Model of analogy as an answer to the Analogy Model Problem. The Healthy Model illustrates for Soncinas, just as it did for Capreolus in his rendering of Aquinas's *In 1 Sent.* description of a specific sort of analogy that explicitly signifies through diverse *ratio-*

---

corruptibili et incorruptibili. Significat enim triuam dimensionem quae est eiusdem rationis in quolibet corpore. Sed in corpore corruptibili habet esse corruptibile, in caelo autem habet esse incorruptibile."

42. Ibid.: "Tertius gradus est quando terminus analogus significat vnam rationem, in qua non parificantur analogata, neque etiam in esse, et hoc modo ens est analogum. Nam entitas habet esse in substantia et accidente, sed perfectius in substantia quam in accidente, et ideo formalis conceptio entis est in substantia et accidente tanquam in fundamento suae veritatis: et habet perfectius fundamentum in substantia quam in accidente. Ratio autem entis, est esse illud, cui contingit esse. Et propter hoc dicit Philosophus et Comm. 7. Metaphy. Com. 2 quod omnia illa dicuntur ens quae aliquo modo habent esse." See the treatment of his passage in Ashworth, "Suárez on the Analogy of Being," 71. See also the parallel passage in Soncinas, *Super Artem* (19rb–va). This *Super Artem* passage does not employ the terms "formal concept" and "objective concept." It adds that analogy of imitation seems to be another mode of analogy but this mode is "perhaps" reducible to another mode.

nes rather than through one *ratio* participated in unequally.⁴³ And, again following Capreolus, the mode of analogy which is suited for the terms of metaphysics and natural theology signifies analogates through one *ratio* unequally.

Soncinas's *AQM*, l. 4, passage differs from Capreolus's parallel treatment by leaving out the words "actually" and "explicitly" from the way that a name expresses a *ratio*. These terms, however, do appear in Soncinas's *Super Artem* rendering of this threefold division of analogy. Even without using these terms, however, the reader of *AQM*, l. 4, can see Soncinas's agreement with Capreolus. Both Capreolus and Soncinas hold that "healthy" actually and explicitly expresses different *rationes* when said of an animal and of urine, and both hold that "being" actually expresses one *ratio* unequally participated when said of substance and of accidents, yet without explicitly signifying one to the exclusion of the other.

I have so far drawn attention to Soncinas's treatment of Aquinas's threefold division of analogy to emphasize how Soncinas parts from Flandrensis and follows Capreolus regarding the *Rationes* Problem. The same passages, however, also reveal one important respect in which Soncinas parts from both Flandrensis and Capreolus. I refer here specifically to Soncinas's claim in both of his parallel passages that the *ratio* of being is "to be that to which it belongs to be."⁴⁴

As noted above, Capreolus attributed greater unity to the formal concept set over analogates than to the objective concept represented through the formal concept. The formal concept is "truly one," whereas, Capreolus says, the objective concept has "unity of attribution or imitation." The "truly one" formal concept represents the analogates unequally because it is abstracted from one analogate and not from the other analogate. Hence, the "truly one" formal concept of "wisdom" formed by abstraction from wise creatures is also the

---

43. *In 1 Sent.*, d. 19, q. 5, a. 2, ad 1.
44. I have not found a text where Soncinas follows Capreolus's example by explicitly invoking analogy of proportionality or by offering any principle for reconciling or privileging one text or another from Aquinas on divine names.

formal concept by which the intellect imperfectly represents the divine wisdom of which creaturely wisdom is an imitation.

Soncinas also attributes greater unity to the formal concept than to the objective concept, yet his account of their unity is quite different from Capreolus's. Beginning with the formal concept's unity, Soncinas describes it as "absolute" and "separate" (*praecisum*). To quote *AMQ*, l. 4, qq. 1–2, on the formal concept of being: "the formal concept of being is absolute. For being [*ens*] is that to which it belongs to be [*esse*],"[45] and "if we speak about the formal concept, it is clear enough that 'being' [*ens*] expresses a separate concept. For the intellect conceiving 'being' says that thing to be a being to which it belongs to be."[46] By Soncinas's account, then, when the intellect conceives being (or other names said analogously of God and creature), it does not rely on a concept that properly signifies one or another of the analogates. The formal concept of being is not identical to the formal concept of substance. Rather, the intellect has a concept distinct from its proper concept of substance through which it signifies being common to substance and accidents. This separate formal concept's signification is analogous rather than univocal because it signifies them unequally, due to the analogates' unequal participation in being. As noted above, Flandrensis presented three ways in which Thomists reject a separate concept of being. His student Soncinas embraces none of these ways. Instead, he affirms a separate formal concept of being.

Soncinas's direct account of the objective concept of being appears in *AMQ*, l. 4, q. 3, where he asks whether "being" explicitly expresses one concept disjunctively. He finds no direct answer to the question in Aquinas's own writings. Thus he turns to the different Thomist views on the unity of the concept of being:

---

45. Soncinas, *AQM*, l. 4, q. 1, ad 3 (3a–b): "Ad tertium dicitur, quod conceptus formalis entis, est absolutus. Nam ens est id cui conuenit esse."
46. Ibid., q. 2 (4a): "Respondeo, quod si loquamur de conceptu formali, satis constat quod ens dicit conceptum praecisum. Intellectus enim concipiens ens, dicit illud esse ens, cui conuenit esse."

The concept can be said to be one in three ways. In one way, by a unity of form, as it is in every generic and specific concept.... And all Thomists deny that "being" has this unity.... Secondly, a concept is said to be one by a unity of analogy and comparison. This occurs when there corresponds to the formal concept immediately as objective concept a multitude of many natures of which one is not called such except in order to another. Third, a concept is said to be one by a unity of disjunction. And this is when there does not correspond to the formal concept either one nature precisely, or a multitude of natures determinately, but properly under a disjunction. Therefore, some say that the concept of being is one in the second way, namely by a unity of analogy because "being" expresses God and creature, and substance and accident such that all those things immediately are expressed by "being," although one of them is only being in order to the other, as accident [is being only] in order to substance, and finite being [only] by analogy to infinite being. But because that mode of speaking does not appear to me as rational as the third, I argue against it.[47]

The first way in which an objective concept can be one is by the unity of form, which all Thomists deny to the objective concept of being, because this would entail univocity. (As noted in chapter 1, it is disputed whether even Scotus himself would attribute such unity to being outside the mind.) The reader of this chapter will notice that the second way of describing the unity of the concept of being identified by Soncinas in this passage is the same as the second Thomist way that Flandrensis identified of rejecting a separate con-

---

47. Ibid., q. 3 (6a): "conceptus potest dici esse vnus tripliciter. Vno modo vnitate formae, sicut est in omni conceptu generico, et specifico: Hominis enim conceptus est humanitas, quae de se est vna natura. Et hanc vnitatem omnes Thomistae, negant ab ente, vt patuit quaestione praecedenti. Secundo dicitur conceptus esse vnus vnitate analogiae et comparationis: et hoc est quando conceptui formali correspondet tanquam conceptus obiectiualis immediate, multitudo plurium naturarum quarum vna non dicitur talis, nisi in ordine ad aliam. Tertio dicitur conceptus esse vnus vnitate disiunctionis, et hoc est quando conceptui formali non correspondet praecise vna natura: nec multitudo naturarum determinate: sed bene sub disiunctione. Dicunt igitur aliqui quod conceptus entis est vnus secundo modo scilicet vnitate analogiae: quia ens dicit Deum et creaturam, et substantiam et accidens. Ita quod omnia ista immediate dicit: sed tamen vnum eorum, non est ens, nisi in ordine ad aliud puta accidens in ordine ad substantiam: et ens finitum, per analogiam ad ens infinitum. Sed quia iste modus dicendi non apparet mihi ita rationalis sicut tertius. Arguo contra ipsum."

cept of being, that is, the way of John Versor.[48] The positions specific to Capreolus and Flandrensis go unmentioned.

Rather than directly arguing against Versor's position, Soncinas proceeds instead to treat the third and more "rational" position, namely, his own position that "being" expresses the disjunction "substance or accident." He does this by showing how unity of disjunction answers standard Scotist objections to analogy, including Scotus's "Certain and Doubtful" Argument. One can be certain that something is a being, while also being doubtful about whether it is a substance or an accident, because to be certain that something is a being is to be certain that it is either a substance or an accident.[49]

We can see that Natalis, Sutton, Dominic of Flanders, and Soncinas all refer to the unity of disjunction when they answer Scotus's "Certain and Doubtful" Argument for the univocity of being. The reader will also have observed that these Thomists integrate unity of disjunction in different ways into their overall solutions to the *Rationes* Problem. In Sutton's and Natalis's accounts, disjunctive unity supports an *ad hoc* rebuttal of Scotus's argument. Flandrensis mentions unity of disjunction specifically as Natalis's way of answering objections, but he does not integrate it at all into his own position. Soncinas, however, not only adopts unity of disjunction into his overall doctrine of analogy, but he explicitly finds it in the objective concept.

In doing so, Soncinas not only parts from Capreolus (who ignores disjunctive unity) and Flandrensis, but also from Hervaeus Natalis. Whereas Natalis used it to deny a single *ratio* in analogy, Soncinas's uses it to permit one. According to Soncinas, the single and separate formal *ratio* of being signifies substance and accidents,

---

48. See note 17 above.
49. Soncinas, *AQM*, l. 4, q. 3 (6b): "iste qui dubitat vtrum A sit substantia vel accidens: non apprehendit A, conceptu proprio: sed conceptu communi ad omnia, scilicet sub hoc disiuncto, substantia vel accidens.... Dubitat tamen quae pars huius disiuncti conueniat ipsi A." (The one who doubts whether A is a substance or an accident does not apprehend A by its proper concept, but by a concept common to all things; namely, under this disjunction: substance or accident.... Nevertheless, this person doubts which part of this disjunction belongs to A itself.)

but not univocally, because the objective concept of being possesses merely disjunctive unity.

For whatever reason, Soncinas does not explicitly apply the disjunctive unity of the concept of being to the case of real being said analogously of God and creatures. His reader is left to wonder whether divine being falls under the disjunct "substance" or whether it is a third disjunct in its own right next to substance and accident. (God only enters into Soncinas's discussion of disjunction as one of the things, such as light, about which one can be certain is a being while being doubtful about whether it is a substance or an accident.)[50] The second option seems more plausible to me.

For one thing, the first option is inconsistent with Soncinas's position in at least two ways. First, by placing God under substance it contradicts Aquinas.[51] Secondly, it would put the being common to God and creatures in the second grade of analogy instead of the third grade. It is likely that Soncinas would notice such an inconsistency. Furthermore, some of Soncinas's statements imply a distinct place for God alongside substance and the accidents in the unity of disjunction. For instance, Soncinas says that a creature of itself is non-being because it only has being from an extrinsic efficient cause. By contrast, God is being. Soncinas notes that the difference between God's natural intrinsic possession of being and a creature's derivative reception of being from an extrinsic efficient cause prevents the

---

50. Ibid.: "Verbi gratia, ille qui dubitat: an Deus sit substantia vel accidens, non habet proprium conceptum diuinitatis: sed habet conceptum entis primi, vel causae primae et habet conceptum substantiae et accidentis: proprie cogniti, et nunc apprehendit aliquas proprietates entis primi: puta infinitatem, simplicitatem, et huiusmodi: et dubitat vtrum istae proprietates sint attribuendum substantiae vel accidenti: et sic per discursum inquirit, an Deus, siue primum ens, sit substantia vel accidens." (For example, the one who doubts whether God is a substance or an accident does not have a proper concept of divinity. Rather, he has a concept of "first-being" or "first cause," and he has a concept of "substance" and of "accident" known properly. And now he apprehends some properties of the first being, for example, infinity, simplicity, and the like. And he doubts whether those properties should be attributed to a substance or to an accident, and so, through discursive reasoning, he inquires whether God (or the first being) is a substance or an accident.) Soncinas gives a similar argument using light as an example on the same page.

51. See Aquinas, *Summa Contra Gentiles* I, c. 25.

univocity of any quiddity for God and creatures.[52] This argument taken together with what has been treated so far suggests that Soncinas recognizes the following disjunction of *per se* being: Being *per se* from itself (God) or being *per se* from another (substance). Combined with the disjunction "substance or accident," Soncinas holds a threefold disjunction of real being: being *per se* from itself (God), or being *per se* from another (substance), or being in another (accident). I do not see another way of reading Soncinas that saves the consistency of his account of the unity of the objective concept of being.

To sum up Soncinas's position on the *Rationes* and Analogy Model Problems, his solutions develop the thought of Natalis and Capreolus in opposition to his teacher Dominic of Flanders. Like Natalis and Capreolus, Soncinas explicitly distinguishes the formal and objective concepts as well as their unity in the case of analogous names. Unlike Capreolus, Soncinas gives a role to unity of disjunction in solving the *Rationes* Problem, but not the role given to it by Natalis, insofar as Soncinas finds unity of disjunction in the objective concept. Following Capreolus, Soncinas uses Aquinas's *In 1 Sent.* to reject the Healthy Model for the Analogy Model Problem, and he uses the same passage (d. 19, q. 5, a. 2, ad 1) to support simple unity for the formal concept in answer to the *Rationes* Problem. Soncinas parts from Capreolus, however, and directly opposes Flandrensis's answer to the problem by proposing that the formal concept in the kind of analogy suited to naming God and creatures is "separate" from the formal concepts proper to the analogates. Below,

---

52. Soncinas, *AQM*, l. 4, q. 4 (8b): "creatura non habet esse, cum non recipiat esse nisi a Deo. Ergo creatura ex se est non ens. Confirmatur. Id quod conuenit alicui ex se per prius conuenit ei, quam id quod conuenit solum per causam extrinsecam. Sed non esse conuenit creaturae ex se, et esse conuenit ei solum per causam extrinsecam efficientem. Ergo, prius natura creatura est non ens, quam ens." (A creature does not have being as it only receives being from God. Therefore, a creature is not a being from itself. This is confirmed because that which belongs to anything from itself belongs [to it] prior to that which belongs only through an extrinsic cause. But nonbeing belongs to a creature from itself and being belongs to it only through an extrinsic cause. Therefore, nonbeing is naturally prior to being in a creature.)

we will see the consequences of the differences between Flandrensis and Soncinas on the *Rationes* and Analogy Model Problems for their solutions to the Equivocation Problem.

FLANDRENSIS AND SONCINAS ON THE EQUIVOCATION PROBLEM

Flandrensis's Solution

Flandrensis takes up the Equivocation Problem directly in three passages: two in his *SDP* and one in his *De Fallaciis*. The two *SDP* passages recite verbatim the words of early fourteenth-century Thomists. The first passage quotes, almost verbatim, a selection from Natalis discussed above in chapter 2.[53] The second passage draws from Natalis's contemporary Thomas Anglicus, who, in the passage in question, explains that the fallacy of equivocation occurs when names are imposed analogously "on account of a certain likeness" but not when they are imposed by a certain ordered relation to one. The example of naming due to likeness is *ridere* said of a human and a field.[54] Below I

---

53. Dominic of Flanders, *SDP*, l. 4, q. 2, a. 3 (152b): "Respondet, quod aliquam demonstationem, procedere ex aequiuoco, potest intelligi dupliciter. Vno modo: quia ignorata distinctione aequiuoca, ex vno sensu alterum concludatur, et sic procedere in aequiuoco, est deceptio fallaciae aequiuocationis. Alio modo, quod nota aequiuocatione, ostenditur illud quod concluditur de aequiuoco, conuenire sibi, secundum communem sensum quem potest habere, et maxime vbi est connexio inter rationes plures, significatas per terminum analogum. Et sic procedere in aequiuocis, non est decipi per fallaciam aequiuocationis sed est demonstrare, et generare scientiam veram, licet illa demonstratio non sit, ita simpliciter vna, sicut illa quae procedit in vniuoco." (He [i.e., Hervaeus Natalis] answers that any demonstration can be understood to proceed from an equivocation in two ways. In one way, because from an unknown distinction in an equivocal term, one concludes from one sense to another. And to proceed in this way in equivocation is the deception of the fallacy of equivocation. In another way, by a known equivocation, it is shown that what is concluded from an equivocal term belongs to it according to a common sense which it can have, and most of all where there is a connection between the many *rationes* signified through the analogous term. And to proceed in this way in equivocals is not to be deceived by the fallacy of equivocation, but it is to demonstrate and generate true science, although that demonstration is not as absolutely one as a demonstration which proceeds in a univocal.) Compare the quotation above to Natalis, *Quodlibet* 2, q. 7 (Venice 1513, 45va–b). See also p. 40n15 above.

54. Dominic of Flanders, *SDP*, l. 4, q. 2, a. 4 (153b): "Respondeo dicendum, quod

focus primarily on the *De Fallaciis* passage where Flandrensis speaks at greater length and seemingly in his own name.

In *De Fallaciis*, q. 9, Flandrensis observes that both univocal names and names said according to analogy signify many through one *ratio*. Analogy differs from univocity only insofar as the many signified by the analogous name agree *per prius et posterius* in the one *ratio*. This passage's rendering of the distinction between analogy and univocity is clearly consistent with Flandrensis's answer to the *Rationes* Problem in the passages of *SDP*, l. 4, discussed above. Here Flandrensis asserts that analogous signification does not cause the fallacy of equivocation because this form of signification is not altogether diverse.[55] He qualifies this claim by distinguishing two kinds of analogy:

---

duplex est analogia. Quaedam est ipsorum conceptuum ad unum nomen tantum, quod scilicet significat vnum conceptum ex impositione, et significat alium, propter quandam similitudinem, non tamen ex impositione, sicut ridere significat risum hominis ex impositione, sed tamen, ex quadam proportione, significat floriditatem prati. Et talis analogia causat fallaciam. Alia est analogia ipsarum rerum ad vnum conceptum, seu conceptuum ad vnum nomen, quod impositum est ad significandum illos conceptus, ordine tamen quodam. Et talis analogiae, triplex est gradus, ut innuit philosophus hic lec. 1 et in 1 Ethic. lec. 7." (I answer that it must be said that analogy is twofold. One [kind of analogy] is of those very concepts which indeed signify one concept for only one name by imposition, and signify another due to a certain likeness, although not from imposition, just as "to laugh" signifies the laughter of a man from imposition, but, nevertheless, from a certain proportion, [also] signifies the flourishing of a field. And this kind of analogy causes a fallacy. The other is the [kind of] analogy of the things themselves to one concept, or of concepts to one name, which is imposed for signifying those concepts by a certain order. And this kind of analogy has three modes, as the Philosopher indicates here in lect. 1 and in Ethics, l. 1, lect. 7.) Flandrensis does not name his source, but compare the above to Thomas Anglicus, *Contra Joannem Scotum primo sententiarum libro*, d. 3, q. 1 (Venice: Erven Octavianus Scotus, 1523), 37va.

55. Dominic of Flanders, *In Diui Thomae Aquinatis fallaciarum opus perutiles quaestiones*, q. 9, in *In D. Thomae Aquinatis Commentaria Super Libris Posteriorum Analyticorum Aristotelis, Quaestiones Perutiles* (Venice, 1587) (hereafter, *De Fallaciis*), 344b–345a: "significat plura secundum quod conueniunt in una ratione analogi, idest secundum prius et posterius. Igitur talis significatio non est penitus diuersa. Vnde non causat fallaciam aequiuocationis si fuerit imposita ad significandum plura per prius et posterius." ([It] signifies many insofar as they agree in one *ratio* of an analogy, that is according to priority and posteriority. Therefore, such signification is not altogether diverse. Hence, it does not cause the fallacy of equivocation if it should be imposed for signifying many by priority and posteriority.)

Analogy is twofold. For there is one [kind of analogy] which signifies many things which agree in one *ratio* according to priority and posteriority, as being [*ens*] signifies the ten categories according to priority and posteriority. Nevertheless, from the imposition it is not such that it causes the fallacy of equivocation except reductively, and with respect of some of the terms which assert a difference between the bearing term [*inferentem*] and the brought forward term [*illatum*]. Otherwise, the first principle would not be the surest, and, although it is called equivocation by design, it is not then called equivocation absolutely. There is another analogy which signifies many, not from the imposition, but it is imposed for signifying one, and it is said transpositively for signifying the rest through some likeness, as laughing from imposition signifies the act of a human, but through likeness it is transposited for signifying the flourishing of a field. And such [an analogy] causes the fallacy of equivocation in the second mode, as will be clear below.[56]

The first of the two kinds of analogy is characterized by primary and secondary signification of a name said of many. The second kind of analogy is what others call metaphor, and, for this metaphorical kind of analogy, Flandrensis provides the same example drawn from Thomas Anglicus in the *SDP* passage cited above.[57] The second (metaphorical) kind of analogy causes the fallacy of equivocation because the name only signifies a certain likeness of one thing to another. That is, the *ratio* of the name is predicated as belonging

---

56. Dominic of Flanders, *De Fallaciis*, q. 9 (Venice, 345a): "quod duplex est analogum. Nam quoddam est quod ex impositione sisinificat [sic] plura, quae conueniunt in una ratione secundum prius et posterius vt ens significat decem praedicamenta secundum prius et posterius. Ex impositione tamen est quod tale non causat fallaciam aequiuocationis nisi reductiue, et respectu aliquorum terminorum qui ponunt differentiam inter terminum inferentem et terminum illatum. Aliter primum principium non esset tutissimum, et licet uocetur aequiuocatio a consimili, non tunc dicitur aequiuocatio simpliciter. Aliud est analogum quod plura significat non ex impositione sed est impositum ad significandum unnm [sic] et transumptiue est dictum est ad significandum reliquum per similitudinem aliquam, sicut ridere ex impositione significat actum hominis, per similitudinem uero est transumptum ad significandum floritionem prati, et tale causat fallaciam aequiuocationis in secundo modo, ut infra patebit." See also my brief treatment of the aforementioned three passages by Flandrensis on the fallacy of equivocation in Domenic D'Ettore, "Some Renaissance Thomists on Analogy in Demonstration," *Angelicum* 93 (2016): 934–39.

57. The same example appears, among other places, in Aquinas, *Summa Theologiae* I, q. 13, a. 6.

to the primary recipient of the name, and only a resemblance to the primary recipient of the name is predicated of the secondary recipient of the name. By contrast with metaphorical analogy, in the other kind of analogy, the name signifies something belonging (albeit by priority and posteriority) to both recipients of the name. The fallacy of equivocation always occurs where a mediating term is metaphorically analogous. But the fallacy of equivocation is only sometimes caused by the other (and nonmetaphorical) kind of analogy.

The fallacy of equivocation occurs with the first mode of analogy when the analogous term asserts a difference between *terminum inferentem* and *terminum illatum*. Presumably, Flandrensis is referring to instances that include the standard example of the fallacy of equivocation: "Every healthy thing is alive, medicine is healthy; ergo, etc." Flandrensis identifies what goes wrong in this invalid demonstration: the term "healthy" asserts one thing in the major premise and something different when it is brought forward (*illatum*) into the minor premise. He denies that this difference between the bearing and brought forward significations of the term occurs in the case of "being" said *per prius et posterius*. Unfortunately, Flandrensis does not explain why.

The obvious objection to Flandrensis's solution—and the one already observed by both Sutton and Capreolus—is that, as a semantic principle, *per prius et posterius* signification fails to consistently preserve demonstration from the fallacy of equivocation. And if *per prius et posterius* signification fails in that semantic task in the mundane cases, such as "Every healthy thing is alive, medicine is healthy; therefore, medicine is alive," it remains to state what principled semantic reason there is for thinking that *per prius et posterius* signification preserves demonstration in metaphysics and natural theology.

Flandrensis's remarks on analogy of proportionality for names said of God and creatures in *SDP*, l. 12, suggest a way of qualifying which sort of *per prius et posterius* signification saves demonstration, but the quotation above from his *De Fallaciis* undermines any systematic application of that qualification to Flandrensis's overall position. In *De Fallaciis*, q. 9, Flandrensis clearly thinks that other forms of analogy than proportionality can also preserve demonstration, as he affirms that "being" said across the categories is an example of a form of analogy that avoids the fallacy of equivocation, and, as we have seen, he considers "being" said across the categories as an instance of determinate proportion, not proportionality. Ultimately, Flandrensis's solution to the Equivocation Problem reduces to that of Natalis and is open to the same criticism. Some demonstrations using analogous terms work because "there is something the same" which is carried over from the first use of the term into the second analogous use of the term in the argument. There is no deception because you can tell the difference between when the *per posterius* signification asserts something different than the *per prius* signification and when it does not.

Soncinas's Solution

Soncinas faces the Equivocation Problem directly in *AQM*, l. 4, where he considers the argument:

> Every proposition must be distinguished in which an analogous or equivocal term is asserted, since it is ambiguous. But "being" is asserted in the first complex principle. Therefore, if "being" is not univocal, it follows that the first principle must be distinguished, and consequently, it is not certain. And since it is present either formally or virtually in every demonstration, it follows that every demonstration will begin from what is uncertain.[58]

This argument draws on the premise that demonstration depends on an unambiguous first principle. The term "being" appears in the

---

58. Soncinas, *AQM*, l. 4, q. 4 (7b): "Omnis propositio in qua ponitur terminus analogus vel aequiuocus, est distinguenda cum sit multiplex, sed in primo principio complexo ponitur ens. Ergo si ens non est vniuocum, sequitur quod primum principium sit distinguendum, et per consequens non est certum. Et cum ingrediatur aut formaliter aut virtualiter omnem demonstrationem, sequitur quod omnis demonstratio sit ex incertis." See the same objection in Capreolus, *Defensiones*, l. 1, d. 2, q. 1, a. 2 (1:130b), and in his source Peter Auriol, *Scriptum in I Sententiarum*, d. 2 (Vatican 1596, 114b–115a). See also my treatment of Soncinas on this point in D'Ettore, "Some Renaissance Thomists on analogy in demonstration," 939–42.

"first complex principle" (i.e., the principle of noncontradiction).[59] If the term "being" is analogous or equivocal, then the first complex principle will be ambiguous, as will be all demonstrations insofar as they contain the first complex principle either formally or virtually. Hence, demonstration requires that "being" is a univocal term. Soncinas answers this argument by noting (as Capreolus did in the face of the same argument) that this objection only applies to the kind of analogy that expresses many *rationes*, and not to the kind of analogy used for "being."[60]

Soncinas provides a fuller account in his *Super Artem* of why, of the three modes of analogy, only the mode of analogy exemplified by the Healthy Model leads to the fallacy of equivocation. After relating the three modes or grades of analogy (discussed above), Soncinas adds that

only the first mode of analogy makes the *rationes* ambiguous, and consequently it causes the fallacy of equivocation, as is clear in this paralogism: "because everything healthy lives, [and] medicine is healthy; therefore, it lives." But the other two modes do not cause such a fallacy ... the analogue taken in the first way is only in one of the analogates through the proper *ratio*.... But the other two modes are in all the analogates.[61]

Soncinas provides the same example of the fallacy of equivocation that we have already seen in Sutton and Capreolus. Following Capreolus's example, Soncinas affirms that the fallacy occurs because the syllogism employs the mode of analogy that explicitly signifies

---

59. Soncinas defends the principle of noncontradiction's claim to be the first complex principle in Paulus Soncinas, *AQM*, l. 4, q. 31 (44a–b).
60. Soncinas, *AQM*, l. 4, q. 4 (9a): "Ad octauum negatur maior nisi illud analogum dicat plures rationes, quale non est ens: vt dictum fuit." (To the eighth, the major premise is denied. Being does not belong to that kind of analogy which expresses many *rationes*, as has been said.)
61. Soncinas, *Super Artem* (19Va): "tantum primus modus analogiae facit rationes multiplicem. Et ex consequenti causat fallatiam equiuocationis: vt patet in hoc paralogismo: quia omne sanum viuit medicina est sana ergo viuit alii autem duo modi non causant talem fallatiam. Differunt tertio quia analogum primo modo acceptum est tantum in vno analogatorum per propriam rationem: sicut patet quod propria ratio sanitatis scilicet adequatio humorum est tantum in animali. Alii autem duo modi sunt in omnibus analogatis."

many *rationes*. I do not find in Capreolus's writings, however, the further explanation that Soncinas offers in the last two lines quoted above.

In these lines, Soncinas marks the difference between the first mode of analogy and the second mode of analogy through the presence or absence of the proper *ratio* in the analogates. The proper *ratio* is present only in one of the analogates in the first mode: "adequation of the humors is only in the animal."[62] But in the second and third modes' analogates, the proper *ratio* is in both analogates; for example, the proper *ratio* of body is present in both heavenly and terrestrial bodies, and the proper *ratio* of being is present in both substance and accidents. At the level of the objective concept, then, the reason why the second and third modes of analogy avoid the fallacy of equivocation and the first mode does not is that the proper *ratio* carries over from one analogate to the next intrinsically in the second and third modes of analogy, but not in the first. The intrinsic presence of the *ratio* objectively makes it possible for a single formal concept to represent each analogate, while the inequality of that objective *ratio* preserves the inequality in the representation and avoids reduction to univocity.

It appears that Soncinas's doctrine of the separate formal concept unequally participated has a uniquely effective answer to the Scotist objector. Soncinas admits to the Scotist that there is without qualification one formal concept—one concept distinct from the proper formal concepts of the analogates—through which the names are signified analogously in a valid demonstration. Such a separate concept would clearly have sufficient unity to ground a contradiction. So any further Scotist objection would have to argue, not that Soncinas has failed to preserve demonstration in metaphysics and natural theology, but that his doctrine of a separate *ratio* participated in unequally reduces the semantics of analogy to univocity.

---

62. Ibid.: "propria ratio sanitatis scilicet adequatio humorum est tantum in animali."

CONCLUSION

Flandrensis and Soncinas model different ways of developing or rejecting their Thomist predecessors' answers to the *Rationes* and Analogy Model Problems. Both of them specifically reject the Healthy Model for the Analogy Model Problem, and turn to their different single *ratio* answers to the *Rationes* Problem in their solutions to the Equivocation Problem. It is much more evident how Soncinas's answer to the *Rationes* Problem, formed in contradiction to Flandrensis's answer, helps to answer the Equivocation Problem than to see how Flandrensis's solution accomplishes the same task. The question remains whether Soncinas's answer to the *Rationes* Problem holds. Flandrensis, as noted above, spoke of three different ways his contemporary Thomists rejected the proposal of a separate concept. The controversy among Thomists over whether there is a separate formal concept does not end with Soncinas, but carries on in the writings of each of the Thomists treated in the remaining chapters of this book. In the following chapter, we will see the critical reception of both Flandrensis and Soncinas from Thomas de Vio Cajetan.

5

Cajetan

Chapter 4 compared the efforts of Dominic of Flanders and his student Paul Soncinas to answer the three problems. For the *Rationes* Problem, both adopt Capreolus's revised definition of univocity, which requires equal participation in a *ratio*, and both hold that there is a single *ratio* common by analogy for being and the other key terms of metaphysics and natural theology. Flandrensis and Soncinas significantly differ on the nature of this single *ratio*. In particular, Flandrensis insists that the single *ratio* is not separate from the proper concepts of the analogates. In the case of being, the one *ratio* of being is the *ratio* of substance. By contrast, Soncinas proposes a separate formal concept. On the Analogy Model Problem, both reject the Healthy Model of analogy. Flandrensis rejects it in favor of the Principle Model, applying the reasoning of Aquinas's *De Veritate*, q. 2, a. 11. Soncinas rejects the Healthy Model by imitating Capreolus's interpretation of Aquinas's *In 1 Sent.*, d. 19. That is, the Healthy Model is unsuited to naming God and creatures because it entails multiple *rationes*, rather than one *ratio* participated in unequally. Both Thomists employ their understandings of a single unequally (or diversely) participated in *ratio* in their solutions to the Equivocation Problem. Flandrensis's solution does not appear to overcome the standard objections. Soncinas's solution to the Equivocation Problem is as strong as his solution to the *Rationes* Problem.

Cajetan 127

The present chapter follows the argument among the Bologna School Thomists into the writings of another of its students and masters, Thomas de Vio Cajetan. Cajetan's *De Nominum Analogia* provides the most sustained and clear account of the semantics of analogy among the authors considered in this study, as well as the most unambiguous answers to the three problems. Indeed, the history of Thomist investigation of these questions (and this study) has been in great part determined by Cajetan's work. The teachings of Cajetan on analogy have been well set out recently in Joshua Hochschild's *The Semantics of Analogy*.[1] This chapter treats Cajetan's answers to the three problems specifically as adaptations or critiques of Capreolus, Flandrensis, and Soncinas. Cajetan's doctrine of analogy in the *De Nominum Analogia* is most famous (or infamous) today for its answer to the Analogy Model Problem, that analogy of "proper proportionality" (as distinct from "metaphorical proportionality") is the mode of analogy suited to metaphysics.[2] In taking this position, Cajetan endorses the answers that we have seen in the works of Thomas Sutton, John Capreolus, and Dominic of Flanders (the latter of whom Cajetan directly follows when he divides analogy of proportionality into its metaphorical and nonmetaphorical species). Cajetan's *De Nominum Analogia* is also known for presenting Aquinas's *In 1 Sent.*, d. 19, threefold division of analogy as the division relevant for metaphysics, which puts Cajetan in continuity

---

1. Hochschild, *The Semantics of Analogy*. For Cajetan's doctrine of analogy, see also Riva, *Analogia e univocità in Tommaso de Vio "Gaetano."*
2. For an emphatic statement by Cajetan on the importance of analogy of proper proportionality, see especially Cajetan, *De Nominum Analogia*, in *Scripta Philosophica*, ed. P. N. Zammit (Rome: Angelicum, 1934), c. 3, n. 29 (29): "Scimus quidem secundum hanc analogiam, rerum intrinsecas entitates, bonitates, veritates etc., quod ex priori analogia non scitur. Unde sine huius analogiae notitia, processus metaphysicales absque arte dicuntur. Acciditque huiusmodi ignorantibus, quod antiquis nescientibus logicam." (Indeed, we know the instrinsic beingness, goodness, truth, etc. of things by this analogy, which is not known from the prior [kind] of analogy. Hence, without knowledge of this kind of analogy, the metaphysical processes are said without art. And what happened to the ancient [philosophers] who did not know logic happens to the ones ignorant of this kind [of analogy].) For a contemporary emphatic criticism of Cajetan as an interpreter of Aquinas's doctrine of analogy, see McInerny, *Aquinas and Analogy*, 3–29.

with Capreolus and Soncinas. Unlike Capreolus, Cajetan explicitly connects the third mode of analogy in this division and *De Veritate*, q. 2, a. 11's analogy of proportionality. On all of these points related to the Analogy Model Problem, Cajetan either simply follows or makes more explicit doctrines taught by his fifteenth-century Thomist predecessors.

CAJETAN'S INTRODUCTORY ANSWER TO THE *RATIONES* AND ANALOGY MODEL PROBLEMS

Prior to composing the *De Nominum Analogia*, Cajetan had already engaged the *Rationes* and Analogy Model Problems in his *In de Ente et Essentia* through his answer to the question: "Whether being is said by priority about substance [and] by posteriority about accident, [or] whether univocally of both?"[3] In this passage Cajetan closely follows Aquinas's *De Veritate*, q. 2, a. 11, answer to the Analogy Model Problem, writing:

Analogates are twofold. Certain ones [are analogous] according to a determinate relation of one to another. Certain [others are analogous] according to proportionality. For example, substance and accident are analogates under being in the first way. But God and creatures [are analogates] in the second way, for there is an infinite distance between God and creature. Now these [modes of analogy] differ very much because analogates in the first mode relate such that the posterior according to the analogous name is defined through its prior: for instance, accident [is defined] as being through substance. But [it is] not [so with] analogates in the second way, for a creature is not defined as being through God.[4]

3. Cajetan, *In de Ente et Essentia*, q. 3, in *Thomae de Vio Caietani Cardinalis Titvlis Sixti, In Praedicabilia Porphyrij, Praedicamenta, Postpraedicamenta, et libros Posteriorvm Analyticorvm Aristotelis castigatissima Commentaria Accesserunt praeterea eiusdem R. Cardinalis doctissima in D. Thomae Aquinatis librum de Ente, et Essentia* (Lyon, 1578), 37: "Num ens per prius de substantia, posterius de accidente dicatur, an de vtroque vniuoce."

4. Cajetan, *In de Ente et Essentia*, q. 3 (Lyon, 43): "Duplicia sunt analogata. Quaedam secundum determinatam habitudinem vnius ad alterum. Quaedam secundum proportionalitatem. Exemplum: Substantia et accidens sunt analogata primo modo sub ente. Deus autem et creatura secondo modo: infinita enim est distantia inter Deum et creaturam. Differunt autem haec plurimum: quoniam analogata primo modo ita se habent: quod posterius secundum nomen analogum diffinitur per suum prius: puta accidens,

The reader can see here continuity both with Aquinas's *De Veritate*, q. 2, a. 11, and with Dominic of Flanders's adaptation of the passage in his *Summa Divinae Philosophiae*, l. 12.[5] There are two modes of analogy. One mode entails determinate proportion, and is illustrated using the Healthy Model. The other mode of analogy entails indeterminate proportion or "proportionality." In the first mode, which is suited to the analogy between substance and accident as being, the posterior analogate is defined by reference to the primary analogate. In the second mode, which is suited to God and creatures, the definition of one analogate does not belong in the definition of the other analogate. Cajetan adds that in the case of the second mode of analogy, "[the analogates] have the same *ratio* relatively on account of the identity of proportion, which is found in them,"[6] which seems to agree with Dominic of Flanders's description of the analogates in the second mode having agreement between two proportions, as opposed to analogates in the first mode which have some determinate proportion between them.[7]

Cajetan does not use "principle"-based examples to illustrate proportionality,[8] but it is evident that he embraces what is here being called the Principle Model of analogy and rejects the Healthy Model for divine names. He even goes beyond Flandrensis in his embrace of proportionality by noting that "being" is said analogously about substance and accident not only in the first (Healthy Model) mode of analogy, but also in the second (Principle Model) mode of analogy.[9]

Stepping out of the Analogy Model Problem into the *Rationes*

---

inquantum ens per substantiam. Analogata vero secondo modo non: creatura enim inquantum ens non diffinitur per Deum."

5. See p. 103n26 above.

6. Cajetan, *In de Ente et Essentia*, q. 3 (Lyon, 43): "sed habent rationem eandem secundum quid propter identitatem proportionis, quae in eis invenitur."

7. See p. 104n27 above.

8. He gives examples of proportionally analogous ways in which diverse things can be called "matter and form" instead.

9. Cajetan, *In de Ente et Essentia*, q. 3 (Lyon, 44): "Ens analogice vtroque modo analogiae dicitur de substantia et accidente." ("Being" is said analogously in both ways about substance and accident.)

Problem in the same passage, Cajetan invokes the language of formal and objective concepts, saying: "The formal concept of being is one unequally representing the being [*esse*] of substance and of accident, of God and of creature, and ... the objective concept has only the unity of determinate proportion from the identity of the term or the unity of proportionability and the identity of the proportions."[10] This statement clearly affirms diverse yet proportionally identical *rationes* at the level of the objective concept. What it means for the unity of the formal concept is less clear. As written, the passage appears ambiguous as to whether the one formal concept of being is separate from the proper concepts of the analogates, or is perhaps one of those proper concepts. Cajetan makes himself clear on these controversial points in his subsequent works, *De Nominum Analogia* and *De Conceptu Entis*.

Although his answer to the Analogy Model Problem has received more attention in the past century, *vis-à-vis* the preceding Thomist tradition, Cajetan's answer to the *Rationes* Problem is more controversial. By affirming that there is one formal concept in names said by analogy of proper proportionality, Cajetan parts from the fourteenth-century Thomists Sutton and Natalis, who deny a single *ratio* in analogy. He also parts from Flandrensis, insofar as the latter does not use the distinction between formal and objective concepts or restrict signification through a single concept to the analogy of proportionality. As discussed in chapter 4, Flandrensis and Soncinas disagree over whether the one concept in analogy is separate from the proper concepts of the analogates. I now compare more fully the position of Cajetan on the *Rationes* Problem with the positions taken by Flandrensis, Soncinas, and Capreolus.

---

10. Ibid.: "Conceptus entis formalis est vnus inaequaliter repraesentans esse substantiae et accidentis Dei et creaturae: et quod conceptus obiectalis non habet nisi vnitatem proportionis determinatae ex identitate termini vel vnitate proportionabilitatis et identitate proportionum."

CAJETAN AND HIS PREDECESSORS ON THE ONE *RATIO* IN ANALOGY

The opening lines of *De Nominum Analogia* criticize three positions held by Cajetan's Thomist predecessors, including the opinion that there is one separate concept unequally participated by the analogates.[11] I take the occasion of this criticism to examine an ambiguity in Capreolus's answer to the *Rationes* Problem, and to compare Cajetan's position closely to those of his fifteenth-century predecessors Capreolus, Flandrensis, and Soncinas, all of whom affirm a one *ratio* solution to the *Rationes* Problem.

Unlike Flandrensis and Soncinas, Capreolus does not specifically raise the question of whether the unequally participated in concept in an analogy is separate from the proper concepts of the analogates. As early as the sixteenth century, however, interpreters of Capreolus's *Defensiones*, including the Jesuit Thomist Peter Fonseca (1528–99), placed Capreolus among the Thomists who hold that both the formal concept of being and the objective concept of being are one and separate from the proper concepts of the analogates.[12]

Now Fonseca merely directs his reader to *Defensiones*, l. 1, d. 2, q. 1, without quoting any passages where Capreolus proposes a separate concept either formally or objectively. The most plausible passages for his interpretation occur within the objections and Capre-

---

11. Cajetan, *De Nominum Analogia*, c. 6, n. 71 (Zammit, 58): "Ex praedictis autem manifeste patet, quod analogum non conceptum disiunctum, nec unum praecisum inaequaliter participatum, nec unum ordine; sed conceptum unum proportione dicit et praedicat." (But from what has been said is manifestly clear that an analogous name does not express and predicate a disjunctive concept, nor one separate unequally participated in [concept], nor one [concept] by [the unity of] order, but one concept [by the unity of] proportion.) For background on this discussion, see E. J. Ashworth, "Petrus Fonseca on Objective Concepts and the Analogy of Being," 48–49, and "Antonius Rubius on Objective Being and Analogy: One of the Routes from Early Fourteenth-Century Discussions to Descartes' Third Meditation," in *Meetings of the Minds: The Relation between Medieval and Classical Modern European Philosophy*, ed. Stephen F. Brown (Turnhout: Brepols, 1998), 48–50.

12. See Petrus Fonseca, *Commentariorvm In Libros Metaphysicorvm Aristotelis Stagiritae*, Tomvs 1, l. 3, c. 2, q. 2, sect. 2 (Frankfurt, 1599), 711D–713A. See also Ashworth, "Suárez on the Analogy of Being," 72n114.

olus's replies concerning the ninth conclusion. For example, in one objection, it is proposed that if the concept of being is identical to the proper concept of substance, then the proposition "A substance is a being" is identical to "A substance is a substance." Likewise, if the concept of being is identical to the proper concept of God, then the proposition "God is a being" is identical to "God is God." However, because these two propositions are not tautologies, there must be different concepts signifying their subjects (substance and God) and their predicate (being).[13]

Fonseca's interpretation of Capreolus could be grounded in Capreolus's reply: "When it is said 'God is a being,' the concept of the predicate is other than the concept of the subject."[14] With these words, Capreolus acknowledges that the concept of being is other than the proper concept of substance and the proper concept of God. Taking these remarks in their wider context, however, reveals their ambiguity. Immediately below the passage quoted above, Capreolus denies "that the concept of being is one from the unity of the understood form except through attribution."[15] It is difficult to see how the concept of being as used in the statements *Deus est ens* and *substantia est ens* can be one by "attribution" and yet also be "separate" from the proper concepts that are attributed one to the other. As even the passages that offer the strongest support for Fonseca's interpretation are ambiguous, I do not think that Fonseca's account of Capreolus has a strong textual foundation.

Moreover, Fonseca's interpretation of Capreolus is directly un-

13. Capreolus, *Defensiones*, l. 1, d. 2, q. 1, a. 2 (1:130a–b).
14. Ibid., 141b. Quoted below in note 15.
15. See Capreolus, *Defensiones*, l. 1, d. 2, q. 1, a. 2 (1:141b): "*Ad sextum* dicitur quod concludit conceptum entis esse alium a conceptu proprio substantiae, et a conceptu proprio Dei, ita quod, dum dicitur: Deus est ens, conceptus praedicati est alius a conceptu subjecti; nec hoc negamus nos; sed solum quod conceptus entis sit unus ab unitate formae intellectae, nisi per attributionem." (To the sixth it is said that it concludes that the concept of being is other than the proper concept of substance and the proper concept of God, such that when one says "God is a being" the concept of the predicate is other than the concept of the subject. We do not deny this conclusion. Rather, [we deny] only that the concept of being is one from the unity of the understood form except through attribution.)

dermined by a number of other passages from *Defensiones*, l. 1, d. 2, q. 1. For example, Capreolus writes:

> Although the question, "whether it is [*an est*]," asks something other than the question, "what is it [*quid est*]," nevertheless, it is not held that the concept of being is distinct from the proper concepts in the way in which a concept that is perfectly one is distinguished from a concept that is perfectly one, but [rather] through the mode in which a concept, having unity of attribution, is distinguished from a concept that is truly one which it includes implicitly.[16]

The concept of "being" is distinct enough from the proper concepts of being (i.e., the concepts proper to substance and accident, God and creature) to avoid making the predication of being to God and to substance tautological. Yet this does not make the concept of being a "perfectly one concept" set apart from the proper concepts of God, substance, and accidents as other "perfectly one" concepts. Rather, the concept of being attributed to God, substance, and accidents is distinct from the proper concepts of God, substance, and accidents only in the way a concept is distinct from another concept which "it includes implicitly." Concepts which are distinct in this way, according to Capreolus, have "unity of attribution."

As discussed in chapter 3, Capreolus sees unity of attribution between concepts in those cases where one concept at once represents one thing perfectly and another imperfectly. For example, the truly one proper formal concept of "human wisdom" represents both human and divine wisdom at once—the human more perfectly and the divine imperfectly. In light of these texts, I think it reasonable to disagree with Fonseca's interpretation and conclude that Capreolus does not hold that there is a separate (analogous) concept from the proper concepts of the analogates when a name is said analogously by the third mode of analogy, which includes "being" said across the

---

16. Ibid., 142a–b: "*Ad decimum quartum* dicitur quod licet quaestio, an est, quaerat aliud quam quaestio, quid est, non tamen habetur quod conceptus entis sit distinctus a propriis conceptibus, illo modo quo conceptus perfecte unus distinguitur a conceptu perfecte uno; sed per modum quo conceptus, habens unitatem attributionis, distinguitur a conceptu vere uno, quem implicite includit."

categories, "being" said of God and creature, and other names said analogously of God and creature.[17]

Moving on to review the positions of Flandrensis and Soncinas, the reader of chapter 4 will recall that Soncinas explicitly affirms what Flandrensis explicitly denies; namely, a separate concept of being. Moreover, Soncinas explicitly denies and Flandrensis explicitly affirms that there is unequal participation in a *ratio* when a name is said of one analogate properly and primarily and of another or others by relation to the primary analogate. Soncinas follows Capreolus by affirming one formal concept and one objective concept of "being" said by analogy of and found in God and creature, substance and accident. Yet Soncinas parts from Capreolus by asserting that the one formal concept of "being" represents "that to which it belongs to be," and that the foundation for the formal concept of being (i.e., the objective concept of being) is one by the unity of disjunction and participated in unequally by the disjuncts. Soncinas's one formal concept is separate, and Capreolus's is not; Soncinas's objective concept has disjunctive unity, and Capreolus's has unity of attribution. It is shown below that Cajetan's own answer to the *Rationes* Problem explicitly rejects the position held by Soncinas without adopting any of the three ways of rejecting this position mentioned by Flandrensis, ultimately bearing a strong resemblance to the position of John Capreolus.[18]

De Nominum Analogia, c. 4, provides the clarification of his answer to the *Rationes* Problem, which Cajetan promised in his *In De Ente et Essentia*, q. 3. After cautioning those who find it written in one place "that analogates agree in one *ratio*" and in another place "that analogates do not agree in one *ratio*,"[19] Cajetan distinguish-

---

17. I discuss my disagreement with Fonseca's interpretation of Capreolus in greater detail in D'Ettore, "The Fifteenth-Century Thomist Dispute over Participation," 252–57.

18. The three ways Flandrensis mentions are unity of disjunction, immediate signification of each analogate, and unity of attribution through the presence of the primary analogate in the signification of the secondary analogates. See pp. 97n15–99n20.

19. Cajetan, *De Nominum Analogia*, c. 4, n. 37 (Zammit, 36): "Propter quod solerti discretione lectorem uti quando invenitur scriptum, quod analogata conveniunt in una ratione, et quando invenitur dictum alibi, quod analogata non conveniunt in una ratione."

es the formal concepts of univocals, which perfectly and adequately represent the many things about which they are said, from the formal concepts of analogates, which represent one analogate perfectly and adequately and the other analogate(s) imperfectly and inadequately. For example, the concept of "animal" answers perfectly and adequately to what is in a human and in a horse, and the concept of "animal" is a different concept from the concepts of "human" and of "horse."[20] By contrast, he says, "there is not one concept that adequately answers to the analogous name and inadequately to the analogates; indeed, such a name would be univocal."[21]

Turning his attention to "being" said of the categories, Cajetan denies that it has any formal concept other than the proper concepts of substance or the other categories. Rather, the formal concept that is proper to one of the categories also represents the other categories insofar as they are proportionally similar. For example, the formal concept of substance represents substance perfectly and quantity imperfectly insofar as substance and quantity are proportionally similar.[22] So, there is a way in which analogates do and a way in which analogates do not agree in one *ratio*. They do not agree in any one *ratio* perfectly. But they do agree in one *ratio* imperfectly by proportionality.

In *De Nominum Analogia*, c. 6, Cajetan explains his answer to the *Rationes* Problem further by distinguishing between two ways of considering the *rationes* of analogates. The individual *rationes* of analogates can be compared to each other either absolutely or pro-

20. Ibid., n. 38 (Zammit, 36): "Est ergo differentia inter analogiam et univocationem quod conceptum mentalem, ita quod univoci et univocatorum ut sic, unus est conceptus perfecte et adaequate eis respondens, ut de conceptu animalis patet." (Therefore, there is a difference pertaining to the mental concept between analogy and univocation, such that, belonging to a univocal name and univocals as such, there is one concept answering to them perfectly and adequately, as is clear about the concept of animal.) See also ibid., c. 8, n. 88 (Zammit, 68–69).
21. Ibid., c. 4, n. 38 (Zammit, 36): "Non tamen ita quod sit unus conceptus adaequate respondens nomini analogo, et inadequate analogatis: quoniam secundum veritatem nomen illud univocum esset."
22. Ibid., n. 40 (Zammit, 37–38). For a treatment of Cajetan on this point, see Hochschild, *The Semantics of Analogy*, 144–48.

portionally. Taken absolutely, the individual *rationes* are found only in one analogate. The formal concept represents determinately one analogate to the exclusion of the other(s). But when the individual *rationes* are compared proportionally, "all the *rationes* of the analogous name are undivided proportionally, and one is the other proportionally."[23] The formal concept of one analogate represents the other analogates precisely insofar as the two *rationes* are proportionally one *ratio*.

Cajetan takes up the issue yet again in his letter *Responsio super duo quaestio De Conceptu Entis ad Fr. Franciscum de Ferraria* (known as *De Conceptu Entis*). Francis Silvestri of Ferrara (whose position is considered in chapter 6) saw an apparent contradiction between the position Cajetan expressed in his *In De Ente et Essentia* and his *De Nominum Analogia* over whether there is "one mental representative concept of being." On Ferrariensis's reading, Cajetan affirms one mental representative concept (i.e., one formal concept) in his earlier work but "seemed to deny this" in *De Nominum Analogia*.[24]

Cajetan's *De Conceptu Entis* professes to explain what he means when he appears to deny that there is numerically one concept that represents analogates. If two things outside the mind are alike to the extent that a concept represents one of them determinately, numerically the same concept will represent the other implicitly. Cajetan applies this principle to the case of God and creatures, saying:

23. Cajetan, *De Nominum Analogia*, c. 6, n. 70 (Zammit, 57): "dupliciter potest secundum singulas rationes ad analogata comparari. *Uno modo* absolute: et sic secundum singulas rationes cum singulis analogatis convertitur; quia nulla omnino una analogi ratio in duobus analogatis invenitur. *Alio modo* secundum identitatem proportionalem, quam habet una cum altera: et sic cum nullo analogato convertitur, quoniam omnes analogi rationes indivisae sunt proportionaliter, et una est altera proportionaliter." (Individual *rationes* can be compared to the analogates in two ways. In one way, absolutely, and, in this way, the individual *rationes* are convertible with the individual analogates because no one *ratio* of the analogous name is found altogether in the two analogates. In another way, [the individual *rationes* can be compared] by the proportional identity which one has with the other. In this way, it [i.e., the analogous name] is convertible with no analogate, because all the *rationes* of the analogous name are undivided proportionally, and one is the other proportionally.)

24. Cajetan, *Responsio super duo quaestio De Conceptu Entis ad Fr. Franciscum de Ferraria*, in *Scripta Philosophica* (Zammit, 97).

"whatever is an image of something similar to another, is also an image of that other to the extent it is similar to the first. And through this, every concept of a creature is a concept of God since every creature is some likeness of God."[25] A mental (formal) concept is an image of what it represents. When the thing the mental concept is an image of through signification is itself an image of some other thing, then the mental concept is an image of that other thing by extension.

In the paragraphs that follow, Cajetan provides a biology example to explain his position. One mental concept represents the determinate nature of bone but also implicitly represents *spinae* insofar as the natures of bone and *spinae* are analogous to each other.[26] Speaking again of numerically one formal concept, he writes, "It does not represent only one nature, but beyond the one which it represents determinately (from which it was impressed), it represents implicitly the remaining things similar to the one represented first." And the way in which the two are similar is, of course, by proportionality.[27] A numerically one concept represents one analogate determinately, and it represents the other analogate to the extent and in the way that the analogates are proportionally similar. So, "when it is found written by me [Cajetan] or by another that an analogue [i.e., a name said analogously] cannot have numerically one mental concept but only analogously one," this must be interpreted as referring to "a perfect or adequate concept explicitly of the analogue."[28]

From the above, it can be seen that Cajetan's answer to the *Ra-*

---

25. Cajetan, *De Conceptu Entis*, n. 3 (Zammit, 98): "quidquid est imago alicuius similis alteri, est etiam imago illius alterius quatenus primo assimilatur. Ac per hoc omnis conceptus creaturae, est conceptus Dei: sicut omnis creatura aliqua est similitudo Dei."

26. The example of analogy between bone and *spinae* is drawn from Aristotle. See *Posterior Analytics* 2.14 (98a20–23) and *Parts of Animals* 2.8 (653b34–37).

27. Cajetan, *De Conceptu Entis*, n. 4 (Zammit, 98–99): "Nec repraesentat unam solam naturam, sed ultra unam, quam determinate repraesentat (a qua est impressus), repraesentat implicite caeteras similes illi primo repraesentatae, secundum id in quo proportionabiliter ei similis est."

28. Ibid., n. 6 (Zammit, 100): "De quo scilicet perfecto seu adaequato explicite conceptu analogi interpretandum est, cum a me vel ab alio scriptum invenitur, quod non potest analogum unum numero mentalem conceptum habere, sed unum analogia tantum."

tiones Problem fundamentally agrees with the answer provided by Capreolus. There is no precise or separate "analogous concept" that is not at once the proper concept of one of the analogates. But the likeness between the analogates themselves serves as the foundation for an imperfectly one objective concept, which makes the proper formal concept of one analogate an imperfect representation of the others. Unlike Capreolus, but not in opposition to him, Cajetan directly invokes analogy of proportionality to explain how a concept proper to one thing can be the imperfect concept of something analogous to it.

CAJETAN ON THE EQUIVOCATION PROBLEM

Cajetan's answer to the Equivocation Problem provides the focal point for Hochschild's study of *De Nominum Analogia*. Hochschild sees *De Nominum Analogia* as primarily directed toward answering the Scotist objection to analogy raised in the opening paragraph of its penultimate chapter. I turn here to that passage in order to consider how Cajetan's solution compares with that of his Thomist predecessors.

Cajetan introduces *De Nominum Analogia*, c. 10, with the observation that some think scientific knowledge cannot be achieved through analogy because an analogous name expresses many *rationes*. Even acknowledging that analogous *rationes* are similar, these figures think that any case of attempting to reason using an analogous name as a medium for demonstration or to reason from the *ratio* of one analogate to a conclusion about another analogate results in the fallacy of equivocation.[29] Cajetan mentions the standard example: "For example, if we assert that wisdom is analogously common to God and to a human from the fact that wisdom, found in a human, taken precisely according to formal *ratio*, expresses an abso-

---

29. Cajetan, *De Nominum Analogia*, c. 10, n. 104 (Zammit, 79). I translate and briefly comment on sections of *De Nominum Analogia*, c. 10, in D'Ettore, "Some Renaissance Thomists," 931–34.

lute perfection, it cannot be concluded 'therefore God is formally wise,' by arguing thus: 'Every absolute perfection is in God; wisdom is an absolute perfection; ergo, etc.'"[30] The reason that this argument would fail is that the syllogism has four terms insofar as the word *sapientia* stands for the proper *ratio* of wisdom in a creature in the minor premise and for the proper *ratio* of divine wisdom in the conclusion. The proper *ratio* of divine wisdom cannot be used in the minor premise, because that would defeat the intention of all the philosophers and theologians, who, Cajetan says, hold that knowledge of God is drawn from knowledge of creatures.[31]

Cajetan claims that those, such as Scotus, who reason in the way of these objectors have recognized the diversity of *rationes* in analogy but not considered their hidden (*latet*) unity and identity. The *rationes* in an analogy can be considered both according to themselves (*secundum se*) and as they are proportionally the same. Taken in the first way, reasoning with them would indeed lead to equivocation, but the second way avoids equivocation "because whatever belongs to one, belongs also to the other proportionally; and whatever is denied about one, also is denied about the other proportionally. [This is] because whatever belongs to a similar thing, in that which [is] similar, also belongs to the one to which it is similar, with proportionality always preserved."[32] Proportional unity does not eliminate diversity, but it is, nonetheless, a real form of similarity such that whatever properties belong to one thing also belong proportionally to whatever is proportionally similar to it.

Continuing his explanation of the demonstration through the

30. Cajetan, *De Nominum Analogia*, c. 10, n. 105 (Zammit, 79): "Verbi gratia: si ponamus *sapientiam* esse analogice communem Deo et homini, ex hoc quod sapientia, in homine inventa, secundum formalem rationem praecise sumpta, dicit perfectionem simpliciter: non potest concludi: ergo Deus est formaliter sapiens, sic arguendo: Omnis perfectio simpliciter in Deo; sapientia est perfectio simpliciter; ergo etc."
31. Ibid. (Zammit, 80).
32. Ibid., n. 106 (Zammit, 80–81): "eo quod quidquid convenit uni, convenit et alteri proportionaliter; et quidquid negatur de una, et de altera negatur proportionaliter: quia quidquid convenit simili, in eo quod simile, convenit etiam illi, cui est simile, proportionalitate semper servata."

analogous term "wise," Cajetan writes: "In the minor premise, the word *sapientia* stands, not for this or that *ratio* of wisdom, but for one wisdom proportionally. That is, [it stands] for each *ratio* of wisdom, not conjunctively or disjunctively, but inasmuch as they are undivided proportionally, and one is the other proportionally, and both constitute one *ratio* proportionally."[33] He adds that "they are signified by the analogous name insofar as they are the same."[34] Cajetan concludes the chapter by criticizing Scotus's definition of a univocal concept (i.e., a concept predicated with sufficient unity for founding a contradiction and mediating a syllogism) for overlooking other forms of identity besides univocal identity. As proportional identity is sufficient to found a contradiction, it follows that unity sufficient for contradiction is broader than univocity.[35]

The key to Cajetan's answer to the Equivocation Problem, then, is the proportional unity of the objective concept. A name can signify through one formal concept not only when the objective concept possesses the unity of nature characteristic of a univocal genus, species, difference, or property, but also when the objective concept possesses only proportional unity. Hence, one can conclude that God is wise employing the formal concept proper to human wisdom because, in the words of Cajetan, "the *ratio* of 'wisdom' is not altogether other, nor altogether this, but this proportionally is in God."[36]

We can now see how Cajetan uses his answer to the *Rationes*

---

33. Ibid., n. 111 (Zammit, 83–84): "in minore ly *sapientia* non stat pro hac vel illa ratione sapientiae, sed pro sapientia una proportionaliter, idest, pro utraque ratione sapientiae non coniunctim vel disiunctim; sed in quantum sunt indivisae proportionaliter, et una est altera proportionaliter, et ambae unam proportionaliter constituunt rationem."

34. Ibid., n. 112 (Zammit, 84): "Significantur enim analogo nomine in quantum eaedem sunt."

35. Ibid., nn. 112–13 (Zammit, 84–85), esp. (85): "non recte igitur univocatio conceptus declarata est esse eam, quae ad contradictionem sufficit, quasi proportionalis identitas ad hoc non sufficiat." (Therefore, univocation of a concept is not rightly declared to be that [identity] which suffices for a contradiction, as though proportional identity does not suffice for this [i.e., for contradiction].)

36. Ibid., n. 110 (Zammit, 83): "sapientiae ratio non omnino alia, nec omnino haec, sed haec proportionaliter est in Deo."

Cajetan 141

TABLE 4. Natalis to Cajetan on the Three Problems

Author	Rationes Problem	Analogy Model Problem	Equivocation Problem
Hervaeus Natalis	Many *rationes*	Healthy Model	There is something that is the same in each analogate
Thomas Sutton	Many *rationes*	Principle Model	Proportional unity is sufficiently close to univocal unity
John Capreolus	One *ratio* by unequal participation	Principle Model	Unequal participation in a perfectly one formal concept proper to one of the analogates
Dominic of Flanders (Flandrensis)	One *ratio* by unequal participation	Principle Model	Unequal participation in a *ratio* which signifies one analogate *per prius* and another analogate *per posterius*
Paul Soncinas	One separate formal *ratio* and one disjunctive objective *ratio*	Not the Healthy Model	Unequal participation in a formal concept which is separate from the proper concepts of the analogates
Thomas de Vio Cajetan	Many *rationes* are proportionally identical	Principle Model	The proportional identity between the analogates is signified through the formal concept proper to one of the analogates.

and Analogy Model Problems to provide a principled answer to the Equivocation Problem, and can turn back to his predecessors' answers for comparison. The resemblance of Cajetan's solution to Sutton's is perhaps the most obvious. Both explicitly invoke the semantic properties of analogy of proportionality. Cajetan's account goes a step beyond Sutton's by addressing how analogy of proportionality can form the foundation of a contradiction—that is, what belongs to one belongs to the other proportionally, and what is denied about one is denied about the other proportionally—thereby showing how proportionality possesses precisely the semantic property that Scotus was seeking in the terms of a valid syllogism. By directly addressing how proportional identity founds a contradiction, Cajetan is also able to more clearly distinguish the unity in analogy of proportionality from the unity in other forms of analogy, and he thereby exceeds Sutton in showing how proportionality is closer than the other forms of analogy to univocity. The semantics of the Healthy Model do not, apparently, found a contradiction. That is, there is no contradiction in saying that medicine is healthy but lacks similarity to an animal or lacks the features whereby an animal is called "healthy," as there is an obvious contradiction between saying that a spring is the principle of a river but lacks the feature through which it is proportionally similar to the foundation of a house, to the starting line of a race, or to the "most known" propositions of a science.

The resemblance of Cajetan's solution to those of Capreolus, Flandrensis, and Soncinas is less obvious. These authors do not mention analogy of proportionality in their direct treatments of the Equivocation Problem, although Capreolus and Flandrensis invoke proportionality to answer the Analogy Model Problem. When addressing the Equivocation Problem directly, Capreolus, Flandrensis, and Soncinas content themselves with unequal participation in a *ratio* as a sufficient semantic principle for preserving demonstration. Flandrensis's use of this principle is most distant from Cajetan's solution, as Flandrensis extends unequal participation to the Healthy Model of analogy. Soncinas also uses unequal participation in a way unacceptable to Cajetan, insofar as Soncinas's unequally participated in formal concept is separate from the proper concepts.

Among his fifteenth-century Thomist predecessors, Capreolus's solution comes closest to Cajetan's. Capreolus presents the perfect unity of the formal concept that represents one analogate perfectly and the other analogate imperfectly as the guarantee of the validity of demonstration through analogous terms. Also, in a separate distinction, which does not address the Equivocation Problem, Capreolus claims that names are said of God and creatures by analogy of proportionality. Cajetan defends demonstration through analogous terms by arguing (with increasing awareness of the need for clarity through his *In De Ente et Essentia*, *De Nominum Analogia*, and *De Conceptu Entis*) that where there is proportional unity between analogates, the formal concept of one analogate is, by proportionality, the formal concept of the other analogate. I see no real opposition between Capreolus's and Cajetan's solutions to the Equivocation Problem. However, for the reasons mentioned above, Cajetan's more explicitly integrated answers represent an improvement over what is at most implicit in the writings of Capreolus.

Reviewing the authors treated to this point with respect to the Equivocation Problem, Natalis offers the least by way of explanation. Sutton provides the most detailed answer to the Equivocation Problem grounded exclusively in his answer to the Analogy Model Problem. Capreolus, Flandrensis, and Soncinas rest their answers to the Equivocation Problem primarily on their solutions to the *Rationes* Problem, and they refer to the Analogy Model Problem only to rule out the Healthy Model either from unequal participation in one *ratio* altogether or from the suitable sort of unequal participation in one *ratio* for divine names. Cajetan's answer to the Equivocation Problem draws on his answers to both the *Rationes* and Analogy Model Problems. One formal concept signifies an objective concept that has proportional unity and can thereby be predicated of both analogates with sufficient unity to establish a contradiction. It can be added here that Cajetan's solutions to the *Rationes* and Analogy Model Problems are not *ad hoc*, but they solve a range of questions through *De Nominum Analogia*, cc. 4–10.

CONCLUSION

To the extent that Cajetan holds (1) a threefold division of analogy derivative from Thomas Aquinas's *In 1 Sent.*, d. 19, q. 5, a. 2, ad 1; (2) that names are said of God and creatures by analogy of proportionality; (3) that one and the same concept can unequally represent analogates; and (4) that Scotus's objection to demonstration through analogous terms must be given a principled response if

Thomist metaphysics is to persist, he can be seen as a Thomist of his time, following ideas present in his fifteenth-century predecessors, especially among the Dominicans at the Bologna *studium*. Cajetan succeeded in making explicit the connections between different aspects of analogy implied by earlier Thomists. His contemporaries and successors would give Cajetan's doctrine a mixed reception, as illustrated in the doctrines of the two figures considered in the following chapter.

6

Early Reception of Cajetan
Chrysostom Javelli and Francis Silvestri of Ferrara

Michael Tavuzzi's 1993 article "Some Renaissance Divisions of Analogy,"[1] notes that Cajetan's *De Nominum Analogia* doctrine of analogy was not universally embraced by his contemporary Dominicans, or even by his contemporary Dominicans at Bologna.[2] This chapter

---

1. Michael Tavuzzi, "Some Renaissance Divisions of Analogy," *Angelicum* 70 (1993): 93–121.

2. Ibid., 107–10, gives special attention to a contemporary critique of Cajetan whose work this study leaves unaddressed, namely Silvestro Mazzolini da Prierio. This contemporary of Cajetan addresses what I have called the *Rationes* and Analogy Model Problems in his *Conflatum ex S. Thoma* commentary on Aquinas's *Summa Theologiae* 1.13.8–9. Regarding the Analogy Model Problem, having observed that "St. Thomas says many things about analogies, and sometimes they are obscure due to the various species of analogies," Silvestro offers a sixfold division of analogy (in opposition to Cajetan's threefold division). Silvestro places names said of God and creatures in two divisions, one of which is proportionality (described as analogy most properly and as proper comparison) and in another division which he calls deficient imitation without proportion properly said. With respect to the *Rationes* Problem, Silvestro proposes that there is one primary *ratio* of an analogous name in relation to which the name is said of all analogates. I have not found Silvestro directly addressing the Equivocation Problem. Because I find that his position on the *Rationes* and Analogy Model Problems have been adequately addressed by Tavuzzi, I leave aside further consideration of Silvestro Mazzolini da Prierio in this study. For Silvestro's position on the *Rationes* and Analogy Model Problems, see Silvestro Mazzolini, *Conflatum ex S. Thoma* (Perugia, 1519), 86v–89v. On the life and

focuses on the early reception of Cajetan's doctrine by two Bologna Dominicans whose careers and doctrines of analogy were partially shaped by Thomas di Vio Cajetan; namely, Chrysostom Javelli and his slightly younger and shorter-lived contemporary Francis Silvestri of Ferrara.[3] Javelli and Ferrariensis present two strikingly different doctrines of analogy and both cite Cajetan as a source for their doctrines while at the same time clearly disagreeing with aspects of Cajetan's answers to the *Rationes* and Analogy Model Problems. As will be shown below, Javelli's differences and implied criticisms of Cajetan are primarily philosophical, whereas Ferrariensis differs from Cajetan primarily as an interpreter of Aquinas's text. I begin with Francis Silvestri, as his relevant works were published several years before Javelli's.

FRANCIS SILVESTRI OF FERRARA

Francis Silvestri of Ferrara offers the most deliberate and detailed attempt of the Thomists considered in this study to solve the *Rationes* and Analogy Model Problems by interpreting and reconciling the varied texts of Aquinas on names said by analogy of God and creatures. Ferrariensis's commentary on Aquinas's *Summa Contra Gentiles* was published in 1523–24, during Ferrariensis's term as inquisitor of Bologna.[4] The work has a similar scope and intention to Cajetan's commentary on the *Summa Theologiae*. It was mentioned in the previous chapter that it was a letter from Ferrariensis that prompted Cajetan's *De Conceptu Entis*. Ferrariensis leaves the

---

works of Silvestro, see Michael Tavuzzi, *Prierias: The Life and Works of Silvestro Mazzolini da Prierio, 1456–1527* (Durham, N.C.: Duke University Press, 1997).

3. See also my treatment of Francis Silvestri's doctrine of analogy in Domenic D'Ettore, "'Not a Little Confusing': Francis Silvestri of Ferrara's Hybrid Thomist Doctrine of Analogy," *American Catholic Philosophical Quarterly* 90 (2016): 101–23.

4. This commentary will hereafter be referred to as *In SCG*. Michael Tavuzzi, *Renaissance Inquisitors: Dominican Inquisitors and Inquisitorial Districts in Northern Italy, 1474–1527*, Studies in the History of Christian Traditions 134 (Leiden: Brill, 2007), 43.

reader of *In SCG* in no doubt about his respect for Cajetan's work, and calls Cajetan *"omnium ingeniossimus hominium."*[5]

FERRARIENSIS ON THE
RATIONES PROBLEM

Ferrariensis's discussion of names said analogously of God and creatures in *In SCG* I, c. 34, is notable for its distinction between three different impositions of the common name. Behind these impositions, he also distinguishes, sometimes implicitly, different concepts for signifying through the name. His remarks on analogy in *In SCG* I, c. 34, build upon his treatment in c. 33 of the role that effect-to-cause relations have in naming. Ferrariensis affirms that the effect to cause relationship a creature has toward God is *a reason* behind naming God and creatures analogously. But he denies that this relationship is *what is signified* by the analogous name. In Ferrariensis's words: "from the considering of such order the same name is imposed to both of the analogates, so that it may be said that the relation of cause to caused is that from which the name is imposed, but not that to which it is imposed as to the thing signified through the name."[6] The name is imposed on both the creaturely and divine

---

5. See Francis Silvestri of Ferrara, *Summa contra Gentiles, quatuor libris comprehensa: commentariis* [...] *Francisci de Sylvestris, Ferrariensis* [...] *illustrata* (Paris, 1552). The quotation appears in the letter dedicating the work to Pope Clement VII. The date of the letter is 1524, and it appears in the 1552 Paris edition. All other references to Francis Silvestri's *In SCG* are taken from Aquinas, *Omnia Opera*, vol. 13.

6. See Ferrariensis, *In SCG* I, c. 33, section I (13:102a–b): "Advertendum quod in nominibus dictis de Deo et creaturis consideratur ordo causae et causati, non quod talis ordo formaliter per ipsa nomina importetur, alioquin omnia essent nomina relativa: sed quia important fundamenta ordinis causae et causati; et ex consideratione ordinis huiusmodi, dum consideratum est hanc perfectionem a Deo sicut a causa dependere, et idcirco esse aliquid in Deo per quod inter ea sit similitudo, et maxime cum nullam importet imperfectionem ex differentiali conceptu, idem nomen et Deo et creaturae est impositum. Unde quod videtur velle Sanctus Thomas in hac ratione, nomen analogum significare unum habere ordinem ad alterum, intelligitur *aut formaliter aut fundamentaliter*: quia in aliquibus formaliter importatur, in aliquibus autem tantum fundamentaliter, ut in sequenti capitulo demonstrabitur. Hoc tamen omnibus commune est, quod ex consideratione talis ordinis idem nomen utrique analogatorum est impositum: ut possit dici

analogates *from* consideration of the order of cause and effect, but the name is not imposed *to signify* the relation of cause to caused.

Turning to the order of the impositions of an analogous name in natural theology, the first imposition signifies the perfection in the creature absolutely. For instance, the first imposition of "wisdom" signifies the creature's wisdom in itself without any reference to divine wisdom as the causal source or exemplar of creaturely wisdom. The second imposition signifies the perfection in God. Continuing with the example of "wisdom," just as the first imposition signifies the creature's wisdom alone or absolutely, without reference to God's wisdom, the second imposition signifies divine wisdom absolutely and without reference to creatures. That is, in the proposition "God is wise," the name "wise" is imposed on God alone, irrespective of creaturely wisdom. The divine wisdom is the primary, and even exclusive, significate of the name. Whereas in a proposition such as "Socrates is wise" (if "wise" is used by its first imposition), the name "wise" is imposed to signify the human wisdom possessed by Socrates, irrespective of any dependence on, or ordering, that human wisdom has to divine wisdom.

The "third imposition" of a name is unlike the first two. Speaking of the third imposition of the name "wise," Ferrariensis says it signifies "human wisdom in order to divine wisdom as to its cause

---

quod habitudo causae ad causatum sit id a quo nomen imponitur, non autem id cui imponitur tanquam rei per nomen significatae." (In names said of God and creatures the order of cause and of caused is considered. This is not because such an order is carried formally through the very names, otherwise all the names would be relative, but because they carry the foundations of the order of cause and of caused. And [it is] from consideration of an order of this kind that the same name is imposed to God and to creature, when it is considered that this perfection depends on God as on the cause, and, therefore, that there is something in God through which there is a likeness among them, and most of all when it carries no imperfection from the differential concept. Consequently, it seems St. Thomas proposes in this reason that the analogous name be understood to signify one having order to another either formally or fundamentally. In some it is carried formally, but in some only fundamentally, as will be demonstrated in the following chapter. Nevertheless, this is common to all, that from the considering of such order the same name is imposed to both of the analogates, so that it may be said that the relation of cause to caused is that from which the name is imposed, but not that to which it is imposed as to the thing signified through the name.)

and exemplar, and in this way it is taken as an analogous and proportional name."[7] Note that Ferrariensis only calls the third imposition of the name analogous. He need not call the first imposition of the name analogous because it refers exclusively to human wisdom, which is said univocally of Aristotle, Avicenna, and Aquinas. The second imposition of the name cannot be analogous because it is said exclusively of God. Only the third imposition of the name entails any order of signification between recipients of the name, as it explicitly refers to creatures as related to God.

Moving to *In SCG* I, c. 34, Ferrariensis introduces three concepts that are roughly, but not exactly, parallel to the three impositions of "wisdom" described above. He writes that, because the human intellect is unable to form a concept of divine wisdom as it is in itself,

we form one concept adequate to the creature, and we form another concept of God proportionally to the concept of the creature which is inadequate to God. Further, because of the likeness of the concept of our wisdom to the concept of divine wisdom, we form one common concept fitting to divine and human wisdom, but imperfect and inadequate to both in which the wisdom of both is assimilated. And so, such a name expresses one inadequate and imperfect concept, not expressing divine wisdom perfectly inasmuch as it is wisdom, but representing each wisdom as they are similar.[8]

---

7. Here is the full quotation listing the three impositions of the name in Ferrariensis, *In SCG* I, c. 34, section IX (13:107a): "Sic est de omnibus divinis nominibus quae proprie et analogice de ipso et creaturis dicuntur. Nam hoc nomen *sapientia* primo attributum est ad significandum *sapientiam humanam absolute*, sicut et primo absolute cognita est; deinde, cognito ipsam esse a sapientia divina exemplatam, impositum est ad significandum *divinam sapientiam*; tum postremo impositum est ad significandum *sapientiam humanam in ordine ad sapientiam divinam tanquam ad causam et exemplar*, et acceptum est tanquam nomen analogum et proportionale. Et simile est de aliis divinis nominibus." (So it is regarding all the divine names which are said properly and analogously about [God] and creatures. For this name "wisdom" is attributed first for signifying human wisdom absolutely, just as [human wisdom] is known first absolutely. Next, when [human wisdom] is known to be modeled from divine wisdom, [the name "wisdom"] is imposed for signifying divine wisdom. Then, lastly, it is imposed for signifying human wisdom in order to divine wisdom as to its cause and exemplar, and in this way it is taken as an analogous and proportional name. And it is similar for the other divine names."

8. Ferrariensis, *In SCG* I, c. 34, section XVI (13:109a): "Similiter diversos conceptus mentales, quorum quilibet uni analogatorum adaequatus esset, importaret, si ipsam sapientiam divinam secundum quod in se est concipere possemus. Sed quia hoc non

In this passage, Ferrariensis gives his reader three formal concepts for using names that alternately signify creatures absolutely, God absolutely, and God and creatures analogously. The first concept of wisdom perfectly and adequately represents the creature. Presumably, this is the proper formal concept signifying human wisdom. The second concept of wisdom imperfectly and inadequately represents divine wisdom by representing divine wisdom precisely insofar as it is proportionally similar to human wisdom. The third concept of wisdom imperfectly and inadequately represents both divine wisdom and human wisdom by representing them precisely insofar as they are similar to each other. Note that Ferrariensis is not proposing that the intellect performs three separate acts of abstraction to acquire these three concepts. Only the first concept (which properly signifies creatures) is abstracted from phantasms. The other two concepts depend on and modify the first concept.

By comparing Ferrariensis's three concepts together with his three impositions, it appears that there is exact agreement between the first two concepts and the first two impositions, but not so for the third concept and imposition. The first imposition employs the name to signify through the first concept. Likewise, the second imposition employs the name to signify the second concept. Yet, although the third concept signifies divine and human wisdom insofar as they are similar, the third imposition of the name signifies through a concept representing the perfection in the creature insofar as it is derived from God. To complete the correspondence between the three concepts and the three impositions, the intellect requires a fourth concept, not mentioned explicitly by Ferrariensis in this text, to signify in the "third imposition" of the name. Likewise, should

---

possumus, formamus quidem conceptum unum creaturae adaequatum, sed alium formamus de Deo proportionaliter ad conceptum creaturae, qui illi est inadaequatus. Et ulterius, propter similitudinem conceptus sapientiae nostrae ad conceptum sapientiae divinae et humanae convenientem, sed imperfectum et inadaequatum utrique, in quo utraque sapientia assimilatur. Et sic dicit tale nomen conceptum unum inadaequatum et imperfectum, non exprimentem divinam sapientiam perfecte inquantum est sapientia, sed utramque sapientiam ut similes sunt repraesentantem."

someone impose a name as signifying divine and human wisdom as they are similar, this would either be a fourth imposition distinct from the three impositions explicitly described by Ferrariensis, or it would be a secondary signification belonging to one of the first two impositions. This point will be returned to below in discussing the *ad mentem Ferrariensis* solution to the Equivocation Problem.

So far, we have seen that Ferrariensis answers the *Rationes* Problem by presenting his reader with (at least) three impositions and (at least) three concepts to account for the different uses of a name used analogously in natural theology. Below, it will be seen that, as a member of the Thomist tradition, Ferrariensis recognizes an obligation to explain whether these three concepts are separate concepts or are somehow reducible to one concept. Hence, he enters into the dispute discussed in chapter 5, which set Flandrensis and Cajetan in opposition to Soncinas over whether there is a concept that is separate from the proper concepts of the analogates.

The reader will recall that (in chronological order), Flandrensis denies a separate concept of being, Soncinas affirms a separate concept, and Cajetan denies it. Ferrariensis explicitly raises the point that this matter is disputed by Thomists:

Concerning this difficulty, there are various positions of Thomists. For certain ones hold ... that "being" and likewise other things said analogously about God and creatures expresses one formal or mental concept [which is] separate from the concepts of other things, although it does not express an objective concept [which is] one and separate, but [is] one only by analogy. But others hold that "being" does not express one adequate mental concept [which is] separate from the concepts of [its] inferiors, just as [it does] not [express] one objective [concept]. Rather, just as it expresses the very analogates as they are one by proportion or as similars, so too all the mental concepts of the analogates express as they are one concept proportionally.[9]

---

9. Ibid., section XII (13:107b): "Circa hanc difficultatem varia est Thomistarum sententia. Tenent enim quidam ... *ens*, et similiter alia analogice dicta de Deo et creaturis, dicere unum conceptum formalem sive mentalem praecisum a conceptibus aliarum rerum, licet non dicat conceptum obiectivalem unum et praecisum, sed unum tantum analogia. Alii vero tenent *ens* non dicere unum conceptum mentalem adaequatum praecisum a

Ferrariensis finds himself drawn to both sides of the question. To the side of Soncinas, he grants a separate concept of being in the following respect:

> If we speak about the imperfect and inadequate concept pertaining to the *quid nominis*, then it is not unfitting to say that "being" expresses one mental concept separate from the others. For from similar things, inasmuch as they are similar, it is not unfitting that one imperfect concept is abstracted, inasmuch as it does not perfectly represent the nature of the foundation of similitude, but only signifies those things as they are similar.[10]

The description of the imperfect concept signifying analogates insofar as they are similar to one another agrees with Ferrariensis's description of the "third concept" described above. Ferrariensis tells his reader that "it is not unfitting" to call this formal (mental) concept "separate from the others." "Being," as used to signify substance and accidents insofar as they are similar, does not signify the foundations for their similarity as such, which would be the nature of substance and the nature of accidents. If it did, then this formal concept of being would not signify substance and accidents insofar as they are similar; on the contrary, it would signify them insofar as they are different because the nature of substance and nature of accidents are different. Hence, Ferrariensis can say that there is a sense in which the formal concept of "being" representing both substance and accidents "abstracts from" and is "separate" from the formal concept of "being" that signifies the being that properly and adequately represents substance, or one that properly and adequately represents accidents. By the same reasoning, this concept would "abstract from" the concept that properly signifies divine being.

---

conceptibus inferiorum, sicut nec unum obiectivalem: sed, sicut dicit ipsa analogata ut sunt unum proportione sive ut similia, ita dicere omnes conceptus mentales analogatorum ut sunt unus conceptus proportionaliter."

10. Ibid., section XV (13:108b): "Si autem loquamur de conceptus imperfecto et inadaequato ad *quid nominis* pertinente, sic non est inconveniens *ens* dicere unum conceptum mentalem ab aliis praecisum. A similibus enim, inquantum similia sunt, non est inconveniens conceptum unum abstrahi imperfectum, utpote qui non perfecte naturam fundamenti similitudinis repraesentet, sed tantum illa significet ut similia sunt."

Ferrariensis affirms the analogous character of the separate, "third" concept by contrasting its foundations with the foundations for a univocal concept:

Whereas it must be considered that *ens* and other analogues [i.e., names said analogously] are distinguished from univocals in this respect: the one and separate mental concept. Although in both cases it [i.e., the mental concept] represents similar and agreeing things, nevertheless [analogues are distinguished from univocals] because the concept of the univocal name represents the foundations of likeness perfectly as they are signified by that name (as in the way the concept of "animal" represents perfectly the nature of animal in a human through which a human is equal to a horse), such that there is no other thing in a human insofar as a human is an animal than there is in a horse insofar as it is an animal (although as "this animal," a human is something different from a horse). But the one concept of an analogue does not represent perfectly the foundations of likeness signified primarily and *per se* by an analogous name. Rather, something belongs to them [the analogates] which is not represented by such a separate concept, as is clear in the case of being.[11]

The unity of the concept in univocal naming is founded on the natures equally contained in the recipients of the name. What it is in human beings, which places humans in the genus of animals, is also in horses placing them in the same genus. By contrast, analogates, insofar as they are analogates, do not have a common nature that can be represented through a concept about each of them perfectly and equally. The unity of the concept in analogy is not founded on the natures of the analogates themselves, but on the similarity of the diverse natures to each other. Consequently, as Ferrariensis goes on to say, "being does not have one perfect and adequate separate mental concept," but "'*quod habet esse*' is the imperfect and inadequate concept belong-

11. Ibid.: "Ubi considerandum est quod *ens* et alia analoga in hoc ab univocis distinguuntur, quantum ad conceptum mentalem unum et praecisum, quia, licet uterque repraesentet similia et convenientia, tamen conceptus nominis univoci repraesentat fundamenta similitudinis perfecte ut illo nomine significantur: sicut conceptus *animalis* repraesentat perfecte naturam animalis in homine, per quam assimilatur equo; ita quod nihil aliud est in homine, ut animal est, quam in equo ut est animal; licet ut *hoc animal*, homo sit aliquid aliud, quod non est equus. Conceptus autem ille unus analogi non repraesentat perfecte fundamenta similitudinis nomine analogo significata primo et per se, sed aliquid convenit ipsis quod tali conceptu praeciso non repraesentatur, sicut patet de *ente*."

ing to beings, representing them as they are similar."¹² The same holds for other names said analogously about God and creatures.¹³

Some of the passages quoted above suggest that Ferrariensis sides with Soncinas in affirming a separate formal concept of being and other analogates. This, however, is not the case. He explicitly raises the question and proclaims that the opinion of Thomists that "being does not have one mental or objective concept separate from the others [i.e., the concepts of substance and the accidents]" is "truer and more in conformity with the doctrine of the philosophers and of St. Thomas."¹⁴ These remarks establish that Ferrariensis disagrees with Soncinas, but they leave open how he understands the third concept, which represents the analogates as they are similar, relates to the proper concepts of the analogates.

Clarity comes to the precise relationship between the third (and

12. See ibid. for the quotation in context: "Dicendum ergo est quod *ens* non habet unum praecisum conceptum mentalem perfectum et adaequatum, sed immediate dicit conceptum substantiae, quantitatis, qualitatis et aliorum, ut sunt unum similitudine et proportione: sicut et ex parte rei omnes illas naturas immediate significat ut proportionales sunt et similes respectu ipsius esse. Et in hoc differt a conceptu univoci: quia conceptus univoci non est multi conceptus ut sunt unus conceptus secundum proportionem, sed est simpliciter unus; sicut et res primo per ipsum significata, si sit univocum metaphysice, est una. Hoc autem quod dicimus, *quod habet esse*, est conceptus entis imperfectus et inadequatus entium, ipsa repraesentans ut sunt similia." (Therefore, it must be said that *ens* does not have one separate, perfect, and adequate mental concept, but it immediately expresses the concept of substance, of quantity, and of the others insofar as they are one by likeness and proportion; just as also on the side of the thing [*ens*] signifies all those natures immediately insofar as they are proportional and similar with respect to their very *esse*. And in this [way], [*ens*] differs from the concept of a univocal name, because the concept of a univocal name is not the concept of many insofar as they are one concept according to proportion, but [the concept of a univocal name] is absolutely one; just as also the thing signified first through [the concept] is one, if it is metaphysically univocal. But we say that this, *quod habet esse*, is the imperfect and inadequate concept belonging to beings, representing them as they are similar.)

13. Ibid., section XVI (13:108b): "Quod dixi de *ente*, similiter intelligendum est de omnibus aliis nominibus convenientibus Deo et creaturae analogice, quantum ad istam unitatem aut multiplicitatem conceptuum." (What I have said about *ens*, must be understood similarly about all other names belonging to God and to creature analogously, regarding their unity or multiplicity of concepts.)

14. See ibid., section XIII (13:107b): "Harum opinionum secunda mihi videtur verior, et conformior doctrinae philosophorum et Sancti Thomae.... sic dico quod *ens* non habet unum conceptum mentalem, sicut nec obiectivalem, ab aliis praecisum."

quasi-separate) concept and the proper concepts of the analogates only in the conclusion of his *In SCG* I, c. 34. There, echoing Cajetan, Ferrariensis affirms the proportional unity of the analogous concepts: "For all analogates and all their concepts are the same by likeness and proportion; and so the concept of one is the concept of the other proportionally."[15] With this statement, Ferrariensis unequivocally rejects the position of Soncinas in favor of Cajetan. There is no concept that is separate from yet standing over the proper concepts of the analogates, even though Ferrariensis at times refers to the third concept as separate from the analogates. Thinking back to his three concepts of wisdom, the reader can now see that Ferrariensis's third and quasi-separate concept of wisdom is not a numerically distinct concept signifying in its own right. Instead, it is numerically identical to either the first concept of wisdom (i.e., the proper concept of human wisdom) or to the second concept of wisdom (i.e., the proper concept of divine wisdom) insofar as one of these concepts is proportionally similar to the other. The proportionally similar foundations for the diverse concepts allow the proper concept of one analogate to represent the other inadequately and imperfectly.

If I have read Ferrariensis rightly, his overall answer to the *Rationes* Problem closely mirrors what he found in the writings of Ca-

15. The quoted line is the last line of Silvestri's *In SCG* I, c. 34, section XVI (13:109b). For greater context, here is the line with its preceding few sentences: "Sed verum est quod *sapientiae* nomen non dicit ipsam sapientiam divinam nisi ut unum proportionaliter cum sapientia creata: nomen autem hoc, *sapientia divina*, significat ipsam absolute et una ratione simpliciter. Ita quod eadem res, ut fundans similitudinem et convenientiam proportionalitatis, nomine analogo significatur: ut autem fundat distantiam et dissimilitudinem, significatur nomine proprio. Propter quod dicitur nomen analogum significare unum proportione: sunt enim omnia analogata, omnesque eorum conceptus, idem similitudine et proportione; et sic conceptus unius est conceptus alterius proportionaliter." (It is true that the name "wisdom" does not express divine wisdom itself except as one proportionally with created wisdom. But the name "divine wisdom" signifies it absolutely and by one *ratio* without qualification. So, that same thing is signified by an analogous name as founding likeness and agreement of proportionality, but it is signified by its proper name as founding distance and dissimilitude. For this reason, it is said that the analogous name signifies one [thing] by proportion. For all analogates and all their concepts are the same by likeness and proportion; and so, the concept of one is the concept of the other proportionally.)

jetan. The intellect can perform an imperfect abstraction from proportionally similar concepts without producing a concept that is numerically distinct or separate from the two similar concepts. Stopping short of complete abstraction from the analogates, the intellect considers one analogate as it is proportionally similar to the other analogate, and vice versa.[16] Consequently, the definition of one analogate is the definition of the other proportionally.[17] As proportionally similar, both analogates are one in concept and in definition.

Ferrariensis agrees with the common fifteenth-century Thomist *una ratio* answer to the *Rationes* Problem. Aware of their disagreement over whether the one formal concept is separate from the proper concepts of the analogates, he proposes that it is separate insofar as it represents the similarity of the analogates. It is not separate in the strict way that univocal concepts are separate, however, as the analogous concept does not perfectly and adequately represent one and same foundation in the analogates, but one or another of the analogates as similar to the other. Ferrariensis adopts the position of Cajetan and Flandrensis against Soncinas, and maintains that the one *ratio* in analogy necessarily is the proper *ratio* of one or another of the analogates.

FERRARIENSIS ON THE ANALOGY MODEL PROBLEM

There are passages within Ferrariensis's *In SCG* I, c. 34, that, taken by themselves, suggest that their author follows Cajetan's solution to the Analogy Model Problem. For example, Ferrariensis writes: "For the name 'wisdom' said about God and creatures immediately signifies diverse natures which, nevertheless, have likeness and proportion among themselves insofar as one is exemplared by the oth-

---

16. See the reference to Cajetan's *De Conceptu Entis*, n. 4, on p. 137n27 and to his *De Nominum Analogia*, c. 10, pp. 139n30–140n36. See also Cajetan, *De Nominum Analogia*, c. 6, n. 70 (Zammit, 57).

17. See especially Cajetan, *De Nominum Analogia*, c. 7, n. 77 (Zammit, 61).

er. For just as by his wisdom God considers the highest causes, but in His own way, so too, the creature in its own way considers the same things through its wisdom."[18] This is the very sort of analogy of proportionality description of the divine names that the reader would expect to find in the writings of a firm proponent of a Principle Model solution to the Analogy Model Problem.[19] The full text of *In SCG* I, c. 34, reveals a more complex position, with strong leanings toward the Healthy Model of analogy.

The passages relating to the Analogy Model Problem appear in sections VII–IX of Ferrariensis's *In SCG* I, c. 34.[20] In Ferrariensis's own terminology, he is addressing the question of the "mode of analogy for divine names."[21] The other Thomists engaged in this study come to this question through philosophical difficulties employing the Healthy Model of analogy in the divine names (as has been shown above). In this respect, Ferrariensis differs from his predecessors. For him, the problem appears to be purely textual; specifically, the problem concerns the apparent conflict between Aquinas's remarks in *Summa Contra Gentiles* I, c. 34, and in *De Veritate*, q. 2, a. 11: "For St. Thomas seems to hold the opposite of this [i.e., the opposite of what he holds in *Summa Contra Gentiles* I, c. 34, about analogy in divine names] in *De Veritate*, q. 2, a. 11. For there he holds that the analogy fitting to God and to creatures is not according to the agreement and proportion of one to another, but according to a certain proportionality."[22] Ferrariensis treats the problem by presenting a series of arguments and counterarguments over how to interpret Aquinas. He does not associate any of

---

18. Ferrariensis, *In SCG* I, c. 34, section XVI (13:108b–109a): "*Sapientiae enim nomen dictum de Deo et creatura diversas naturas immediate significat, habentes tamen inter se similitudinem et proportionem, secundum quod una ab altera exemplatur: sicut enim sua sapientia Deus altissimas considerat causas, sed suo modo, ita et creatura suo modo per suam sapientiam easdem considerat.*"

19. Compare this passage to Sutton's remarks in *Quaestiones Ordinariae* 33 (Schmaus, 77–78).

20. Ferrariensis, *In SCG* I, c. 34, sections VII–IX (13:105b–107a).

21. Ibid., section III (13:104b).

22. Ibid.: "*Oppositum enim eius videtur tenere Sanctus Thomas Ver.*, q. II, a. 11. *Ibi enim tenet quod analogia conveniens Deo et creaturis non est secundum convenientiam et proportionem unius ad alterum, sed secundum quandam proportionalitatem.*"

these arguments with particular Thomists, but the reader of this study may recognize a number of them from Sutton, Capreolus, Flandrensis, and Cajetan, where they treat the significance of analogy of proportionality for the divine names.

Ferrariensis gives particular attention to a point drawn out of *De Veritate*, q. 2, a. 11, by Capreolus and Flandrensis about the difference between the indeterminate mode of analogy (illustrated by the examples of "principle" and "sight") and the determinate analogy of one to another (illustrated by the example of "healthy"); namely, in the determinate mode, but not in the indeterminate mode, the primary analogate is in the definition of the secondary analogate.[23] Ferrariensis recites the same texts from Aquinas as his aforementioned predecessors, but he does not agree with their conclusion. On the contrary, according to Ferrariensis: "It can be responded [to these arguments] ... and better, in my judgment, to the mind of St. Thomas, that in every mode of analogy it is true that the prior is posited in the definition of the posterior, inasmuch as it is considered and signified analogously."[24]

23. For the positions of Capreolus, Flandrensis, and Cajetan, see *Defensiones* 1, d. 35, q. 2, a. 2 (2:399a–b), Dominic of Flanders, *SDP*, l. 12, q. 8, a. 4, ad 3 (778a–b), and Cajetan, *In Primam Partem* 13.6, III–IV (Leonine, 4:151a). On Cajetan's position, see especially *In Primam Partem*, q. 13, a. 6, section III (Leonine, 4:151a): "Tum quia ex dictis patet sapientiam analogice dici de Deo et aliis: et tamen creatura non dicitur sapiens in ordine ad Deum, nec e converso, ut patet, sed uterque dicitur sapiens absolute. Tum quia in ratione hominis ut sapiens, non clauditur sapientia Dei; nec in ratione Dei ut sapiens est, clauditur sapientia hominis. Ergo." (Then because from what has been said it is clear that wisdom is said analogously about God and others, and, nevertheless, a creature is not called "wise" in order to God, nor the reverse, as is clear, but each one is called "wise" absolutely. Then the wisdom of God is not included in the definition of a human as wise, nor is the wisdom of a human included in the definition of God as He is wise. Therefore.) According to Tavuzzi, "Some Renaissance Thomist Divisions of Analogy," 110–11, Ferrariensis was not alone among his Dominican Thomist contemporaries in arguing for the universality of the rule that one analogate is in the definition of the other. Tavuzzi says that Silvestro Mazzolini da Prierio takes a similar position in his commentary on *Summa Theologiae* I, q. 13, a. 9. See Mazzolini, *Conflatum ex S. Thoma*, 88r. By my own reading of the passage, although Silvestro faults Cajetan's reasons, Silvestro still objects to the rule on other grounds. I take up this dispute between Flandrensis, Cajetan, Silvestro, and Ferrariensis in detail in Domenic D'Ettore, "One Is in the Definition of All: The Renaissance Thomist Controversy Over a 'Rule' for Names Said by Analogy," *The Thomist* 82 (2018, forthcoming).

24. Ferrariensis, *In SCG* I, c. 34, section IX (13:106b): "Potest secundo responderi,

Javelli and Ferrariensis 159

With this Ferrariensis informs his reader that he disagrees with at least one aspect of the solution to the Analogy Model Problem provided by Cajetan and Cajetan's predecessors Capreolus and Flandrensis.[25] For the purposes of giving a more complete answer to an existing disputed question in the Thomist tradition, it would have been useful for Ferrariensis to have explained and given some nonmetaphysical and nontheological examples of the primary analogate in the definition of the secondary in an analogy of proportionality. He does not do this. Instead, he justifies his interpretation of Aquinas by employing his distinction between the three impositions of an analogous name.

As mentioned in the previous section of this chapter, the first imposition of a name said analogously of God and creatures signifies the creaturely perfection absolutely. The second imposition signifies God absolutely, and the third imposition signifies the creaturely perfection as ordered to the divine perfection. With respect to one analogate's place in the definition of the other analogate, Ferrariensis writes:

And so according to the first imposition, the first analogate is not posited in the definition of the other, because then the name is not taken as analogous but as univocal. But insofar as it is taken analogously, which belongs to it [i.e., to the name] according to the third imposition, the divine perfection is posited in the definition of the perfection of the creature as it is signified by the same name.[26]

---

et melius, meo iudicio, ad mentem Sancti Thomae, quod in omni modo analogiae verum est quod prius ponitur in definitione posterioris, inquantum analogice consideratur et significatur."

25. Ralph McInerny gives an interpretation of proportionality which agrees with Ferrariensis's, in *Aquinas and Analogy*, 111–14. A more developed but, likewise, overall agreeing account can be found in Santiago Ramirez, *De Analogia*, in *Opera Omnia* (Madrid: Instituto de Filosofia "Luis Vives," 1970–72), 2.3:1399–1460; see 1415–16, where Ramirez expresses his disagreement with Cajetan very bluntly, but respectfully.

26. Ferrariensis, *In SCG* I, c. 34, section IX (13:107a): "Secundum itaque primam impositionem, primum analogatum non ponitur in definitione alterius: quia non accipitur tunc nomen ut analogum, sed ut univocum. Secundum autem quod analogice sumitur, quod convenit sibi secundum tertiam impositionem, perfectio divina ponitur in definitione perfectionis creaturae ut eodem nomine significatur."

Ferrariensis's solution avoids the problem of affirming that the creaturely perfection is in the definition of the divine perfection, which like his Thomist predecessors (and Aquinas himself in *Summa Contra Gentiles* I, c. 34, and *Summa Theologiae* I, q. 13, a. 6), he regards to be impossible because then the names would be said *per prius* of the creature and *per posterius* about God. Ferrariensis's solution likewise sidesteps his predecessors' objections, which were based on the order of the imposition of names, to placing the divine perfection in the definition of the perfection of the creature. Ferrariensis admits that the divine perfection is not in the definition of the creaturely perfection in the "first imposition" of the name. Rather, the divine perfection only enters the definition of the creaturely perfection in the "third imposition." And it is in its "third imposition" alone that the name is said analogously.

I do not find Ferrariensis's own remarks to be sufficiently clear regarding how one analogate is in the definition of the other in an analogy of proportionality.[27] My own best guess at how Ferrariensis could reconcile this approach with analogy of proportionality without reducing it to the determinate mode of analogy of one to another is to appeal back to his claim that "for all analogates and all their concepts are the same by likeness and proportion; and so the concept of one is the concept of the other proportionally."[28] If the

---

27. For where Ferrariensis discusses how one analogate is in the definition of the other when names are said analogously of God and creatures, see ibid.: "Cum hoc tamen stat quod in analogis omnibus, inquantum analoga sunt, semper unum ponitur in definitione aliorum: aut scilicet illud cui primo imponitur nomen absolute; aut id cui secundario nomen imponitur. In nominibus enim divinis primum secundum rem, posterius autem secundum impositionem nominis, ponitur in definitione aliorum inquantum analoga sunt: nam homo analogice dicitur *sapiens*, quia habet perfectionem secundum quam divinam sapientiam imitatur; et sic de aliis." (Although it holds that in all analogous names, insofar as they are analogous names, one is always affirmed in the definition of the others—either, of course, that to which the name is first imposed absolutely, or that to which the name is imposed secondarily. For in divine names, what is prior according to reality but posterior according to imposition of the name, is affirmed in the definition of the others insofar as they are analogous names. For a human is called "wise" because he has the perfection insofar as he imitates divine wisdom; and it is the same for the other [names said analogously about God and creatures].)

28. Ibid., section XVI (13:109b), quoted in full in note 15 above.

concept of one is proportionally the concept of the other analogate, then there is some sense in which the concept and definition of one analogate can serve as the definition of the other analogate. If this is all that Ferrariensis is claiming in proposing that analogy of proportionality is no exception to the rule of one analogate in the definition of the others, then there may be only an apparent conflict between Ferrariensis's position and the positions of Capreolus, Flandrensis, and Cajetan. Nonetheless, even if Ferrariensis's method of applying the rule that "the primary analogate is in the definition of the other(s)" to analogy of proportionality is reconcilable with his predecessors' positions, Ferrariensis's overall answer to the Analogy Model Problem differs significantly both in content and in approach.

With respect to content, Ferrariensis uniquely appeals to multiple impositions of a name in order to account for the divine names, and he uniquely takes the position that analogous naming occurs only when the name is imposed on the creature for the second time (i.e., in the name's third imposition). Ferrariensis's approach (which leads to and justifies the content of his solution) is through the variations found in the texts of Aquinas, especially the variations between *De Veritate*, q. 2, a. 11, and parallel passages in *Summa Contra Gentiles* I, cc. 32–34, and *Summa Theologiae* I, q. 13. By distinguishing the second imposition and the second concept from the first imposition and the first concept, Ferrariensis avoids putting the definition of the creature in the definition of God, thereby satisfying the rule found in *Summa Theologiae* I, q. 13, a. 2, that names are said of God formally and not only relationally. The third concept, which represents the human perfection and divine perfection as proportionally identical to each other, nods to the *De Veritate*, q. 2, a. 11, condition that the names are said of God and of creatures by proportionality. The third imposition gives Ferrariensis an instance wherein the divine analogate is in the definition of the name said of the creature, thereby both satisfying the assertions in *Summa Theologiae* I, q. 13, a. 6, that one analogate is in the definition of the other and that the names are said of God *per prius*, and justifying Aquinas's use of Healthy Model analogies in those texts.

FERRARIENSIS ON THE EQUIVOCATION PROBLEM

Ferrariensis explicitly directs the reader of *In SCG* I, c. 34, to Cajetan's *De Nominum Analogia* for the resolution of "other difficulties which occur concerning analogy of names."[29] Ferrariensis's silence on the Equivocation Problem suggests that it is one of those difficulties. I propose here to offer a solution to the problem of the fallacy of equivocation in a demonstration using analogous terms *ad mentem Ferrariensis*. Given Ferrariensis's silence on the question and his reference to Cajetan for solutions to problems concerning analogy, as well as the differences between Ferrariensis's and Cajetan's positions on the Analogy Model Problem, I assume that such a solution would (1) attempt to satisfy Cajetan's standards for solving the Equivocation Problem and (2) be consistent with and follow from Ferrariensis's own answers to the *Rationes* and Analogy Model Problems.

Consider, once again, the syllogism "All simple perfections are in God, and wisdom is a simple perfection; therefore, wisdom is in God." To proceed by way of elimination using Ferrariensis's three impositions and their corresponding concepts, the first imposition of "wisdom" can be excluded as a candidate for use in the argument's conclusion because the definition of "wisdom" signified "absolutely" of a creature includes its genus as a quality. Hence, to employ the first imposition of "wisdom" in the conclusion of the argument above would be to say that "wisdom, an accident in the category of quality, is present in God." The divine simplicity excludes this option. The name "wisdom" cannot be said according to its second imposition in the argument's minor premise. If it were, then the minor premise could be paraphrased as "the wisdom proportionally similar to yet more eminent than creaturely wisdom is a simple perfection."

---

29. See ibid., section XI (13:107a): "Alias difficultates quae circa nominum analogiam occurrunt, si ad plenum vis intelligere, vide ingeniosissimum opus *de Nominum Analogia* Reverendissimi Thomae Gaietani, Cardinalis Sancti Sixti."

TABLE 5. Solution to the Equivocation Problem *ad mentem Ferrariensis*

	Statement	Imposition of the Name "Wisdom"
Major Premise	All simple perfections are in God	[Not addressed by Ferrariensis]
Minor Premise	Wisdom is a simple perfection	First imposition (creaturely wisdom absolutely)
Conclusion	Wisdom is in God	Second imposition (divine wisdom absolutely)

Because the argument claims to establish that there is such a thing as a higher form of wisdom proportionally similar to creaturely wisdom, employing knowledge of this wisdom in the minor premise would be question-begging. The argument would also fail to reason to God from creatures.

The word "wisdom" cannot be used according to the third imposition in the minor premise because this imposition is only generated in the first place by the argument's conclusion. That is to say, the name "wisdom" cannot be said of a creature to signify the dependence of creaturely wisdom on divine wisdom in a premise of an argument attempting to establish the existence of divine wisdom without begging the question. The third imposition is also excluded from the argument's conclusion, this time, because the conclusion predicates the name of God absolutely, which is proper to the name's second imposition. Having excluded the other options, we are left with using "wisdom" by Ferrariensis's first imposition in the minor premise and by his second imposition in the conclusion.

This approach to the imposition of names in the demonstration has merit by Cajetan's standards. To recall, Cajetan invokes Scotus's requirement for valid demonstration: the mediating terms must be said in both parts of the syllogism with sufficient unity for a contradiction. Taken by themselves, the concepts through which the first and second impositions are made are too diverse to establish a contradiction. There is no contradiction in saying "the quality of wisdom is a simple perfection but nonqualitative divine wisdom is not a simple perfection." Nor is there any contradiction in saying "God is nonqualitative wisdom and God is not qualitative wisdom." However, because Ferrariensis recognizes proportional similarity between the objects of the first and second impositions, and he maintains that the intellect forms an imprecise third concept representing these diverse objects insofar as they are proportionally similar (in this case divine and human wisdom insofar as they are proportionally similar), Ferrariensis could maintain, using Cajetan's account of proportional unity, that it would be a contradiction to both affirm and deny proportional likeness between the object of a first imposition and the object of the second imposition of the same name. Ferrariensis's differences with Cajetan's account of analogy, including his dispute over the Analogy Model Problem, do not seem to prevent him from embracing a basically Cajetanian solution to the Equivocation Problem.

CHRYSOSTOM JAVELLI

Moving from one inquisitor to another, the final figure to be treated in this study is another reader of Cajetan, Chrysostom Javelli, who composed a series of commentaries on the works of Aristotle while serving his appointment as inquisitor at Piacenza and Cremona in 1515–43.[30] His primary treatments of the three problems appear in his *Quaestiones in Metaphysicam Aristotelis*, first published in 1532.[31] The issues are also discussed in his *In Logicam Aristotelis*, published posthumously in 1555.[32]

As mentioned in the introduction, Javelli studied at Bologna and received his appointment as inquisitor from Cajetan. Javelli's QMA

---

30. Tavuzzi, *Renaissance Inquisitors*, 43.
31. This text will hereafter be referred to as QMA. All references to this work are taken from Chrysostom Iavellus, *In Libros Metaphysicos Aristotelis*, in *Quaestiones, In Metaphysicam Aristotelis: Ab innumeris mendis repurgatae & in gratiam Philosophiae studiosorum denuo editae Accessit in hac editione, Tractatus de natura Metaphysices ex Epitome Metaphysica eiusdem autoris huc translatus, & duplex Index [...]* (Wittenberg: Selfischius, 1609). See Lohr, "Renaissance Latin Aristotle Commentaries: Authors G–K," 732.
32. Ibid., 733.

reveals him to be a close reader and critic of Dominic of Flanders's *Summa Divinae Philosophiae*, which is frequently cited as presenting the main Thomist alternative to Javelli's own position. Notably for the topic at hand, Javelli argues against Flandrensis's position on the unity of the concept of being, and, that, as a consequence of his errors about the concept of being, Flandrensis makes other mistakes pertinent to the subject matter of metaphysics and to being "as first known."

Javelli's more extended treatment of "being as first known" appears in his treatise *De Transcendentibus*, where he reveals himself to be a close reader of Cajetan's *In de Ente et Essentia*, despite the fact that he never mentions Cajetan there by name. The first question of this text, addressing the first concept of being, is in many respects an abbreviation of Cajetan's *In de Ente et Essentia*, q. 1, on "whether being is the first known in the order and way of origin." Javelli goes through the same set of arguments from Scotus and Scotists as Cajetan, provides a simplified version of Cajetan's fourfold division of cognition, and takes Cajetan's responses to Scotus and the Scotists for his own.[33] In the end, however, Javelli parts from Cajetan on what being as first known is. Whereas Cajetan informed his reader that "concrete being belonging to a sensible quiddity is the first known in actual confused cognition,"[34] Javelli holds that the intellect's first concept (likewise held in actual confused cognition) expresses "*cui debetur esse*."[35] This phrase suggests the influence of Paul Soncinas, who, as seen in chapter 4, proposed "*cui debetur esse*" for the separate formal concept of being, and was criticized by Cajetan for doing so.

Javelli's discussion of the *Rationes* Problem represents an attempt to revive Soncinas's separate formal concept (but not his disjunctive

---

33. See Chrysostom Javelli, *De Transcendentibus*, c. 1, in *Epitome Chrysostom Iavelli Canapitii Ord. Praedicatorum, in universam Aristotelis philosophiam, tam naturalem, quam transnaturalem* (Venice, 1567).

34. Cajetan, *In De Ente et Essentia*, q. 1 (Lyon, 9): "Ens concretum quidditati sensibili est primum cognitum cognitione actuali confusa."

35. Javelli, *De Transcendentibus*, c. 1 (Venice, 1567), 150–51.

objective concept) despite the criticisms of Flandrensis and Cajetan. Although he would surely have been familiar with proportionality as discussed by Flandrensis and Cajetan (at least in Cajetan's *In de Ente et Essentia*), Javelli leaves it out altogether from his own treatment of the Analogy Model Problem, and gives instead a modified version of Soncinas's solution.

JAVELLI ON THE *RATIONES* PROBLEM

Javelli addresses the *Rationes* and Analogy Model Problems together in his *QMA*, l. 4, q. 1.[36] The question begins with a brief enumeration of historical answers to whether "being" is said univocally, equivocally, or analogously.[37] Javelli begins with Averroes and ends, fittingly, with Cajetan. He credits Capreolus, Soncinas, and Cajetan with rightly presenting the doctrine of Aquinas on the question. Specifically, Javelli affirms that Aquinas "holds that it [i.e., being] is analogous by the analogy which is one to another, and not by the analogy which is of many to one, such as is the analogy of the name 'healthy.'"[38] Javelli concludes his introduction to the question with a list of five goals he intends to achieve. These are: (1) to identify what is required for real univocity, (2) to identify what is required for logical univocity, (3) to draw some responsive conclusions, (4) to show that there is not real disagreement between Scotus's opinion and that of Aquinas, and (5) to answer the arguments of Scotus that seem most to go against Javelli's own judgment.[39] Javelli's answers to

---

36. I draw from *QMA*, l. 4, q. 1, to point out Javelli's disagreement with Dominic of Flanders over whether there is a separate concept of being in Domenic D'Ettore, "A Thomist Re-consideration of the Subject Matter of Metaphysics: Chrysostom Iavelli on What is Included in Being as Being," *Proceedings of the American Catholic Philosophical Association* 89 (2015): 215–17.

37. Javelli, *QMA*, l. 4, q. 1 (Selfischius, 94): "An ens sit univocum, vel analogum. Ens multis modis dicitur, sed ad unum etc."

38. Ibid. (95): "similiter manifestum est, quod B. Thom. tenet ipsum esse analogum analogia, quae est unius ad alterum, et non analogia, quae est plurium ad unum, qualis est analogia hujus nominis sanum, et hoc videre poteris in Capreolo in 1, d. 2., q. 1..., et in Paulo Soncinate in 4 metaph. q. 4, et in Thoma Cajetano, super de ente et essentia."

39. Ibid.: "Volo autem pro hujus quaesiti evidentia, agere quinque. Primo, quid

the three problems are scattered within his treatment of these five goals, but primarily in the first and third.

Drawing on the authority of Aristotle and Simplicius, Javelli observes that real univocity entails comparing how the concept of a name applies to diverse recipients of the name.[40] To defend his point, he adds:

> From these things, I elicit that if "animal" is considered precisely in itself, as it expresses one concept, before it is compared to its inferiors, it is not univocal, nor equivocal, nor analogous. I say the same about "being," if it is considered precisely in itself, as it expresses one concept, for instance, "being is that to which it is owed to be," and it is not compared to subject and accident, to God and creature. In that first and absolute consideration, it will not be univocal nor analogous, etc.[41]

With these remarks, Javelli introduces a consideration absent from (or at most implied by) the texts of the other authors treated in this study when addressing the *Rationes* Problem; namely, consideration of being as first known, and, consequently, the concept of being (and other terms said analogously) considered by itself prior to being said of many.

The grounds for the aforementioned condition for real univocity go back to Aristotle's introduction of the terms "univocal" and "equivocal" in the *Categories*. The philosopher writes that terms have the characteristics of being univocal or equivocal depending on whether the many to which the term is predicated share both in the common name and in a common nature. Javelli observes that in the

---

requiratur ad univocum reale. Secundo quid ad univocum logicum. Tertio ponentur aliquae conclusiones responsivae. Quarto ostendam quod opinio Scoti non discordat in re ab opinione B. Tho. Quinto solventur argumenta Scoti, et maxime quae videbuntur repugnare contra determinationem, quam facturi sumus."

40. Ibid.

41. Ibid.: "Ex his elicio, quod si consideretur animal praecise in se, ut dicit unum conceptum, antequam comparetur ad sua inferiora, non est univocum, nec aequivocum nec analogum. Idem dico de ente, si in se praecise consideretur, ut dicit unum conceptum, puta, ens est, cui debetur esse, et non comparetur ad subjectum et accidens, ad Deum et creaturam, in illa prima et absoluta consideratione, non erit univocum nec analogum, etc."

absence of the comparison between how a name is said of one thing and how it is said of another, the concept through which the name is predicated lacks univocity, analogy, or equivocity. And this is the case for the name "animal" as much as it is for the name "being." I have not found this point made explicitly by the earlier Thomist authors (or even in contemporary Thomist works). Soncinas's separate formal concept seems to come closest to anticipating it, and Javelli does indeed treat the first and prior absolute concept as separate from the proper concepts, which emerge only after the intellect compares its diverse applications of a common name.

Javelli proceeds to give three arguments for a prior and separate concept of being which is neither univocal, equivocal, nor analogous:

About each thing we can consider first that it is a being before what sort of being it is, for instance a substance or an accident. Therefore, in that prior [consideration], "being" expresses one concept before it is compared to its contents.

Further, the absolute concept is prior to the relative concept. But the concept of "being" in itself is absolute, but when it is compared to its contents, it is relative, for it regards the inferiors about which it is predicated. Therefore, one concept of "being" can be held before it is compared to its inferiors.

Further, if the first which falls on our intellect is being, clearly before I know about anything that it is substance or accident, first, I know that it is being. But I would not know that it is a being unless in that prior [knowledge] I had a concept of "being."[42]

The first and third arguments above appeal in different ways to the order of knowing. The first argument is derivative of Scotus's "Cer-

---

42. Ibid. (96): "De quolibet possumus considerare primus quod sit ens, quam quod sit tale ens, puta substantia vel accidens. Ergo in illo priori ens dicit unum conceptum antequam comparetur ad sua contenta. Praeterea conceptus absolutus prior est conceptu relativo. Sed conceptus entis in se est absolutus, cum autem comparatur suis contentis, sit relativus, respicit enim inferiora, de quibus praedicatur, ergo potest haberi de ente unus conceptus, antequam comparetur suis inferioribus. Praeterea, si primum quod cadit in nostro intellectu est ens, patet quod antequam sciam de aliquo, quod sit substantia vel accidens, prius scio quod est ens, nescirem ipsum esse ens nisi in illo priori haberem conceptum entis."

tain and Doubtful" Argument for the univocity of being, a connection Javelli makes explicitly in his fifth "responsive conclusion."[43] The intellect can be certain that something is a being prior to discovering whether the thing in question is a substance or an accident, a finite being or an infinite being. Consequently, the intellect must have a concept of being through which it makes the prior judgment, and that concept must be different from the concept through which it makes the latter judgment that the object in question is a substance or accident, finite or infinite. Natalis, Sutton, and Soncinas appealed to unity of disjunction to solve this difficulty for analogy, and Capreolus distinguished the unity of the formal and objective concepts, but Javelli admits that the intellect in this case does indeed judge that the object in question is a being through a concept of being that is separate from its concepts of substance and its concepts of accidents. Javelli does not see this, however, as a fatal blow to denying a univocal concept of being across the categories, etc. On the contrary, unlike Scotus or the other Thomists considered in this study, Javelli proposes that the concept of being, which is employed by the one who is certain that something is being and doubtful whether it is a substance or whether it is an accident, is neither a univocal concept, nor an equivocal concept, nor an analogous concept.

43. See ibid. (102): "Respondeo. Scotus deceptus fuit in hac consequentia, ens dicit unum conceptum, alium a conceptibus suorum contentorum. Ergo est univocum, negatur consequentia, quoniam ut diximus in corpore quaestionis, ad univocum non sufficit unitas conceptus, sed requiritur quod illud commune habeat unum conceptum, non solum in se considerato, sed ut respicit inferiora, et quod ille conceptus aequaliter participetur a suis inferioribus. Quorum secundum deficit in ente, quoniam conceptus ejus non convenit accidenti nisi in ordine ad substantiam, nec enti creato nisi in ordine ad ens increatum." (I answer. Scotus was deceived in this consequence: "being" expresses one concept other than the concepts of its contents; therefore, it is univocal. The consequence is denied because, as we have said in the body of the question, unity of concept does not suffice for univocity. Rather, [univocity] requires that this commonality has one concept, not only when [the concept is] considered in itself, but as [the concept] regards its inferiors, and that the concept is participated in equally by its inferiors. Of these [conditions], the second is lacking in "being," because its concept does not belong to accident except in order to substance, nor [does it belong] to created being except in order to uncreated being.)

Javelli joins his Thomist brethren in affirming that being is said analogously across the categories and of God and creatures by locating the analogy in the comparison which follows the prior judgment that the object in question is a being. That is, the initial concept of being is found to apply analogously when it is said of substance and accident (or indeed when something is affirmed to be a substance as distinct from an accident, or vice versa, or when something is affirmed to be one accident rather than another accident).

The third argument quoted above appeals to the Avicennian dictum, repeated by Aquinas, that being is that which first falls upon the intellect.[44] This argument is introduced as support for the previous two arguments by affirming the intellect's awareness of being prior to its awareness of the relative modes of being. The concept of being is the intellect's very first concept. In Javelli's words, "this is the order in the intellect, that it first conceives *ens commune* in itself, by which it compares [*ens commune*] to its contents."[45] In the first of his "responsive conclusions" he writes: "But being so considered in that first [concept], is not compared to its contents, for first I consider being as being, then being as substance, or accident; therefore, as such, it is not univocal, nor equivocal, nor analogous."[46] Javelli repeats and defends his claim that the possible intellect's first concept is being in other texts such as his 1534 *De Anima* commentary, adding there that the concept of being is first in the orders of time, generation, and resolution.[47] As was mentioned in the introduction to

---

44. See Avicenna, *Metaphysics of the Healing*, l. 1, c. 5, n. 1, trans. Michael E. Marmura (Provo, Utah: Brigham Young University Press, 2005), 22; Aquinas, *De Veritate*, q. 1, a. 1, and q. 21, a. 1.

45. Javelli, *QMA*, l. 4, q. 1 (Selfischius, 96): "Sed quod iste est ordo in intellectu, ut prius concipiat ens commune in se, quo comparet ipsum suis contentis."

46. Ibid. (98): "Sed ens sic consideratum in illo priori, non comparatur suis contentis, prius enim considero ens ut ens, quam ens ut substantia, vel accidens, ergo ut sic, non est univocum, nec aequivocum nec analogum."

47. See Chrysostom Iavellus, *Super tres libros Aristotelis de Anima*, l. 3 (Bonellus, 1568), 171r–v, especially the following: "Ens vt ens, id est vniuersalissimo modo sumptum prout in se comprehendit omnes modos entis, est primum obiectum intellectus primitate adaequationis, et temporis, siue generationis, et resolutionis, sed non perfectionis." (Being as being, that is, taken in the most universal way insofar as it comprehends all

Javelli above, he follows the example of Cajetan's *In de Ente et Essentia* and defends the priority of the concept of being at length in his *De Transcendentibus*, c. 1.[48]

On the *Rationes* Problem, then, Javelli clearly belongs with Soncinas among those who hold that not only is there a single concept through which names are said analogously of God and creatures, but that this concept is separate from the concepts proper to the analogates. This concept is not predicated univocally of God and creatures, however, because they participate in it unequally. For Javelli, this means that when the intellect compares what it means to say that God is "wise," etc., to what it means to say that a creature is "wise," etc., it finds that the word "wisdom" does not signify a common nature found in both God and creatures. Javelli explains how the comparison is analogous in the course of his answer to the *Rationes* and Analogy Model Problems.

JAVELLI ON THE ANALOGY MODEL AND EQUIVOCATION PROBLEMS

As noted above, Javelli's intention in *QMA*, l. 4, q. 1, is to show that there is no real disagreement between Aquinas and Scotus on names said analogously of God and creatures. In pursuit of this point, Javelli quotes Scotus's definition of univocity through the possession of unity sufficient for contradiction and for mediating a syllogism without committing the fallacy of equivocation.[49] Echoing Cajetan,

---

modes of being, is the first object of the intellect by the primacy of adequation, and of time or generation, and of resolution, but not of perfection.) Javelli claims that this is Aquinas's position in *De Veritate*, q. 1, a. 1. On the 1534 date of this commentary's first publication, see Lohr, "Renaissance Latin Aristotle Commentaries: Authors G–K," 732.

48. See Javelli, *De Transcendentibus*, c. 1 (Venice, 1567), 149–64. This text is discussed in Daniel Heider, "Suárez and Javelli on transcendentals and divisions of being," in *Universalità della ragione: pluralità delle filosofie nel Medioevo: XII Congresso internazionale di filosofia medievale, Palermo, 17–22 settembre 2007*, ed. Alessandro Musco (Palermo: Officina di studi medievali, 2012), 2.2:851–52.

49. See Javelli, *QMA*, l. 4, q. 1 (Selfischius, 100). See also my translations and brief comments on Javelli's answer to the Equivocation Problem in D'Ettore, "Some Renaissance Thomists on analogy in demonstration," 945–49.

Javelli states that a certain mode of analogy also has this unity.[50] Javelli continues by giving his own variation of Aquinas's *In 1 Sent.*, d. 19, threefold division of analogy. Tavuzzi has suggested Soncinas as Javelli's obvious source in this passage,[51] and the similarity between Javelli's explanation and use of Aquinas to Soncinas's makes Tavuzzi's suggestion plausible. Here I will draw attention to the particularities of Javelli's version of Aquinas's threefold division of analogy as distinct from the renderings of it by Capreolus, Soncinas, and Cajetan.

Consider therefore, according to the Thomist doctrine, as is clear through Blessed Thomas's *In 1 Sent.*, d. 19, [q. 5, a. 2, ad 1], that analogy is threefold. The first [mode of analogy] is when the analogue expresses many *rationes* and its significate is found only in one analogate. For example, "healthy," which by one *ratio* is predicated about an animal, and by another about medicine, and another about diet, but its significate is saved only in the animal, although the analogy stands because the thing conservative, causative, [or] indicative of health relates to the healthy animal, and

---

50. See ibid. (100–101): "Ex quibus patet quod Scotus conatur ponere tantum unitatem in ente, quanta sufficiat ad contradictionem ponendam, et ut sit medium efficax in syllogismo. Sed non solum univocum sufficit ad hoc, imo, et analogum, illo quidem modo analogiae, in quo ponimus ens. Quod ergo Scotus dicit univocum, B. Tho. dicit analogum." (From which it is clear that Scotus tried to affirm as much unity in being as suffices for affirming a contradiction and that it may be an effective medium in a syllogism. But not only a univocal name suffices for this, on the contrary, so does an analogous name, at least in that mode of analogy in which we put "being.")

51. See Tavuzzi, "Some Renaissance Divisions of Analogy," 116: "It is obviously dependent on the corresponding passage in Soncinas even though Iavelli's initial claim that for Aquinas the analogy of being is exclusively a matter of proportionality and in no way of attribution might well be indicative of Cajetan's influence. Yet at the beginning of the question in which the passage is set Iavelli refers his readers on the theme of analogy to the works of Capreolus and Soncinas and to Cajetan's *De Ente et Essentia* but does not mention the *De Nominum Analogia*." I quote these two sentences to note a difference between my own reading of the text and Tavuzzi's. As quoted, Tavuzzi refers to Javelli saying that the analogy of being for Aquinas is "exclusively a matter of proportionality and in no way of attribution." I have not been able to locate what Tavuzzi calls "Iavelli's initial claim." At the beginning of the question under discussion, as quoted by Tavuzzi (ibid., 117), Javelli affirms that Thomas holds that being is analogous by analogy of one to another and not by analogy of many to one: "Bl. Thomas tenet ipsum esse analogum analogia, quae est unius ad alterum, et non analogia, quae est plurium ad unum." Javelli, *QMA*, l. 4, q. 1 (Selfischius, 95). I have not so far found Javelli treating proportionality as a distinct mode of analogy.

what is said analogously in this way is closest to the equivocal. Therefore, it makes a proposition ambiguous and takes away contradiction, because both of these [propositions] are true, "an animal is healthy," "medicine is not healthy," namely by the healthiness which is subjectively in an animal.⁵²

Following the example of Aquinas and the Thomists Capreolus, Soncinas, and Cajetan, Javelli observes that the first mode of analogy is represented by the Healthy Model. As to why this mode will not serve demonstrative purposes, Javelli turns to Scotus's point about contradiction. A term can be a medium for demonstration only when it is used in such a way that it would be a contradiction to affirm and deny it of something or to affirm and deny some property about it. But the Healthy Model does not meet these conditions. For example, it is true that "medicine is healthy," but it is no contradiction to say "medicine is not healthy" using one of the other analogous meanings of "healthy."

The passage continues:

The second [mode of analogy] is when the analogue expresses one *ratio* and, nevertheless, it has diverse and non-uniform being [*esse*] in the analogates. For example, [take] "body" when it is predicated of a heavenly body and of an inferior one. For although they agree in the *ratio* of bodiliness, nevertheless, they do not agree in being [*esse*], since the being [*esse*] of a heavenly body is incorruptible, but the being [*esse*] of an inferior body is corruptible. And this mode does not take away contradiction. Indeed, it asserts [contradiction]. For this always is true, "an element is a body," and this always is false, "the heavenly object is not a body," because the *ratio* of "body" belongs to both, even though it does not agree in [their] being [*esse*].⁵³

---

52. Javelli, *QMA*, l. 4, q. 1 (Selfischius, 101): "Adverte igitur, secundum doctrinam Thomisticam, ut patet per B. Thom. in 1 Sent., d. 19. q. [sic], a. 2, ad idem, quod triplex est analogia, prima est quando analogum dicit plures rationes et ejus significatum solum in primo analogato reperitur. Sicut sanum, quod alia ratione praedicatur de animali, et alia de medicina, et alia de dieta, suum autem significatum, tantum in animali salvatur, stat tamen analogia quoniam conservativum, causativum, indicativum, sanitatis respiciunt animal sanum, et hoc modo dictum analogum, est propinquissimum, aequivoco, ideo facit propositionem multiplicem et aufert contradictionem, quoniam utraque harum est vera, animal est sanum, medicina non est sana, scilicet sanitate, quae subjective est in animali."

53. Ibid.: "Secunda est quando analogum dicit unam rationem et tamen diversum esse et difforme habet in analogatis. Sicut corpus dum praedicatur de coelesti, et

Javelli's explanation of the second mode follows the same pattern of looking for the ability to found a contradiction with statements using the term analogously in this mode. The second mode does carry contradiction. Despite their diverse ways of being bodies, "this is always true, an element is a body, and this is always false, a heavenly object is not a body, because the *ratio* of 'body' belongs to both."[54]

As for the third mode of analogy, Javelli writes:

The third [mode of analogy] is when the analogue expresses only one *ratio* in which the analogates are not made equal, nor [are they made equal] in the being [*esse*] carried through that *ratio*, because that *ratio* is found in one analogate, and its being [*esse*] has connection with another analogate. For example, an accident is a being [*ens*] as it has connection to substance, and not the reverse, and a creature is a being [*ens*], not from itself but it participates in being [*esse*] from God to whom being [*esse*] belongs first and *per se*, and being [*ens*] is analogous in this third mode. And this third mode asserts contradiction and is efficacious in a syllogism. For if this conclusion is asserted, "hot and cold are not in the same thing," and it is proven in this way, "no opposite beings [*entia*] are in the same thing, hot and cold are opposites, therefore, etc.," clearly that major [premise] is absolutely true, and under it there can be a distributive descent both in substances and in accidents. From these things it is clear that the opinion of Scotus on the matter does not disagree with Blessed Thomas, for what Scotus says is univocal being [*ens*], Blessed Thomas says is analogous in the third mode.[55]

---

de inferiori, licet enim conveniant in ratione corporeitatis, tamen non conveniunt in esse, cum esse coeli sit incorruptibile, esse autem corporis inferioris est corruptibile, et hic modus non aufert, imo ponit contradictionem. Nam haec semper est vera, elementum est corpus, et haec semper est falsa coelum non est corpus, eo quod ratio corporis utrique convenit, licet non conveniat in esse."

54. Ibid. (101), quoted above.

55. Ibid. (101–2): "Tertia est quando analogum dicit tantum, unam rationem, in qua non parificantur analogata, nec in esse importato per illam rationem, eo quod in uno analogato reperitur illa ratio, et illius esse connexionem habet cum alio analogato. Sicut accidens est ens, ut habet connexionem ad substantiam, et non econverso, et creatura est ens, non ex se, sed ut participat esse a Deo, cui primo et per se competit esse, et hoc tertio modo ens est analogum, et hic tertius modus, ponit contradictionem, et est medium efficax in syllogismo, si enim ponatur haec conclusio, calidum et frigidum, non sunt in eodem, et probatur sic, nulla entia opposita sunt in eodem, calidum et frigidum sunt opposita, ergo etc. Patet quod illa major est absolute vera, et potest sub ea fieri descensus distributive, tam in substantiis, quam in accidentibus. Ex his igitur patet, quod opinio

Javelli stresses that in the third mode of analogy one analogate relies on another analogate for its possession of the feature signified by the common name: "As an accident is a being [ens] as it has connection to substance, and not the reverse, and a creature is a being [ens], not from itself, but as it participates in being [esse] from God, to whom being [esse] belongs first and *per se*."[56] The causal dependence of the secondary analogates on the primary, as distinct from any order of signification, appears to be the key feature of Javelli's third mode of analogy.

This text shows that Javelli follows the example of Capreolus and Soncinas by introducing the threefold division of analogy from Aquinas's *In 1 Sent.*, d. 19, to meet the objection that analogous terms cannot mediate a valid demonstrative syllogism. He likewise follows Soncinas in using this text to reject the Healthy Model for names said analogously of God and creatures without actually selecting the Principle Model as the alternative. Indeed, he provides no reference to analogy of proportionality, a conspicuous absence given Javelli's familiarity with the work of both Flandrensis and Cajetan.

Turning directly to the Equivocation Problem, consider now Javelli's argument that the third mode of analogy meets Scotus's definition of univocity. Javelli offers as an example of a demonstration using the term "being" analogously by the third mode. I paraphrase it as "No opposites are in the same thing, and heat and cold are opposites; therefore, heat and cold are not in the same thing."[57] Javelli informs his reader that the major premise is clearly true, and that it can be applied to both substance and to accidents.[58] That is, whether the opposites in question are substantial or accidental predicates, they are not in the same thing. The minor premise in the example gives a qualitative mode of being for the minor term (i.e., heat and

---

Scoti quoad rem non discordat a B. Tho. nam quod dicit Scotus ens esse univocum, dicit B. Tho. esse analogum tertio modo."

56. Ibid. (101), quoted above.

57. Ibid. (101–2), quoted above. It is a valid Celarent syllogism unless it has four terms.

58. See ibid. (102), quoted above.

cold). However, if a minor premise were substituted in which the minor term was different accidental mode of being than quality or was even a substantial mode of being, then the major premise would still generate a valid conclusion. This kind of substitution is possible because the different modes of being all share in the separate and absolute concept of "being" discussed at length earlier in the question.

There is a closely resembling treatment of the Equivocation Problem in Javelli's *In Logicam Aristotelis*. In this logical treatise, Javelli writes that a term is analogous which "under distinct *rationes* or under one unequally participated in [*ratio*], signifies many natures by a certain order of prior and posterior."[59] He gives the Healthy Model example for signifying distinct *rationes* and the example of "being" said of substance and accident for unequal participation by an order of prior and posterior. The accident participates unequally in the *ratio* of being because it depends for its being on substance. Javelli goes on to say that "if an analogous term expresses only one *ratio*, but [it is] unequally participated in (such as 'being' is in the *via Thomistica*), then [the analogous term] does not impede, but rather is a true medium" for a syllogism.[60] His example of a syllogism

---

59. Chrysostom Iavellus, *In Logicam Aristotelis*, Tractatus 2, c. 1 (Lyon, 1555), 32: "Analogus est, qui sub distinctis rationibus vel sub vna inaequaliter participata plures naturas quodam ordine prioris, et posterioris significat."

60. For fuller context, see ibid., Tractatus 6, c. 6, 284: "nunquam medium sit terminis aequiuocus, nec analogus, analogia plurium rationum, et propterea hic syllogismus non valet 'Omnis canis latrat, Stella est canis, ergo stella latrat,' neque iste valet 'Omne sanum est animal, vrina est sana, ergo vrina est animal.' Dixi analogus, analogia plurium rationum: quoniam si analogum dicat tantum vnam rationem, sed inaequaliter participatam, quale est ens in via Thomistica, non impedit, quin sit verum medium, et verus syllogismus, vt hic cuilibet enti debetur esse. Substantia est ens, ergo substantiae debetur esse. Idem concluditur de accidente. Necesse est ergo medium esse vniuocum, vel analogum, analogia vnius rationis inaequaliter participatae." (A medium [for a syllogism] is never an equivocal term, nor an analogous term, by the analogy of many *rationes*, and, therefore, this syllogism is not valid: "Every dog barks, the Star is [the] Dog; therefore, the star barks." Nor is this one valid: "Every healthy thing is an animal, the urine is healthy; therefore, the urine is an animal." The analogous term that I meant is an analogy of many *rationes*, because if an analogous term expresses only one *ratio*, but [it is] unequally participated in (such as "being" is in the *via Thomistica*), then [the analogous term] does not impede, but rather is a true medium. And this is a true syllogism: "*Esse* belongs to each being, a substance is a being; therefore, *esse* belongs to substance." The same is concluded

mediated through an unequally participated concept of being is the following: "*Esse* belongs to each being, a substance is a being; therefore, *esse* belongs to substance." He adds that "accident" could be substituted for "substance" in the argument.[61]

In both his logical and metaphysical treatises, then, we find three key elements to Javelli's defense of demonstration using analogous terms: (1) unequal participation in a *ratio*, (2) an ontological order of prior and posterior (specifically, order of efficient or exemplar cause to effect) as the foundation for unequal participation in the *ratio*, and (3) an example of a demonstration where the major premise is proposed to work indifferently with either a minor premise employing substantial predicates or a minor premise employing accidental predicates. Combining these three elements together, the ontological dependence of one analogate on another allows the intellect's one *ratio* (i.e., its formal concept) of the perfection signified by the name to mediate a demonstration, whether it is being applied to the ontologically prior recipient of the name (which participates in the signified perfection more perfectly) or to the ontologically posterior recipient of the name (which participates in the signified perfection less perfectly).

Among the Thomists considered in this study, Javelli's solution to the Equivocation Problem is perhaps the most unique. Scotus had challenged the defenders of analogy in demonstration to show how anything other than a univocal term could be the foundation for a contradiction and, consequently, a mediating term in a syllogism. Rather than following the example of the Thomists treated in this study and attempting to show that the concept through which the demonstration occurs is itself analogous yet sufficiently one for contradiction and demonstration, Javelli turns his attention to what he takes to be a more fundamental question; namely, the nature of the intellect's first concept and the origins of equivocation, univocity,

---

about an accident. Therefore, it is necessary that a medium [for a syllogism] is a univocal term or an analogous term by the analogy of one *ratio* participated in unequally.)

61. Ibid. See quotation in note above.

and analogy. Having concluded that the intellect's first concept of being is absolute, he proceeds to argue that it is neither univocal, equivocal, nor even analogous considered in itself. Rather, it takes on these features only insofar as its diverse predications are compared to each other. In the case of "being" said across the categories or of names said of God and creatures, the names are said analogously insofar as, when the different predications of the name are compared, the intellect discovers that one analogate depends on another for its possession of the signified perfection. This prompts the intellect to recognize that the diverse recipients of the name possess the *ratio* signified unequally; and the application of the intellect's absolute concept of the perfection is unequal in the two (or more) cases. Still, as the predications are analogous only insofar as one concept applies unequally in two or more cases, it would be a contradiction to affirm and to deny the one (absolute) concept about the same thing.

To use an example from the divine names, there is not one concept of being for divine being and a different concept of being for created being until the intellect has compared the applications of its first concept of being (i.e., being as first known) to divine being and created being. Likewise, there are not different concepts of wisdom for divine wisdom and human wisdom until the intellect has compared its first and absolute concept of wisdom (i.e., wisdom as first known) to how that concept applies to God and how it applies to creatures. Even after this comparison has been made, it would still be a contradiction to affirm and deny about God or about creatures that they have the being or wisdom signified through the intellect's first and absolute concepts of being or wisdom.

CONCLUSION

Cajetan offered a principled semantic answer to the Scotist objection to demonstration with analogous terms, developing the Principle Model approach to the Analogy Model and Equivocation Problems first presented by Sutton, while incorporating the fifteenth-century Thomist "unequal participation" answer to the *Rationes* Problem. Cajetan's younger Dominican contemporaries, Ferrariensis and Javelli, both partially follow and partially reject what they received from Cajetan.

Ferrariensis joins Cajetan in rejecting a truly separate concept predicated analogously of God and creatures. Yet Ferrariensis downplays the significance of proportionality, while he carries out his intention to show that names are said analogously of God and creatures in such a way that the definition of the name as imposed absolutely on God falls in the definition of the name as said of creatures, *contra* Cajetan, Soncinas, Flandrensis, and Capreolus.

Javelli affirms a separate concept and ignores proportionality altogether in his solutions to the three problems. Although Javelli expressly follows Cajetan in rejecting the Healthy Model for the Analogy Model and Equivocation Problems, Javelli's own solution to the Equivocation Problem partially resembles the solution proposed by Hervaeus Natalis on the side of the objective concept insofar as it refers to connection between the analogates themselves. Javelli specifies that the connection between the analogates is one of causal dependency of one analogate on the other. So, although Javelli rejects Healthy Hodel, he still adopts analogy of one to another for his solutions to the Analogy Model and Equivocation Problems. On the side of the formal concept, Javelli's solution imitates Soncinas's. There is one concept numerically for the diverse analogates, just as a numerically one concept signifies univocals. Unlike Soncinas, Javelli directly appeals to his doctrine of being as first known to support his answer to the *Rationes* Problem. Insofar as Javelli's arguments for his understanding of being as first known are derivative from Cajetan, Javelli takes this doctrine in a different direction than the one intended and assented to by his master general.

It is a merit of Ferrariensis's account that it engages many texts from Aquinas himself and a range of views from other Thomists in the tradition, including Cajetan. It is a demerit of Javelli's account that he does not directly engage his disagreement with Cajetan's position, even though he is clearly aware of it. Even granting that, as Tavuzzi has pointed out, Javelli cites Cajetan's earlier work *In De Ente et Essentia* rather than the *De Nominum Analogia*, it is very unlikely that Javelli was unaware that significant figures in Thomism had attempted to solve the problems he addressed by appeal to analogy of proportionality, and it is likewise unlikely that he was unaware of Cajetan's rejection of a separate concept of being as a solution to the *Rationes* Problem. It is beyond the scope of this work to judge whether Javelli's development of Cajetan's doctrine of being as first known is justified.

Conclusion

Etienne Gilson remarked about the history of scholarship on Thomas Aquinas's doctrine of analogy: "Judging from the numerous articles, papers and volumes devoted to this subject, we might easily think that St. Thomas had explained himself at length. But this is not so."[1] Perhaps if Aquinas had dedicated a work directly to analogy and to the problems it gives rise to in logic and science, he would have explicitly addressed the three problems discussed in this study.

In such a work, Aquinas might have told his readers exactly what he meant when he spoke of one *ratio* in analogy and what he meant when he spoke elsewhere of diverse *rationes* in analogy. Perhaps he would even have integrated his distinction between the *ratio* in the intellect and *ratio* in *re* into this discussion. Such a work would have provided a forum for Aquinas to have given his fundamental division of analogy and to have explained the relationship between his various fourfold, threefold, and twofold divisions of analogy. There could have been an article titled "Whether names are said of God and creatures in the way that 'healthy' is said of medicine and an animal," followed by an article titled "Whether names are said of God and creatures in the way that 'principle' is said of a spring, unity, and a point." (I expect the answers to both would be a qualified "yes.") The question containing these articles would have fittingly asked "Whether names said by any modes of analogy cause the fallacy of

---

1. Etienne Gilson, *The Christian Philosophy of Thomas Aquinas*, trans. L. K. Shook (Notre Dame, Ind.: University of Notre Dame Press, 1994), 105.

equivocation" or, perhaps just as fittingly, "Does analogy have unity sufficient to establish a contradiction?"

These questions, however, do not seem to have occurred to Aquinas, or at least not with sufficient urgency for him to have made his own thoughts on the matter as clear as his successors would make theirs. The writings of Scotus forced Aquinas's disciples to search their master's texts for answers to questions he was not considering. On the whole, these Thomists seemed to have come away satisfied that implied answers were there in Aquinas's texts to be found. As this study has shown, however, Aquinas's successors were far from being of one mind about the *mente S. Thomae*.

CHRONOLOGICAL REVIEW

Scotus gave a series of arguments aimed at showing that the key terms of metaphysics and natural theology are predicated univocally, rather than analogously, across the categories and of God and creatures. For Scotus, this means that the names are said through one and the same *ratio* or concept, that the name has sufficient unity to serve as the foundation for a contradiction, and (consequently) that it has sufficient unity to mediate a valid demonstration without generating the fallacy of equivocation. The arguments of Scotus and the Scotists motivated the Thomists to answer the three problems treated in this study more deliberately than Aquinas himself. This study has shown that, in each case, the Thomists' answers to the Equivocation Problem are either products of (or productive of) their answers to the *Rationes* and Analogy Model Problems.

In the case of Hervaeus Natalis, his answers to the *Rationes* and Analogy Model Problems set the limits for his answer to the Equivocation Problem. Natalis rejects a single *ratio* for names said of God and creatures (the *Rationes* Problem), and he only considers the Healthy Model when he takes up names said analogously of God and creatures (the Analogy Model Problem). These answers to the *Rationes* and Analogy Model Problems leave Natalis looking for some feature of the diverse *rationes* of the analogates that would preserve demonstration from one analogate to the other. He proposes that there is something that is the same in each case where a name is said of one by priority, and of another by its reference to the first, but he is unclear on what this same thing may be or why it preserves demonstration from the fallacy of equivocation. If the something that is the same in each case is the *ratio* of the prime analogate, the standard objections to demonstration using analogous terms are left standing—for example, the argument "All simple perfections are in God, and wisdom is a simple perfection; therefore, wisdom is in God," would seem to have the same logical flaws as the argument "All healthy things are alive, and this urine is healthy; therefore, this urine is alive."

Thomas Sutton's doctrine of analogy reverses the order of priority in answering the three problems. He identifies *proportio* (i.e., Principle Model or proportionality) as the only mode of analogy that contains the necessary semantic properties to mediate a demonstration. This observation controls his answer to the Analogy Model Problem. Because names said analogously by the Healthy Model cannot mediate demonstration, but names said by the Principle Model can—and because natural theology demonstrations occur using names analogously—it follows that names are said analogously of God and creatures by the Principle Model of analogy. Insofar as Sutton agrees with Natalis on the answer to the *Rationes* Problem, Sutton maintains that it is precisely the greater unity that obtains between the diverse *rationes* in *proportio* analogy than the unity between *rationes* in the other modes of analogy that grants to *proportio* analogy the semantic properties necessary for demonstration. Sutton writes with greater awareness than Natalis of the objections to demonstration with analogous terms, and Sutton offers those objections a clear and challenging response.

For John Capreolus as well, it is the demands of the logic of demonstration that set the order for answering the three problems. Capreolus is the first of the Thomists to secure demonstration with analogous terms using numerically one *ratio*. Having accepted the arguments of Scotus and others that there really is in some sense a single concept for all terms mediating demonstrations, Capreolus identifies the single concept as the formal concept. A formal concept signified through a name said according to the "third mode" of analogy (i.e., the mode whereby "the analogous term . . . expresses one *ratio* actually in which the analogates are not made equal, and they are not made equal in their *esse* either") properly signifies one analogate and at the same time imperfectly signifies another. To the inequality of representation, there stands a corresponding inequality in the real order (objective) participation in the *ratio*. Because the Healthy Model of analogy necessarily requires diverse formal concepts for its analogates, it cannot serve as the mode of analogy suited for naming God and creatures (the Analogy Model Problem) in a valid demonstration of the divine attributes (the Equivocation Problem). These considerations lead him to adopt *In 1 Sent.*, d. 19, q. 5, a. 2, ad 1, and *De Veritate*, q. 2, a. 11, as the principal texts for expressing the mind of Aquinas on analogy. Capreolus sets a precedent followed by the rest of the Thomists taken up in this study by finding a way to accommodate Scotus's arguments for a single *ratio* of being into his doctrine of analogy. To the extent to which he is able to affirm the unity of the formal and objective concepts of names said analogously of God and creatures and across the categories, Capreolus addresses Scotus's concern that these names be predicated with sufficient unity for contradiction and for mediating a syllogism.

Among the fifteenth-century Thomists, it is most difficult to the see the overall integration between Dominic of Flanders's answers to the three problems. He solves the Equivocation Problem without reference to the Analogy Model Problem. Unlike Capreolus and Sutton, Flandrensis rejects the Healthy Model in the Analogy Model Problem, not because of its implications for the Equivocation Problem, but only to avoid putting the *ratio* of a creature into the *ratio* of God or vice versa. Demonstration can proceed through analogous names because, as in univocity, there is one *ratio* in analogous nam-

Conclusion 185

ing (the *Rationes* Problem). This one *ratio* does not produce univocity because it is unequally participated by an order of prior and posterior signification of the name. He insists that this applies at the level of the categories, which are analogous by the Healthy Model of analogy. Presumably, he maintains the same position for the names said analogously of God and creatures, which are analogous by the Principle/Sight Model of analogy and not by the Healthy Model. Flandrensis goes beyond one of his sources (namely, Natalis) for solving the Equivocation Problem by pointing out a reason why demonstration sometimes fails to proceed in analogy: there can be a difference between the *terminum inferentem* and *terminum illatum*. Unfortunately, like Natalis before him, Flandrensis does not explain why it is that sharing in a *ratio* which signifies one analogate *per prius* and another *per posterius* ever preserves the unity necessary for mediating a demonstration. Consequently, the standard fallacy of equivocation objections to demonstration using analogous terms remain unanswered by Flandrensis.

Paul Soncinas's doctrines are integrated in an explicitly similar way to Capreolus's, with the answer to the Equivocation Problem dictating the answers to the *Rationes* and Analogy Model Problems. Soncinas modifies Capreolus's answer to the *Rationes* Problem by distinguishing and separating the single formal concept in analogy from the proper concepts of the analogates. While Capreolus had defended demonstration with analogous terms on the grounds that the proper formal concept of one analogate imperfectly represents another analogate, Soncinas maintains that the inequality of representation occurs because the intellect possesses a formal concept that is separate from the concepts through which it properly signifies the analogates. By taking this approach, Soncinas proposes an even greater unity for the kind of analogy suited to demonstration than his Thomist predecessors allowed or recognized. If the key terms of metaphysics and natural theology have the unity that Soncinas attributes to them—which is to say that if Soncinas's solutions to the *Rationes* and Analogy Model Problems are sound—then he at least satisfies the standard lines of objection to demonstration using analogous terms (the Equivocation Problem).

Thomas de Vio Cajetan produced the most thoroughly integrated answers to the three problems. His introduction to the modes of analogy using Aquinas's *In 1 Sent.*, d. 19, indicates continuity with Capreolus and Soncinas in making the answer to the Equivocation Problem the primary point of reference for answering the *Rationes* and Analogy Model Problems. Like Sutton, Cajetan finds that analogy of proportionality has the semantic features closest to univocity among the modes of analogy, and that these features make proportionality the uniquely suited mode of analogy for predicating names of God and creatures and mediating demonstrations in metaphysics and natural theology (the Analogy Model and Equivocation Problems). He differs from Sutton by maintaining that, in analogy of proportionality, the *ratio* proper to one analogate is imperfectly the *ratio* of the other analogate (the *Rationes* Problem). If Sutton gives a satisfying response to the Equivocation Problem, then Cajetan's answer is more satisfying yet.

Francis Silvestri of Ferrara developed a hybrid of the earlier Thomist positions, with Cajetan's position serving as the primary point of reference. Contrary to his fifteenth-century Thomist predecessors but like Natalis, Ferrariensis gives primacy to the Healthy Model in his answer to the Analogy Model Problem. He avoids the issues with this model observed by the likes of Sutton, Capreolus, Soncinas, and Cajetan by distinguishing between three different impositions of a name. According to Ferrariensis names are said analogously of God and creatures according to the Healthy Model when they are imposed to signify the presence of a perfection in a creature specifically as derivative from the creator. But this (third and) analogous imposition of the name occurs only after demonstration has shown that the name that was first imposed on creatures can also be imposed on God. As the Healthy Model analogy occurs only posterior to demonstration, it is no obstacle to accounting for demonstration using analogous terms (the Equivocation Problem). Fer-

TABLE 6. Thomists on the Three Problems

Author	Rationes Problem	Analogy Model Problem	Equivocation Problem
Hervaeus Natalis	Many *rationes*	Healthy Model	There is something the same in each analogate
Thomas Sutton	Many *rationes*	Principle Model	Proportional unity is sufficiently close to univocal unity
John Capreolus	One *ratio* by unequal participation	Principle Model	Unequal participation in a perfectly one formal concept proper to one of the analogates
Dominic of Flanders (Flandrensis)	One *ratio* diversely participated	Principle Model	Diverse participation in a *ratio* which signifies one analogate *per prius* and another analogate *per posterius*
Paul Soncinas	One separate formal *ratio* and one disjunctive objective *ratio*	Not the Healthy Model	Unequal participation in a formal concept which is separate from the proper concepts of the analogates
Thomas de Vio Cajetan	Many *rationes* are proportionally identical	Principle Model	The proportional identity between the analogates is signified through the formal concept proper to one of the analogates
Francis Silvestri of Ferrara (Ferrariensis)	Many *rationes* are proportionally identical	Healthy Model for third imposition, but not for the first or second imposition	Proportional identity between objects of the first and second imposition of the name represented in a nonseparate formal concept
Chrysostom Javelli	One separate formal *ratio* unequally participated	Not the Healthy Model	Unequal participation in a formal concept which is separate from the proper concepts of analogates, where one analogate is causally dependent on the other analogate

rariensis shows continuity with Cajetan's answers to the *Rationes* and Analogy Model Problems by maintaining that there is proportional unity between the objects of the first and second impositions of a name, and that this proportionality can be signified by a single, nonseparate formal concept. I have argued that, although Ferrariensis does not specifically address the Equivocation Problem, his answers to the *Rationes* and Analogy Model Problems are consistent with a Cajetanian answer to the Equivocation Problem, and I justified this approach through Ferrariensis's own referral of his readers to Cajetan's work for answers to problems about analogy that he does not address.

Chrysostom Javelli provides an alternative to Cajetan's development of Capreolus and Soncinas. Like Cajetan, Javelli opens his treatment of the topic with Aquinas's *In 1 Sent.*, d. 19, threefold division of analogy. As Capreolus, Soncinas, and Cajetan had done before him, Javelli observes that the third mode of analogy possesses the specific semantic attributes that permit demonstration through a logically (and metaphysically) analogous term, that is, one *ratio* participated in unequally. Uniquely among these Thomists, Javelli integrates his understanding of being as first known into his doctrine of names said analogously across the categories and of God and creatures. This leads him, *contra* Cajetan, to embrace Soncinas's separate *ratio* answer to the *Rationes* Problem. To the extent that Javelli's answers are like Soncinas's, they share in the merits and demerits of Soncinas's answers. Insofar as Javelli explicitly links his answers to a wider set of issues than Soncinas does, Javelli either exceeds or falls short of his predecessor, depending on whether he rightly or mistakenly joined these issues.

ASSESSMENT

It may be asked fairly which one of these Thomists produces a doctrine that is closest to the writings of Aquinas. While I refrain from making a firm judgment on the question, I think it is likely that the answer would be Natalis and Flandrensis. Very little of what these authors say regarding the three problems cannot be found written by Aquinas himself. What they say explicitly (and which Aquinas leaves unsaid) is that there is "something the same" and "no deception" in some cases of demonstration through terms signifying *per prius et posterius*. Like Aquinas, they do not explain what it is about analogous terms that allows deception and fallacy of equivocation to occur in some cases of demonstration with analogous terms but not in the particular demonstrations relevant to metaphysics and natural theology, and they are blind to any issues with the Healthy Model of analogy for the logic of demonstration. Flandrensis's overall account is superior to Natalis's insofar as Flandrensis attempts to address more of Aquinas's texts on analogy (including *De Veritate*, q. 2, a. 11).

I hope, however, that the history related in this book has indicated that answering questions *ad literam vel ad mentem Thomae* is not the only measure of the quality of an author's Thomism. To the extent that Aquinas himself in fact said too little on the questions to resolve them, he left to his successors the task of developing answers which he may not himself have anticipated in his own works. And Aquinas did leave unresolved issues when he affirmed that analogous terms can mediate valid demonstrations because they are between univocity and pure equivocation, despite the fact that the second species of the fallacy of equivocation applies to terms that fall between univocity and pure equivocation. To resolve such issues, Thomists could draw from Aquinas, but they could not limit themselves to answering from his own words.

The Thomists who were more selective in drawing from what Aquinas himself said, or who even added distinctions never explicitly made by Aquinas himself, provided the more satisfactory defenses of Aquinas's metaphysics. A prime example of this is seen as early as the first decade of the fourteenth century in the difference between Natalis and Sutton over the Analogy Model Problem. Arguably, in his rejection the Healthy Model in favor of the Principle Model, Sutton is the Thomist who is less faithful to at least the majority of Aquinas's passages addressing names said of God and creatures. Nonetheless, as has been illustrated through this study, Sutton found in the Principle Model of analogy a semantic foundation for solving the Equivocation Problem. By contrast, the Healthy Model provides the prime example of the second species of the fallacy of equivocation ("Everything healthy is alive, medicine [or urine, or food] is healthy; therefore, medicine [or urine, or food] is alive"). In the absence of some careful qualifications about how the Healthy Model can apply to names said analogously of God and creatures (such as the qualifications provided by Ferrariensis), its use for explaining Aquinas's doctrine of analogy appears to leave that doctrine open to devastating criticism. Appeal to the proportional unity illustrated by the Principle Model of analogy at the very least requires a counterargument from a critic of demonstration using analogous terms, and it directly challenges Scotist critics insofar as Scotus himself acknowledges proportional unity.[2]

The fifteenth- and sixteenth-century Thomists' *una ratio* answers to the *Rationes* Problem are arguably less in keeping with the majority (and the most mature writings) of Aquinas than the fourteenth-century Thomists' *diversae rationes* answers. The *una ratio* answers certainly grant more to Scotus, and they compel the Thomists to redefine univocity in a way that is at best implied by Aquinas's remarks in *In 1 Sent.*, d. 19, q. 5, a. 2, ad 1. Accordingly, this passage from the beginning of Aquinas's corpus takes on greater significance for these Thomists than it perhaps deserves in light of his subsequent writings. But as we have seen, the fifteenth- and sixteenth-century Thomists illustrated a variety of ways in which they could affirm the diversity of analogates' proper *rationes* while at the same time maintaining that, in some sense, the analogates share in one *ratio*. This approach allows them to draw on the qualified unity of *ratio* between analogates when faced with Scotist objections, including the Equivocation Problem.

2. See the references on p. 59n61. I hope in the future to engage texts by later Scotists attempting such counterarguments. I am currently interested in the arguments of the seventeenth-century Scotist Bartholomaeus Mastrius, contained in his *Disputationes ad mentem Scoti in duodicem Aristotelis Stagiritae Libros Metaphysicorum*, disputatio secunda, "De Natura entis."

Conclusion

So, are there one or many *rationes* involved in analogous naming? What kind or kinds of analogy are used in metaphysics and natural theology? Which semantic attribute or attributes allow demonstration through analogous terms? Is there only one mode of analogy that possesses these semantic features? I believe that the way forward within the Thomist tradition on these questions involves exploring the formation and development of concepts, beginning with the initial abstraction of concepts from phantasms and proceeding through the development of concepts by the possible intellect.

If, by Aquinas's account, the initial concept abstracted from the phantasms is numerically distinct from concepts that the intellect develops and applies later to some of the same things, then perhaps Aquinas really does provide grounds for affirming a separate first concept of the sort described by Soncinas and Javelli.[3] If not, then at least one proposed route to answering these questions from Aquinas's own principles could be ruled out. Examination of the varied acts that the intellect performs to refine its concepts and compare its judgments should uncover the diverse modes of analogy, including which mode or modes apply in one context or another to names said across the categories or of God and creatures. In short, the path to a Thomist solution to the three problems considered in this study lies through Aquinas's texts on the operations on the intellect. In themselves, these texts are no less challenging than his texts on analogy. However, because they address the prior questions to the questions about analogy, solutions to problems in analogy, including solutions *ad literam et mentem Thomae*, must proceed through them.

---

3. Take Aristotle's example of children calling all men "father." The child's first concept of father is presumably in some respects different from the concept that the same child has later when he or she no longer calls all men "father." Furthermore, the concept through which the child calls some men "father" (e.g., priests, founders, etc.) seems to be different in some respect from the one through which the child calls only one man "father" (e.g., the child's biological father or foster father). How many concepts really are involved in these different predications? Has the child developed new concepts of "father," or is the child simply using the original concept differently? Is the original concept separate from the concept or concepts developed or used later?

Selected Bibliography

PRIMARY SOURCES

Anicii Manlii Severini Boethius. *In Categorias Aristotelis.* PL 64. Paris, 1891.

Aristotle. *The Complete Works of Aristotle: The Revised Oxford Translation.* Edited by Jonathan Barnes. Translated by R. P. Hardie and R. K. Gaye. 2 volumes. Bollingen Series LXXI. Princeton, N.J.: Princeton University Press, 1984.

Avicenna. *The Metaphysics of The Healing.* Translated by Michael E. Marmura. Provo, Utah: Brigham Young University Press, 2005.

Chrysostom Iavellus. *De Transcendentibus.* In *Epitome Chrysostomi Javelli Canapitii Ord. Praedicatorum, in universam Aristotelis philosophiam, tam naturalem, quam transnaturalem.* Venice, 1567.

———. *In Logicam Aristotelis.* Lyon, 1555.

———. *Quaestiones, In Metaphysicam Aristotelis: Ab innumeris mendis repurgatae & in gratiam Philosophiae studiosorum denuo editae Accessit in hac editione, Tractatus de natura Metaphysices ex Epitome Metaphysica eiusdem autoris huc translatus, & duplex Index* [...]. Wittenberg: Selfischius, 1609.

———. *Super tres libros Aristotelis de Anima.* Venice, 1568.

Dominic of Flanders. *In Diui Thomae Aquinatis fallaciarum opus perutiles quaestiones.* In *In D. Thomae Aquinatis Commentaria Super Libris Posteriorum Analyticorum Aristotelis, Quaestiones Perutiles.* Venice, 1587.

———. *In duodecim libros Metaphysicae Aristotelis, secundum expositionem eiusdem Angelici Doctoris, lucidissimae atque utilissimae quaestiones.* Cologne: Ordo, 1621.

Francis Silvestri of Ferrara. *Commentaria Ferrariensis.* In *Omnia Opera,* vol. 13. Rome: Leonine Commission, 1882–.

———. *Summa contra Gentiles, quatuor libris comprehensa: commentariis ... Francisci de Sylvestris, Ferrariensis ... illustrata.* Paris, 1552.

Henry of Ghent. *Summa questionum ordinarium.* In *Henry of Ghent's Summa: the questions on God's existence and essence (articles 21–24)*, translated by Jos Decorte and Roland J. Teske. Leuven: Peeters, 2005.

Henry of Harclay. *Questiones Ordinariae*. In *Henry of Harclay: Ordinary Questions I–XIV, XV–XXIX*, Auctores Britannici Medii Aevi, edited by M. Henninger, translated by R. Edwards and M. Henninger. 2 volumes. Oxford: Oxford University Press, 2010.

Hervaeus Natalis. *Quolibeta Heruei: subtillissima Heruei Natalis Britonis.* Venice, 1513; reprinted in Ridgewood, N.J.: Gregg, 1966.

Johannes Versor. *Quaestiones super metaphysicam Aristotelis.* Cologne, 1494; reprinted in Frankfurt am Main: Minerva GmbH, 1967.

John Capreolus. *Defensiones Theologiae Divi Thomae Aquinatis.* Edited by Ceslaus Paban and Thomas Pegues. 7 volumes. Tours: Alfred Cattier, 1900–1908; reprinted in Frankfurt: Minerva GmbH, 1967.

John Duns Scotus. *Opera Omnia.* Paris: Vives, 1891.

———. *Opera Omnia.* Edited by the Scotistic Commission. Vatican City: Typis Polyglottis Vaticanis, 1950–.

———. *Opera Philosophica.* Edited by R. Andrews, G. Etzkorn, G. Gal, R. Green, F. Kelley, G. Marcil, T. Noone, and R. Wood. St. Bonaventure, N.Y.: Franciscan Institute, 1997.

Paulus Soncinas. *Elegantissima Expositio Super Artem.* Venice, 1499.

———. *Pauli Soncinatis ordinis praedicatorum, Quæstiones metaphysicales acutissimæ: nunc demum summo studio, et accuratius quàm antehac vnquam castigatæ, repurgatæ, & multis in locis illustratæ. Cum triplici earum indice, quorum primus, quæstionum titulos promiscuè: secundus, ad hos, iuxta librorum & alphabeti seriem simul materiam: tertius verò digna notatu circa hæc omnia, demonstrat.* Lyon: Sumptibus Petri Landry, 1579.

Peter of Spain. *Tractatus* (or *Summule Logicales*). Edited by L. M. de Rijk. Assen: Van Gorcum, 1972.

Petrus Aureoli. *Commentariorum in Primum Librum Sententiarum.* Rome: Vaticana, 1596.

———. "Petrus Aureoli: De unitate conceptus entis (Reportatio Parisiensis in I Sententiarum, dist. 2, p. 1, qq. 1–3 et p. 2, qq. 1–2)." *Traditio* 50 (1995): 199–248.

Petrus Fonseca. *Commentariorvm In Libros Metaphysicorvm Aristotelis Stagiritae.* Frankfurt, 1599.

Silvestro Mazzolini. *Conflatum ex S. Thoma.* Perugia, 1519.

Thomas Anglicus. *Contra Joannem Scotum primo sententiarum libro.* Venice: Erven Octavianus Scotus, 1523.

Thomas Aquinas. *De Fallaciis.* In *Opuscula Philosophica.* Edited by R. M. Spiazzi. Turin: Marietti, 1954.

———. *In Aristotelis Libros Peri Hermeneias et Posteriorum Analyticorum Expositio.* Edited by R. M. Spiazzi. Second edition. Turin: Marietti, 1964.

———. *In Duodecim Libros Metaphysicorum Aristotelis Expositio.* Edited by R. M. Spiazzi. Turin: Marietti, 1950.

———. *Quaestiones Disputatae de Potentia.* Edited by R. P. Pauli and M. Pession. Turin: Marietti, 1965.

Selected Bibliography 195

———. *Sancti Thomae de Aquino Opera omnia*. Rome: Leonine Commission, 1882–.

———. *Scriptum super libros Sententiarum*. Edited by P. Mandonnet and M. F. Moss. 4 volumes. Paris: Lethielleux, 1929–47.

Thomas de Vio Cajetan. *De Nominum Analogia* and *Responsio super duo quaestio De Conceptu Entis ad Fr. Franciscum de Ferraria*. In *Scripta Philosophica*, edited by P. N. Zammit. Rome: Angelicum, 1934.

———. *In Primam Partem*. In *Opera Omnia*, vol. 4. Rome: Leonine Commission, 1882–.

———. *Thomae de Vio Caietani Cardinalis Titvlis Sixti, In Praedicabilia Porphyrij, Praedicamenta, Postpraedicamenta, et libros Posteriorvm Analyticorvm Aristotelis castigatissima Commentaria Accesserunt praeterea eiusdem R. Cardinalis doctissima in D. Thomae Aquinatis librum de Ente, et Essentia*. Lyon, 1578.

Thomas Sutton. *Quaestiones Ordinariae*. In *Zur Diskussion uber das Problem der Univozitat in Umkreis des Johannes Duns Skotus*, edited by Michael Schmaus. Munich: Bayerische Akademie der Wissenschaften, 1957.

———. *Quodlibeta*. Edited by Michael Schmaus. Munich: Bayerische Akademie der Wissenschaften, 1969.

SECONDARY SOURCES

Anderson, James F. *The Bond of Being: An Essay on Analogy and Existence*. St. Louis, Mo.: Herder, 1949.

Ashworth, E. J. "Signification and Modes of Signifying in Thirteenth-Century Logic: A Preface to Aquinas on Analogy." *Medieval Philosophy and Theology* 1 (1991): 39–67.

———. "Analogical Concepts: The Fourteenth-Century Background to Cajetan." *Dialogue: Canadian Philosophical Review* 31 (1992): 399–413.

———. "Analogy and Equivocation in Thirteenth-Century Logic: Aquinas in Context." *Mediaeval Studies* 54 (1992): 94–135.

———. "Suárez on the Analogy of Being: Some Historical Background." *Vivarium* 33 (1995): 50–75.

———. "Analogy, Univocation, and Equivocation in Some Early Fourteeth-Century Authors." In *Aristotle in Britain during the Middle Ages*, edited by John Marenbon, 233–47. Turnhout: Brepols, 1996.

———. "Analogy and equivocation in Thomas Sutton O.P." In *Vestigia, Imagines, Verba: Semiotics and Logic in Medieval Theological Texts (XIIth–XIV Century). Acts of the XIth Symposium on Medieval logic and semantics. San Marino, 24–28 May 1994*, edited by Marmo Costantino, 289–303. Turnhout: Brepols, 1997.

———. "Petrus Fonseca on Objective Concepts and the Analogy of Being." In *Logic and the Workings of the Mind: The Logic of Ideas and Faculty Psychology in Early Modern Philosophy*, edited by Easton Patricia, 47–63. Atascadero: Ridgeview, 1997.

———. "Antonius Rubius on Objective Being and Analogy: One of the Routes from Early Fourteenth-Century Discussions to Descartes' Third Meditation." In *Meetings of the Minds. The Relation between Medieval and Classical Modern European Philosophy*, edited by Stephen F. Brown, 43–62. Turnhout: Brepols, 1998.

———. "Metaphor and the Logicians from Aristotle to Cajetan." *Vivarium* 45 (2007): 311–27.

———. *Les theories de l'analogie du XIIe au XVIe siecle*. Paris: Vrin, 2008.

———. "Medieval Theories of Analogy." *Stanford Encyclopedia of Philosophy*, 2013. Available at plato.stanford.edu/entries/analogy-medieval/#3.

Bonino, S.-T. "Le concept d'étant et la connaissance de Dieu d'après Jean Cabrol (Capreolus)." *Revue Thomiste* 95 (1995): 109–36.

Boulnois, Olivier. "Duns Scot, Theoricien De L'Analogie de L'Etre." In *John Duns Scotus, Metaphysics and Ethics*, edited by L. Honnefelder, R. Wood, and M. Dreyer, 293–315. Leiden: Brill, 1996.

Brown, Stephen. "The Unity of the Concept of Being in Peter Aureoli's Scriptum and Commentarium (with a critical edition of the Commentarium text)." PhD diss., University of Louvain, 1964.

———. "Scotus's Univocity in the Fourteenth Century." *De doctrina Ioannis Duns Scoti: Acta Congressus Scotistici Internationalis*, 35–41. Rome: Scotist Commission, 1968.

Cesario, Romanus. *A Short History of Thomism*. Washington, D.C.: The Catholic University of America Press, 2005.

Clarke, Norris. "Analogy and the Meaningfulness of Language about God." In his *Explorations in Metaphysics: Being–God–Person*. Notre Dame, Ind.: University of Notre Dame Press, 1994.

Conti, Alessandro D. "La composizione metafisica dell'ente finito corporeo nell'ontologia di Tommaso Sutton." *Documenti e studi sulla tradizione filosofica medievale* 2 (1991): 317–60.

Cross, Richard. *Duns Scotus*. Cary, N.C.: Oxford University Press, 1999.

———. "Univocity and Mystery." In *New Essays on Metaphysics as Scientia Transcendens*, edited by R. H. Pich, 115–44. Textes Et Etudes Du Moyen Âge 43. Louvain-La-Neuve: Fédération Internationale des Instituts d'Études Médiévales, 2007.

———. "Duns Scotus and Analogy: A Brief Note." *The Modern Schoolman* 89 (2012): 147–54.

D'Ettore, Domenic. "John Capreolus on Names said Analogously of God and Creatures." *The Thomist* 77 (2013): 395–418.

———. "The Fifteenth-Century Thomist Dispute Over Participation in an Analogous Concept: John Capreolus, Dominic of Flanders, and Paul Soncinas." *Mediaeval Studies* 76 (2014): 241–73.

———. "The Semantic Unity of the Analogous Concept according to John Capreolus." In *Maimonides on God and Duns Scotus on Logic and Metaphysics (Volume 12: Proceedings of the Society of Medieval Logic and Metaphysics)*, edited by Gyula Klima and Alexander W. Hall, 133–54. Newcastle upon Tyne: Cambridge Scholars Publishing, 2015.

———. "A Thomist Re-consideration of the Subject Matter of Metaphysics: Chrysostom Iavelli on What Is Included in Being as Being." *Proceedings of the American Catholic Philosophical Association* 89 (2015): 209–23.

———. "'Not a Little Confusing': Francis Silvestri of Ferrara's Hybrid Thomist Doctrine of Analogy." *American Catholic Philosophical Quarterly* 90 (2016): 101–23.

———. "Some Renaissance Thomists on Analogy in Demonstration." *Angelicum* 93 (2016): 927–50.

———. "Thomas Sutton's Doctrine of Analogy: Revisiting a Continuator of Thomas Aquinas." *Nova et Vetera* (English Edition) 14 (2016): 831–52.

———. "Dominic of Flanders' Critique of John Duns Scotus's Primary Argument for the Univocity of Being." *Vivarium* 56 (2018, forthcoming).

———. "One Is in the Definition of All: The Renaissance Thomist Controversy over a 'Rule' for Names Said by Analogy." *The Thomist* 82 (2018, forthcoming).

De Boni, Luis Alberto. "Duns Scotus and the Univocity of the Concept of Being." In *New Essays on Metaphysics as Scientia Transcendens*, edited by Roberto Hofmeister Pich, 91–114. Textes et Etudes du Moyen Âge 43. Louvain-La-Neuve: Fédération Internationale des Instituts d'Études Médiévales, 2007.

Decorte, Jos. "Henry of Ghent on Analogy: Critical Reflections on Jean Paulus." In *Henry of Ghent: Proceedings of the International Colloquium on the Occasion of the 700th Anniversary of His Death (1293)*, edited by W. Vanhamel, 71–105. Leuven: Leuven University Press, 1996.

Dewan, Lawrence. "Does Being Have a Nature? (Or: Metaphysics as a Science of the Real)." In *Approaches to Metaphysics*, edited by William Sweet, 23–59. Dordrecht: Kluwer, 2004.

Dondaine, Antoine. "Saint Thomas et la dispute des attributs divins (I Sent., d. 2, a. 3): authenticité et origine." *Archivum Fratrum Praedicatorum* 8 (1938): 253–62.

Dreyer, Mechtild, and Mary Beth Ingham. *Philosophical Vision of John Duns Scotus: An Introduction*. Washington, D.C.: The Catholic University of America Press, 2004.

Dumont, Stephen. "The Univocal Concept of Being in the Fourteenth Century: I. John Duns Scotus and William of Alnwick." *Mediaeval Studies* 49 (1987): 1–75.

———. "Transcendental Being: Scotus and the Scotists." *Topoi* 11 (1992): 135–48.

———. "John Duns Scotus." In *A Companion to Philosophy in the Middle Ages*, edited by Jorge Gracia and Timothy Noone, 353–69. Malden, Mass.: Blackwell, 2006.

Fabro, Cornelio. *Participation et causalite selon S. Thomas d'Aquin*. Louvain: Publications universitaires de Louvain, 1961.

Gilson, Etienne. "Avicenne et le point de départ de Duns Scot." *Archives d'Histoire doctrinale et littéraire du Moyen Age* 2 (1927): 89–150.

———. *Jean Duns Scot: Introduction à ses positions fondamentales*. Paris: J. Vrin, 1952.

———. *The Christian Philosophy of Thomas Aquinas*. Translated by L. K. Shook. Notre Dame, Ind.: University of Notre Dame Press, 1994.

Goris, Wouter. "Implicit Knowledge: Being as First Known in Peter of Oriel." *Recherches de Theologie et Philosophie Medievales* 69 (2002): 33–65.

Hall, Alexander. "Confused Univocity." *Proceedings of the Society for Medieval Logic and Metaphysics* 7 (2007): 18–31.

———. *Thomas Aquinas and John Duns Scotus: Natural Theology in the High Middle Ages*. Continuum Studies in Philosophy. London: Continuum, 2007.

Heider, Daniel. "Suárez and Javelli on Transcendentals and Divisions of Being." In *Universalità della ragione: pluralità delle filosofie nel Medioevo: XII Congresso internazionale di filosofia medievale, Palermo, 17–22 settembre 2007*, edited by Alessandro Musco, 2.2:849–60. 3 volumes. Palermo: Officina di studi medievali, 2012.

Henninger, Mark G. "Henry of Harclay." In *A Companion to Philosophy in the Middle Ages*, edited by Jorge Gracia and Timothy Noone, 305–13. Malden, Mass.: Blackwell, 2006.

———. "Thomas Sutton on Univocation, Equivocation, and Analogy." *The Thomist* 70 (2006): 537–75.

Hochschild, Joshua. "Did Aquinas Answer Cajetan's Question? Aquinas's Semantic Rules for Analogy and the Interpretation of De Nominum Analogia." *Proceedings of the American Catholic Philosophical Association* 77 (2003): 273–88.

———. *The Semantics of Analogy: Rereading Cajetan's De Nominum Analogia*. Notre Dame, Ind.: University of Notre Dame Press, 2010.

———. "Proportionality and Divine Naming: Did St. Thomas Change His Mind About Analogy?" *The Thomist* 77 (2013): 531–58.

Irwin, Terence H. *Aristotle's First Principles*. Oxford: Clarendon Press, 2002.

Jindráček, Efrem. "Soncino, Paulo Barbo." In *Encyclopedia of Renaissance Philosophy*. Springer International Publishing Switzerland, 2015.

Kappes, Christiaan W. *The Immaculate Conception: Why Thomas Aquinas Denied, while John Duns Scotus, Gregory of Palamas, and Mark Eugenicus Professed the Absolute Immaculate Existence of Mary*. Bedford, Mass.: Academy of the Immaculate, 2014.

Klima, Gyula. "The Semantic Principles underlying Saint Thomas Aquinas's Metaphysics of Being." *Medieval Philosophy and Theology* 5 (1996): 87–141.

———. "Peter of Spain." In *A Companion to Philosophy in the Middle Ages*, edited by Jorge Gracia and Timothy Noone, 526–31. Malden, Mass.: Blackwell, 2006.

———. "Thomas of Sutton." In *A Companion to Philosophy in the Middle Ages*, edited by Jorge Gracia and Timothy Noone, 664–65. Malden, Mass.: Blackwell, 2006.

Selected Bibliography 199

Klubertanz, George P. *St. Thomas Aquinas on Analogy: A Textual Analysis and Systematic Synthesis*. Chicago: Loyola University Press, 1960.

Krempel, Anton. *La Doctrine de la Relation chez Saint Thomas: Exposé historique et systématique*. Paris: J. Vrin, 1952.

Lauge, O. Nielsen. "Peter Auriol." In *A Companion to Philosophy in the Middle Ages*, edited by Jorge Gracia and Timothy Noone, 494–503. Malden, Mass.: Blackwell, 2006.

Livesey, Steven J. *Antonius de Carlenis, O.P.: Four Questions on the Subalternation of Sciences*. Transactions of the American Philosophical Society 84.4. Philadelphia: American Philosophical Society, 1994.

Lohr, Charles H. "Renaissance Latin Aristotle Commentaries: Authors C." *Renaissance Quarterly* 28 (1975): 689–741.

———. "Renaissance Latin Aristotle Commentaries: Authors G–K." *Renaissance Quarterly* 30 (1977): 681–741.

Mahieu, Léon. *Dominique de Flandre (XVe siècle) sa métaphysique*. Paris: J. Vrin, 1942.

Maurer, Armand. "Henry of Harclay's Question on the Univocity of Being." In his *Being and Knowing: Studies in Thomas Aquinas and Later Medieval Philosophers*, 203–28. Toronto: Pontifical Institute of Mediaeval Studies, 1990.

———. "St. Thomas and the Analogy of Genus." In his *Being and Knowing: Studies in Thomas Aquinas and Later Medieval Philosophers*, 19–32. Toronto: Pontifical Institute of Mediaeval Studies, 1990.

McInerny, Ralph. "Scotus and Univocity." In *De doctrina Ioannis Duns Scoti: Acta Congressus Scotistici Internationalis Oxonii et Edimburgi 11–17 sept. 1966 celebrati*, 115–22. Rome: Commissio Scotisticae, 1968.

———. *Aquinas and Analogy*. Washington, D.C.: The Catholic University of America Press, 1996.

Montagnes, Bernard. *The Doctrine of the Analogy of Being according to Thomas Aquinas*. Translated by E. M. Macierowski. Edited by Andrew Tallon. Milwaukee, Wis.: Marquette University Press, 2004.

Pasnau, Robert. "Cognition." In *The Cambridge Companion to Duns Scotus*, edited by Thomas Williams, 285–311. Cambridge: Cambridge University Press, 2003.

Pelster, Franz. "Thomas von Sutton O. Pr., ein Oxforder Verteidiger der thomistischen Lehre." *Zeitschrift für kath. Theol.* 46 (1922): 361–401.

Pini, Giorgio. "Species, Concept, and Thing: Theories of Signification in the Second Half of the Thirteenth Century." *Medieval Philosophy and Theology* 8 (1999): 21–52.

Przezdziecki, Joseph J. "Thomas of Sutton's Critique of the Doctrine of Univocity." In *An Etienne Gilson Tribute*, edited by Charles O'Neil, 189–208. Milwaukee, Wis.: Marquette University Press, 1959.

Ramirez, Santiago. *De Analogia*. In *Opera Omnia*. 4 volumes. Madrid: Instituto de Filosofia "Luis Vives," 1970–72.

Riva, Franco. "L'Analogia Dell'ente in Domenico di Fiandra." *Rivista di Filosofia Neo-Scolastica* 86 (1994): 287–322.

———. *Analogia e univocità in Tommaso de Vio "Gaetano."* Milan: Vita e Pensiero, 1995.
Roensch, Frederick. *Early Thomistic School.* Dubuque, Iowa: Priory Press, 1964.
Ross, J. F. *Portraying Analogy.* Cambridge: Cambridge University Press, 1981.
Rutten, Pepijin. "'*Secundum processum et mentem Versoris*': John Versor and His Relation to the Schools of Thought Reconsidered." *Vivarium* 43 (2005): 292–329.
Simon, Yves R. "Order in Analogical Sets." In *Philosopher at Work: Essays by Yves R. Simon*, ed. Anthony O. Simon, 135–71. Lanham, Md.: Rowman and Littlefield, 1999.
Tavuzzi, Michael. "Hervaeus Natalis and the Philosophical Logic of the Thomism of the Renaissance." *Doctor Communis* 45 (1992): 132–52.
———. "Some Renaissance Divisions of Analogy." *Angelicum* 70 (1993): 93–121.
———. *Prierias: The Life and Works of Silvestro Mazzolini da Prierio, 1456–1527.* Durham, N.C.: Duke University Press, 1997.
———. "Silvestri, Francesco (1474–1528)." *Concise Routledge Encyclopedia of Philosophy.* London: Routledge, 2000.
———. *Renaissance Inquisitors: Dominican Inquisitors and Inquisitorial Districts in Northern Italy, 1474–1527.* Studies in the History of Christian Traditions 134. Leiden: Brill, 2007.
Teske, Ronald J. "Hervaeus Natalis." In *A Companion to Philosophy in the Middle Ages*, edited by Jorge Gracia and Timothy Noone, 314–15. Malden, Mass.: Blackwell, 2006.
Torrell, J. P. *Saint Thomas Aquinas, Volume 1: The Person and His Work.* Revised edition. Translated by Robert Royal. Washington, D.C.: The Catholic University of America Press, 2005.
van der Lecq, Ria. "Logic and Theories of Meaning in the Late 13th and Early 14th Century Including the Modistae." In *Mediaeval and Renaissance Logic*, edited by Dov M. Gabbay and John Woods, 2:347–88. Amsterdam: North Holland, 2007.
Wielockx, Robert. "Henry of Ghent." In *A Companion to Philosophy in the Middle Ages*, edited by Jorge Gracia and Timothy Noone, 296–304. Malden, Mass.: Blackwell, 2006.
Wippel, John. *The Metaphysical Thought of Thomas Aquinas: From Finite Being to Uncreated Being.* Monographs for the Society for Medieval and Renaissance Philosophy 1. Washington, D.C.: The Catholic University of America Press, 2000.

Index

abstraction, act of, 27n18, 35, 40, 73, 85, 104n28, 112, 150, 152, 156, 191. *See also* categories of being

accident, categories of, 15, 35–37, 41, 43–44, 46, 52, 62n14, 68–69, 70n16, 74n26, 78, 90–91, 96n12, 97, 99–100, 103n26, 108–9, 111–17, 124, 128–30, 133–34, 152, 154, 162, 167–70, 174–77

agreement: between analogates, 104, 129; analogous, 30; generic, 48; of proportion (*proportio*) or proportionality, 48, 57, 104, 129, 155n15, 157; univocal, 20, 30, 57

Analogous. *See* analogy

Analogy: *ab uno*, 3–4, 47, 49, 55, 95t3; *ad unum*, 3–4, 7, 47, 49, 51–52, 55, 69, 86, 95t3, 107n33, 166, 172; of attribution, 9, 52, 70n16, 79–80, 100n22, 172n51; properly speaking, 47; *proportio* or proportionality, 3–4, 9, 15, 34, 47–53, 55–60, 81–82, 84–87, 93–95, 101, 103–8, 112n44, 121–22, 127–30, 135, 138, 141–43, 145n2, 158–61, 172n51, 175, 179–80, 183, 186–87; semantics of, 1, 17, 26, 30–32, 41–42, 55, 75n27, 77, 100, 121, 124, 127, 141–42, 178, 183, 186, 188, 190–91; *similitudo*, 3–4, 47–48, 50, 53, 55. *See also* Analogy Model Problem; demonstration; equivocation; Healthy Model; Henry of Ghent; participation in *ratio*; Principle Model; *ratio*; *Rationes* Problem;

Scotus; univocation; and *individual Thomists by name*

Analogy Model Problem, 10, 13–17, 31, 33, 35, 37, 39, 46, 58–63, 78, 80–81, 85–86, 88–90, 102, 108–9, 111, 117–18, 125–30, 141–43, 145n2, 146, 156–57, 159, 161–62, 164, 166, 171, 178–79, 182–89. *See also* Scotus; and *individual Thomists by name*

Anderson, James F., 55n54

Antonius Andreas, 59n61

Antonius de Carlensis, 97n13

Aquinas. *See* Thomas Aquinas

Aristotle, 7, 28, 63n3, 73, 104, 109, 149, 164, 191n3; on analogy, univocation, and equivocation, 2–4, 10n23, 45, 66t2; *Categories*, 3–4, 19n3, 45, 47, 64, 167; on demonstrative science, 4–5, 31; *De Interpretatione*, 2n1; *Metaphysics*, 4, 5n8, 16–17, 47, 57–59, 90, 109, 111; *Nicomachean Ethics*, 9, 94n8; *Parts of Animals*, 137n26; *Physics*, 48; *Posterior Analytics*, 4, 59, 137n26; *Topics*, 103n26

Ashworth, E. J., 2n1, 3n2, 5n10, 12n28, 13–14, 28, 33–34, 45n25, 46, 48n33, 50n45, 52–53, 67n14, 98n18, 100n22, 111n42, 131n11–12

Auriol, Peter. *See* Peter Auriol

Averroes, 166

Avicenna, 149, 170

201

Index

Bartholomaeus Mastrius, 190n2
being: not a genus, 5; subject of metaphysics, 5, 6. *See also* accident; Analogy Model Problem; categories; concept of being; divine; *Rationes* Problem; substance
Boethius, 3–4, 7, 9, 47, 85–86, 94n8, 95t3
Bonino, S., 62n1, 65n10, 67n14, 78n31, 82n35
Boulnois, Olivier, 28
Brown, Stephen, 64n8

Cajetan. *See* Thomas de Vio Cajetan
Capreolus. *See* John Capreolus
categories of being, 6, 9, 18, 36, 37n12, 43–45, 47, 53, 58, 63, 66t2, 69, 81, 89, 96n12, 98–99, 120, 122, 134–35, 169–70, 178, 182, 185, 188, 191. *See also* accident; concept of being; substance
Cesario, Romanus, 13
Chrysostom Javelli (Iavellus), 15–17, 145–46, 164, 180, 191; on Analogy Model Problem, 166, 171–79, 187–88; on Equivocation Problem, 171–79, 187–88; on *Rationes* Problem, 165–71, 179, 187–88
Clarke, Norris, 51n46
concept: disjunctive, 37–39, 46, 91, 97–98, 108–9, 115–17, 131n11, 134, 165–66, 169, 187t6; distinct vs. indistinct (confused), 64–65; formal vs. objective, 33, 35–39, 41–42, 46, 63, 67–70, 72, 74, 77–81, 84–89, 101–2, 108–9, 111–17, 124–26, 130–31, 133–38, 140–43, 150–52, 154, 156, 165–66, 168–69, 177, 179, 184–85, 187–88; as likeness of things, 2; simple vs. complex, 20, 22, 24, 30–31, 37, 46, 71–75, 97. *See also* concept of being; *ratio*; *Rationes* Problem
concept of being (*ratio* of being): of categories, 18, 36, 63, 91, 96–100, 113–17, 124, 126, 130, 132–33, 152, 154, 168–70, 176, 178, 184; first, 165, 167–68, 170–71, 178; formal vs. objective, 35–36, 70, 112–16, 124, 126, 130–31, 134, 136, 152, 154, 165, 169, 184; of God and creatures, 19n3, 21–22, 27, 29, 36, 45, 63, 75, 116–17, 126, 130, 132–33, 170, 178, 184; Henry of Ghent on, 21–22; Peter Auriol on, 63–66; Scotus on, 22–29, 64–65; separate, 96–99, 108, 113–14, 131, 134, 151–52, 154, 165, 166n36, 169, 180; simple vs. composite, 24, 73, 75, 96–97. *See also Rationes* Problem
Conti, Alessandro D., 53
Cross, Richard, 11, 19, 28–31, 75n27

De Boni, Luis Alberto, 23n12
Decorte, Jos, 22n9
demonstration, 1, 4n7, 42, 89, 163, 173; and analogy, 2, 7–8, 10–11, 18, 32–33, 39–40, 55, 60–61, 80–81, 86–88, 118n53, 121–24, 138–40, 142–43, 162, 175, 177–78, 182–91; and univocity, 5–6, 19, 26, 29, 32, 39–40, 64, 79n31, 88, 118n53, 177–78, 182–90. *See also* Equivocation problem; fallacy of equivocation
D'Ettore, Domenic, 30n27, 34n5, 63n4, 70n17, 79n31, 82n37, 90n2, 102n25, 109n37, 120n56, 166n36, 171n49
Dewan, Lawrence, 10n23, 62n1, 67n14, 79n31
divine: analogate, 87, 147–48, 161; attributes, 6, 24, 26, 53, 57, 70, 106n32, 184; being, 21, 116, 152, 178; essence or nature, 71, 83, 84n42, 96n12; intelligence, 107; knowledge, 103; names, 51–53, 82, 112n44, 129, 143, 149n7, 157–58, 160n27, 161, 178; perfection, 71, 84–85, 159–61; simplicity, 162; will, 82n36; wisdom, 38–39, 42, 67, 76n30, 77, 105, 107, 113, 133, 139, 148–51, 155, 160n27, 163–64, 178. *See also* God
Dominic of Flanders (Flandrensis), 12, 16, 33, 40, 52n48, 63n4, 89, 165–66; on Analogy Model Problem, 102–8, 111–12, 125–27, 129–30, 141–43, 158–59, 161, 175, 179, 182–85, 187t6, 189; on Equivocation Problem, 118–22, 125–26, 141–43, 175, 184–85, 187t6, 189; on *Rationes* Problem, 90–102, 111–12, 115, 117, 125–26, 131, 134, 141t4, 143, 151, 156, 184–85, 187t6, 189
Dondaine, Antoine, 2n1

Index

Dreyer, Mechthild, 19, 23n12, 28
Dumont, Stephen D., 11n25, 19, 22n9, 28n19

Equivocation Problem, 10, 13, 15, 17, 33, 39–43, 54, 57–58, 60–62, 86, 88–90, 118, 122, 125–26, 138, 140–43, 145, 151, 162–64, 171, 175–79, 182, 184–88, 190. *See also individual Thomists by name*
equivocation: by chance, 3, 47; by design, 3–5, 7, 9, 47–49, 51, 52n49, 55, 94n8, 120; *pros hen*, 4; pure, 3, 5, 8. *See also* analogy; Equivocation Problem; fallacy of equivocation

Fabro, Cornelio, 94n10
fallacy of equivocation, 2, 5–7, 10, 25, 39–43, 53–55, 59, 61, 64, 80–81, 86, 88, 118–24, 138, 162, 171, 182–83, 185, 189–90; in definition of univocation (Scotus), 19–20
Ferrariensis (Francis Silvestri of Ferrara). *See* Francis Silvestri of Ferrara.
Flandrensis. *See Dominic of Flanders*
Fonseca, Peter. *See* Peter Fonseca.
Francis Silvestri of Ferrara (Ferrariensis), 16–17, 136, 145–46, 190; on Analogy Problem, 156–61, 179, 186–88; on Equivocation Problem, 151, 162–64, 186–88; on *Rationes* Problem, 147–56, 186–88; on three impositions, 147–51, 159–64

genus, 4–5, 37, 48, 69–70n16, 95, 103n26, 140, 153, 162
Gilson, Etienne, 21n6, 28, 181
God. *See* Analogy Model Problem; concept of being; divine; *Rationes* Problem
Goris, Wouter, 64

Hall, Alexander, 21n6, 27n18
Healthy Model of Analogy, 7, 10, 13, 38, 41, 51, 58, 60–62, 65, 78–79, 81, 85–86, 88, 92, 101–2, 105–6, 108, 111, 117, 123, 125–26, 129, 141–43, 157, 161, 173, 175–76, 179, 182–87, 189–90. *See also* Analogy Model Problem

Heider, Daniel, 171n48
Henninger, Mark G., 13, 34, 44n22, 45n24, 46, 50n44, 53
Henry of Ghent, 21–25, 31
Henry of Harclay, 34n6, 44, 45n24–25
Hervaeus Natalis, 12, 16, 33–34, 88–89; on Analogy Model Problem, 37–39, 49, 58–62, 141t4, 182–83, 186–87, 189; on Equivocation Problem, 39–43, 58–61, 118, 122, 141t4, 143, 179, 182–83, 185, 187t6, 189; on *Rationes* Problem, 35–39, 46, 58–61, 67, 75, 96–98, 108n34, 115, 117, 130, 141t4, 182–83, 187t6, 189
Hochschild, Joshua, xi, 8n18, 9n22, 29, 30n26, 49n42, 127, 135n22, 138

imposition, 2, 3n2, 8, 70–71, 96, 99, 100–101, 118–120, 147–51, 159–64, 179, 186–88. *See also* Francis Silvestri
Ingham, Mary Beth, 19, 23n12, 28
intentions: first vs. second, 2n1, 12n26; as synonym for *rationes* or concepts, 14, 66, 80
intelligible species, 25, 83
Irwin, Terence H., 4n7

Javelli, Chrysostom. *See* Chrysostom Javelli (Iavellus)
Jindráček, Efrem 16n36, 109n35
John Capreolus, 13–17, 30n27, 52n48, 60–61, 90–93, 126–28, 183; on Analogy Model Problem; 78–86, 88–89, 96, 111–12, 117, 141t4, 143, 158–59, 161, 166, 172–73, 175, 179, 184–88; on Equivocation Problem, 86–89, 121–24, 141–43, 175, 184–87; on *Rationes* Problem, 62–77, 88–89, 101–2, 108–9, 111–13, 115, 117, 130–34, 138, 141t4, 143, 184–87
John Duns Scotus, 11, 33, 35, 45, 55, 59, 63–68, 76n30, 77, 86, 89, 98, 115, 139–41, 143, 163, 165–66, 171–75, 177, 182, 184, 190; "Certain and Doubtful" Argument, 23–24, 36, 37, 41–42, 46, 60, 75, 97, 98n15, 115, 168–69; criticism of analogy, 21–26, 31–32; definition of univocity, 18–20; semantics of analogy, 30–32, 75n27; on univocity of being, 22–29

John Versor (Johannes Versor), 98–100, 115

Kappes, Christiaan W., 12
Klima, Gyula, 2, 6n12, 13n29, 35
Klubertanz, George P., 8, 10n22–23, 11n24
Krempel, Anton, 12n27

Livesey, Steven J., 97n13
Lohr, Charles H., 16n38–39, 164n31, 171n47

Mahieu, Léon, 16n36, 104n26
Maurer, Armand, 44, 48n34
McInerny, Ralph, xi, 10n22, 11n24, 41n16, 127n2, 159n25
metaphysics, science of, 5–7, 9–10, 18, 21, 26, 33, 58, 61, 68, 80–81, 90–91, 108, 112, 121, 124, 126–27, 144, 165, 182, 185–86, 189, 191
Montagnes, Bernard, 10n22, 11n24, 34, 82

Natalis. *See* Hervaeus Natalis
natural theology, science of, 1, 5–7, 9, 11, 13–14, 21–22, 25–26, 29–30, 42, 55–58, 60–61, 80–81, 86, 88, 91, 108, 112, 123–24, 126, 148, 151, 182–83, 185–86, 189, 191
Nielsen, Lauge O., 14n32

participation in *ratio*: equal vs. unequal (diverse), 63, 65–68, 75, 77, 84, 90–93, 100–102, 105, 107–9, 111, 113, 126, 134, 141–43, 176–77, 179, 187t6; perfect vs. imperfect, 66, 83, 184–87
Pasnau, Robert, 24n14
Paul Soncinas, 15–17, 52n48, 89–90, 108, 126–28, 156, 169, 191; on Analogy Model Problem, 109–18, 141–43, 166, 172–73, 175, 179, 185–87; on Equivocation Problem, 122–25, 141–43, 175, 185–87; *Rationes Problem*, 109–18, 130–31, 134, 141t4, 143, 151–52, 154–55, 165–66, 168, 171, 179, 185–88
Paul, Saint (Apostle), 5
Pelster, Franz, 44n23
Peter Auriol, 14, 33, 63–66, 73–77, 82n36, 122n58

Peter Fonseca (Petrus Fonseca), 131–33, 134n17
Peter of Spain, 6, 54n53
physics, science of, 81
Pini, Giorgio, 2n1, 83n40
Principle Model of Analogy, 10, 13, 47, 51, 53, 58, 61–62, 65, 78, 81–82, 85–86, 89, 126, 129, 141t4, 157, 175–78, 183, 187t6, 189–90. *See also* Analogy Model Problem
proportion. *See* analogy; proportional identity; proportionally similar; unity
proportional identity, 136, 139–42, 187t6
proportionality. *See* analogy; unity
proportionally similar, 51, 85, 87, 135, 137, 139, 142, 150, 155–56, 162–64
Przezdziecki, Joseph J., 13, 34

Ramirez, Santiago, 159n25
ratio: in intellect (mind) vs. in thing, 35, 38–39, 46, 60, 181. *See also* concept; participation; *Rationes* Problem
ratio entis. *See* concept of being
Rationes Problem, 10, 11n24, 13, 16–17, 21–23, 31, 33, 35, 38–39, 43, 45, 58, 60–63, 68, 88–91, 101–2, 112, 115, 117, 119, 125–26, 130–31, 134–35, 141t4, 143, 145, 147, 151, 155–56, 165–67, 171, 179–80, 182–83, 185–88, 190; in Aquinas 8–9, 11n24. *See also individual Thomists by name*
Riva, Franco, 16n36, 90n1, 127n1
Roensch, Frederick, 12n26–27, 33, 34n6
Ross, J. F., 51n46
Rutten, Pepijin, 98n16

Scotist (adj.), 7, 115, 124, 138, 178, 190
Scotist (noun), 28, 59, 77, 88, 108n34, 124, 165, 182, 190
Scotus. *See* John Duns Scotus
signification of a name, 2–3, 20, 43, 49–51, 52n49, 60, 72, 94, 113, 119–22, 130, 134n18, 137, 149, 151, 175; analogous (Scotus), 31–32; primary vs. secondary, 8, 100–102, 105; prior vs. posterior, 6, 92, 96–97, 100, 120–22, 185
Simon, Yves R., 30n26
Simplicius, 167

Index

Soncinas, Paul. *See* Paul Soncinas
Suarez, 12, 100n22
substance, 15, 19n3, 27n18, 36–37, 41, 43–44, 46–47, 52, 69, 70n16, 72n22, 78, 90, 95t3, 96n12, 97, 99–100, 103n26, 108–9, 111–17, 124, 128–30, 132–35, 152, 154, 168–70, 174–77
Sutton. *See* Thomas Sutton
syllogism, 6, 19n3, 20, 31, 39, 41–42, 54–55, 57–58, 66, 79–80, 86, 88, 123, 139–41, 162–63, 171, 172n50, 174–77, 184

Tavuzzi, Michael, 12n26, 17n39, 65n10, 145, 146n2n, 146n4, 158n23, 164n30, 172, 180
Teske, Ronald J., 12n26
theology, science of, 13, 18, 26, 63n3
Thomas Anglicus, 12, 118–20
Thomas Aquinas: *De Potentia*, 7, 38, 49, 62, 82, 85; *De Veritate*, 9, 10n23, 15, 62, 81–82, 84–85, 88, 94n8, 101–3, 108, 126, 128–29, 157–58, 161, 170n44, 171n47, 184, 189; *In Aristotelis Libros Posteriorum Analyticorum*, 4n7, 7; *In Duodecim Libros Metaphysicorum*, 2n1; *In Peri Hermeneias*, 2n1, 95n11; *In Physic.*, 48n33; *In Sent.*, 2n1, 6n11, 14, 15n33, 35, 62, 66, 67n12, 77, 79, 82, 86, 88, 96, 104n26, 110–11, 112n43, 117, 126–27, 143, 172, 173n52, 175, 184, 186, 188, 190; *Sententia Libri Ethicorum*, 9, 94; *Summa Contra Gentiles*, 7–9, 17, 38, 49, 51n46, 62, 82, 85, 104n26, 106n32, 116n51, 146, 147n5, 157, 160–161; *Summa Theologiae*, 2n1, 6n11, 7–9, 15, 38, 49, 62, 82, 85, 100–102, 104n26, 107n33, 120n57, 145n2, 146, 158n23, 160–61
Thomas de Vio Cajetan, xi, 1–2, 15–17, 52n48, 125–28, 144–47, 162–65; on Analogy Model Problem, 128–30, 141–43, 156, 158–59, 161, 166, 171–73, 175, 178–80, 186–88; on Equivocation Problem, 138–43, 171–72, 175, 178–79, 186–88; on *Rationes* Problem, 128–31, 134–38, 141t4, 143, 151, 155–56, 179–80, 186–88
Thomas Sutton (Thomas of Sutton), 12, 16, 33–34, 62–63, 75–77, 82, 85, 88, 94, 96–98, 121, 123, 127, 130, 169; on Analogy Model Problem, 46–61, 141–43, 157n19, 158, 179, 183–84, 186–90; on Equivocation Problem, 54–60, 61, 86, 141t4, 143, 179, 183–84, 186–87, 190; on *Rationes* Problem, 43–46, 58–61, 115, 141t4, 186–87
Torrell, J. P., 54n53, 82n34

unity: analogous, 7, 30, 34, 46, 58n59, 98, 100n22, 114; of attribution, 112, 133–34; disjunctive, 33, 37–39, 41–42, 45–46, 60, 75, 91, 97–98, 108–9, 113–17, 131n11, 134, 140–41, 165–66, 169, 187t6; of formal or objective concept, 68–70, 77–81, 85–88, 101–2, 112–14, 117, 130–33, 140, 142–43, 153–55, 169, 184–85; as principle of number, 4, 9, 47–48, 50, 59, 181; proportional, 57–61, 97, 102, 130, 131n11, 136, 139–41, 143, 155, 164, 187–88, 190; of science of metaphysics, 4–5; sufficient for contradiction, 19–20, 64, 66, 124, 140–43, 163–64, 171–74, 177–78, 182, 184
univocal. *See* univocation
univocation, 3, 66t2; as defined by Auriol, 64–66; as defined by Scotus, 18–20, 64–66, 171, 175; logical vs. metaphysical, 26–29, 48n34, 80–81, 96, 154n12, 166–67, 188; as necessary for demonstration, 5, 171. *See also* participation in *ratio*; and *individual Thomists by name*
univocity. *See* univocation

van der Lecq, Ria, 2n1
Versor, John. *See* John Versor

Wielockx, Robert, 21n7
Wippel, John F., 10n22, 11n24
Wolter, Allen, 64n5

ALSO IN THE
THOMISTIC RESSOURCEMENT SERIES

Series Editors: Matthew Levering
Thomas Joseph White, OP

The Metaphysical Foundations of Love
Aquinas on Participation, Unity, and Union
Anthony T. Flood

The Cleansing of the Heart
The Sacraments as Instrumental Causes in the Thomistic Tradition
Reginald M. Lynch, OP

The Ideal Bishop
Aquinas's Commentaries on the Pastoral Epistles
Michael G. Sirilla

Aquinas and the Theology of the Body
The Thomistic Foundations of John Paul II's Anthropology
Thomas Petri, OP

Angels and Demons
A Catholic Introduction
Serge-Thomas Bonino, OP
Translated by Michael J. Miller

The Incarnate Lord
A Thomistic Study in Christology
Thomas Joseph White, OP

www.ingramcontent.com/pod-product-compliance
Lightning Source LLC
Chambersburg PA
CBHW020320010526
44107CB00054B/1918